10/29/11
Chad,

Your courage
Makes a difference

FACE IT!

12 Obstacles that Hold You Back on the Job

Your courage!

Sandra Ford Walston

"Make courage your daily legacy."

iii

Endorsements for FACE IT!

- Courage is the virtue that has to be activated within us, and Sandra Walston is an activator extraordinaire! *FACE IT!* is more than a book, it is a gift. By reading this book, you'll have access to a refined perspective of your everyday courage and how it applies to your advancement at work. And that's a gift truly worth sharing.
  — **Bill Treasurer, author of** *Courage Goes to Work*

- If the world seems to be conspiring against you, your problems are solved with *FACE IT!*. Sandra Walston gently dynamites every obstacle that your own mind conjures up to stall your career and hold you back. This book is a marvel of pragmatics and philosophy, immediate help and inspiring history. The working world is a far better place with Sandra Walston in it.
  — **Harriet Rubin, author of** *The Princessa*

- This well researched, thoughtful book, guides the reader to a fuller life. We can't say that about many books. Sandra Ford Walston is at her best when she goes into depth about words and situations that most of us mortals do not even discuss with our closest friends. For example, her analysis of how "intimidation" stops us day in and day out, and how "courage" unleashes our true potential, is spot on. Reading this book can make you more than a little uncomfortable, but if you have a good, clean mirror to view yourself, you will be able to see the image in the mirror improve, as you improve, by reading this book.
  — **Herb Rubenstein, Lead Author,** *Leadership Development for Educators*

- One opportunity in your work life you will never regret is having and applying more courage. Sandra Ford Walston's insightful research explains how to combine the components of overcoming stuck thinking with courageous work behaviors to face the obstacles in your career.
  — **D. A. Benton,** *CEO Material: How to Be a Leader in Any Organization*

- *FACE IT!* is Sandra Walston's excellent follow-up book to *STUCK* written for people in all professions. This third unique guide demonstrates how any person can achieve life-changing personal and professional breakthroughs by recognizing the thinking that keeps them stuck at work and then how they can claim and manifest their everyday courage that is always available. With thought-provoking charts, tips and questions, and powerful stories of women and men who made courage their foundational value, this book is recommended for those of us at work all levels—we all know where we need to face the obstacles that hinder us on the job!
  — **Gail Evans, author of** *She Wins You Win and Play Like a Man, Win Like a Woman*

- Rich in insight and real-life stories that overcome the obstacles that keep us stuck, *FACE IT!* demonstrates that courage in the workplace springs from the courage for self-examination and exploring what truly matters in your life as much as your career. Sandra Ford Walston offers valuable information and inspiration to help you cultivate the courage that already exists within you.

  — Sylvia L. Lovely author of *New Cities in America: The Little Blue Book of Big Ideas*

- *FACE IT!* should be required reading for all working men and women. Why? For working woman, many are going to be crossed by deceitful, controlling, hyperaggressive individuals seemingly hell bent on derailing her career. For workers at all levels, paralysis that shows up in a stalled career is the result of failing to act while hoping the destructive people and bad events will evaporate. *FACE IT!* communicates the truth—failing to respond with authentic courage is the only truly risky act.

  Courageous actions free the trapped person, empowering them to accomplish boundless success. Courage is transformative. Consequently, timid followers who witness everyday courage firsthand are inspired. The paradox is true—the worst imagined risks from taking action pale in comparison to the real risks endured by doing nothing. Take charge and live more fully and successfully with this book as your guide.

  — Dr. Gary Namie, Workplace Bullying Institute, Co-Author, *The Bully At Work*

- Sandra Ford Walston does not write run-of-the-mill 'how to' books. *FACE IT!* is replete with erudition, insight and wit. It is a celebration of our human spirit's potential, a pleasure to read and then read again.

  — Anne B. Zill, President, Women's Center for Ethics in Action

- I love this book! Its message provides the same encouragement I would give myself when I find myself stuck in the quagmire of my thoughts. If you have ever fallen into the trap of believing that the 'smart thing' requires you to shrink at work from being courageous, you will relish this book's flood of great reasons to respect your inner leadership abilities. Here is a way to experience how 'courage consciousness' can create your new world.

  — Rennie Davis, President, Foundation for a New Humanity and author of *The Great Turning*

- This book is an invaluable resource for those women and men who desire to be true to their own courageous instincts in business environments by offering both inspirational insights that keep us in stuck-thinking and courage coaching for taking action. Walston does not focus on the aggressive habits of command-and-control that so often ape courage nowadays. Courageously she focuses on the true nature of courage. She provides carefully researched and thought-through suggestions for embodying courage as effectively in business as a few noted women and men have consistently done in the rest of their lives. This book is both inspiring and enabling.

— Harold G. Nelson, Ph.D., Consultant and President of Advanced Design Institute and co-author of *The Design Way*

- In this world rendered insecure and uncertain by terrorism, natural disasters, economic turbulence and situational ethics, it is easy to be afraid. Once, even in the most fearful times, we could look to role models in public, intellectual and corporate life, to inspire us and to reassure us that our courageous instincts were not wrong, naïve or futile. No more.

We have seen courage without intelligence, as Robert E. Lee said of Confederate General John Bell Hood, 'All lion and no fox'—possessed of great courage but little wisdom. Men and women die in spirit and sometimes in fact in the company of such leaders. They are not our new heroes. Thus we are fortunate that Sandra Ford Walston has summoned her courage to invite and guide our courageous instincts, to show us a path, to be our guide and counselor on this often lonely but always rewarding journey to our personal greatness.

Philosopher Jacob Needleman observes that all the big things in life, save birth and death, are really comprised of small things. Sandra reveals how twelve obstacles hold us back on the job rather than embracing twelve courage actions as we summon our hearts and minds to fully express who we are and what we want. Sandra speaks and writes from her experience, so she is our fellow traveler. When you want to be stronger to life's journey and more available to its gifts, invite Sandra's everyday courage and wisdom into your life.

— Louis L. Marines, President, Advanced Management Institute, author of *The Language of Leadership: Stories and Studies in Courage, Wisdom and Sacrifice*

- "My cynical tendencies get revealed by authors of so-called self-help books who themselves haven't 'taken the journey'. Not so with Sandra, she lives what she writes about. Wonderfully researched, thoughtfully organized, passionately written, FACE IT! will touch many through its emphasis on being something--not just doing something. This book will be especially useful for those who feel a gut-level need for change in their lives. For a select few, it will help them stop chasing 'shiny objects' and get on with their life's work."

— Bill Wiersma, Author of *The Big AHA* **and** *The Power of Professionalism*

FACE IT!

12 Obstacles that Hold You Back on the Job

Walston, Sandra Ford—FACE IT! 12 Obstacles that Hold You Back on the Job/Sandra Ford Walston.—1st ed.

Cover Design by Lauren Hildebrand, M.A. and graphic designer Christopher Bohnet

Technical and typesetting layout by R. (Rahja) McKee-Cray

ISBN-13: 978-1453729847

ISBN-10: 1453729844
BISAC: Business & Economics/Management

Printed in the USA

Doesn't everything die at last, and too soon?

Tell me, what is it you plan to do

with your one wild and precious life?

-- Mary Oliver, American poet, "The Summer Day"

Dedicated to the everyday

person that demonstrates

everyday courage

in spite of the circumstances.

Related titles also by

Sandra Ford Walston:

COURAGE

The Heart and Spirit of Every Woman

Reclaiming the Forgotten Virtue

STUCK

12 Steps Up the Leadership Ladder

FACE IT!
TABLE OF CONTENTS

No one has looked back sadly on a life full of experiences,
but many look back wishing they had had the courage to do more.

— Anonymous

Foreword

The backdrop for *FACE IT!* is the professional environment, but its application reaches far beyond that setting. Its ultimate impact is at the human level, not the employee level. As you read it, I suggest you use your job as a point of reference, not as a boundary to stay within. This book is an invitation to explore courage in all aspects of your life, not just where you are employed. Although there is indeed truth in advertising here, in the sense that this book will help you address issues hindering professional advancement; however, that is not why I was attracted to it. I enthusiastically recommend what is presented here because of its broader message: The world is in desperate need of more courageous people to serve as the architects for humanity's future. It's not easy, but it's doable, and we must get on with it.

Sandra has done us all a service by crafting this marvelous book on courage. She combined penetrating insight with a reader-friendly style to create a resource that furthers our understanding of courage and its place in our lives. I'm particularly struck by how she wove the threads of her discourse in such a way that the reader is both galvanized by the notion of becoming more courageous and sobered by how difficult the journey is.

Look elsewhere if you seek an easy path to follow—Sandra doesn't offer one. This book is a significant contribution to the courage literature precisely because it doesn't shy away from the subject's true essence nor succumb to a simplistic formula for its attainment. It is informative and inspiring, but not in lieu of being confrontive and challenging. She includes all four elements in her recipe for this compelling cake:

- Her thorough research of the subject will leave most readers much better *informed.*

- She does this in a way that makes courage seem like a real, yet doable, stretch, which means for those who are ready to pay the price, this is an *inspiring* read.

- The most *confrontive* action you can do with someone is to hold up a mirror so they see something about themselves that is less than flattering in their own eyes. This book invites you to look deep within yourself to see what aspects of courage may or may not be prevalent.

- If you finish this book and aren't taken by how formidable it is to live up to the twelve courageous actions outlined, then go back and start over. Sandra describes a *challenging* path, but if it was a commodity everyone was capable of, it wouldn't be the differentiator we all believe it truly is.

The basic premise of this book is that what holds you back on the job is the same as what hinders achievement of any important aspiration—the reluctance to face and live a courageous life. Given how important courage

1

is to our well-being, it is surprising how few resources exist on the subject. Sandra Walston provides welcome relief through this carefully-laid-out exploration into the true nature of courage. She presents the pursuit of courage as a worthwhile endeavor without sugarcoating its inherent challenges...something many others have tried, yet failed, to accomplish.

In my opinion, there are far too many speeches, seminars, webinars, podcasts, articles, and books about courage that not only tout it as a laudable characteristic but also claim how easy it is to access. Isn't it fascinating how our species will conspire to make any coveted attribute easy to acquire? The trouble is, whatever the trait, if it's highly valued, it's also inherently scarce. That doesn't stop us, however—we want to maintain a high value on our aspirations while also ensuring widespread access for everyone. It rarely works out as intended. This means, while courage remains a "potential" for everyone, it becomes a "reality" for only those willing to pay the price.

Take MBAs, for example. There was a time when having an MBA meant a job applicant would be exceptionally well prepared, enormously qualified and highly sought after. Then they became so commonplace that they were no longer differentiating but, rather, expected. Were students really better prepared, or were requirements relaxed somewhat, allowing more people through the gate without as much effort as formerly required?

When the goal becomes having more people carrying a label at the expense of the designation's integrity, the attribute becomes commoditized. Of course, with commoditization comes devaluation of the label being applied. I fear we have done this with our overuse of the term *courage*.

One way to judge whether a cherished characteristic has been devalued is to notice how often it's mentioned. Case in point: It is hard to absorb more than a half hour of TV or radio programming without hearing commentary about someone's courageous behavior. It is common now to hear an individual described as "courageous" when he or she actually did something difficult, adventuresome, or even bold. Upon close examination, however, the circumstance didn't require much actual courage. That is, the action taken never really put the person much at risk.

Courage means acting despite unsafe circumstances and is in no way associated with security and assurances. Sometimes the situation involves external intimidators (people, things, new ideas, etc.). Other times, it's something inside us that's terrifying...anxieties and distress that reside just below the surface or that may be buried deep within our psyche. Regardless of the point of origin, courage is about knowing the obstacles that hold you back, and then taking action.

People who find the courage to move forward face a difficulty such as two examples from the book: challenging an uncomfortable truth or instilling self-discipline. They choose to do so because of an overriding need to live up to an internal image they have of themselves. They don't lack awareness of the consequence they face; they are simply more driven to be the person they aspire to be.

2

In our effort to make it easier to be courageous, we run the risk of discounting the concept to the point that it is unrecognizable. It may be that the only thing in shorter supply than courage itself is a proper understanding of what it really is. Reading *FACE IT!* will close this gap.

Daryl Conner

Daryl R. Conner is chairman of Conner Partners®, an Atlanta-based consulting firm that specializes in transformation implementation. He is an internationally recognized leader in organizational change and serves as an advisor and mentor to senior executives around the globe. His work is built on a strong foundation of research, extensive consulting experience, a master's degree in psychology, and a deep spiritual focus. He has authored three books—*Managing at the Speed of Change* (Random House, 1993), *Leading at the Edge of Chaos* (John Wiley & Sons, 1998) and *Project Change Management* (McGraw-Hill: New York, 2000).

February 2011

Preface

As for courage and will—we cannot measure how much of each lies within us,
we can only trust there will be sufficient to carry through trials which may lie ahead.
— Andre Norton

Sophie was shocked ... and disappointed. She had just discovered that one of her hospital's employees had been skipping steps in the surgical sterilization process. This threatened patients, not to mention the integrity of the entire institution. As CEO of this community hospital, this information had arrived through the whistle-blower mechanism she had put in place months before. Ninety patients were exposed to potential cross-infection from this lack of adherence to safety procedures. Now it was up to her to deal with this breach of protocol and decide how to convey the news to those affected. How was she going to face it?

Fortunately for the public, the CEO and the whistle-blower demonstrated true courage. "If we screw up," Sophie said, "we are going to tell you in an appropriate and timely disclosure. Regardless of the devastating PR and lack of confidence the public could have with our facility, we create a workplace culture that supports reporting errors at all levels. We care about the patients and chose not to hide behind risk-management." She trusted that her forthrightness would establish trust with their patients in the event that they discovered a positive exposure. The hospital took the most courageous step they could by personally contacting every patient. "No 800 number in a form letter for our patients," Sophie said proudly, "we contacted them all. We treated patients individually, and we gave the institution a face, a name and a resource that they could contact because we used one nurse." How would you handle a situation like this?

True practitioners of everyday courage, like Sophie, do not allow obstacles they face on the job to prevent them from establishing and achieving high standards. They trust their own abilities, demonstrate their talents and create opportunities for advancement in life as well as on the job. Without the strength of her innate courage, Sophie could not have stepped up to the challenge and taken the risky course of action that allowed her to achieve community and board approval.

During fourteen years of research, I have discovered that certain obstacles can become an endless series of dramas holding us back in our personal and professional lives. When people face these impediments, the natural tendency is to stay stalled in a mental comfort zone ... and stagnate. A selection of the men and women I interviewed had learned to overcome this psychological paralysis even in very challenging circumstances. Conquering their StuckThinking™, they discovered a crucial source of self-actuated motivation—courage! Unfortunately, most people mistakenly equate courage with perilous situations requiring feats of heroic bravery. This view fails to recognize the everyday courage required to explore new ideas, create innovative businesses, break from consensus, transcend rejection, keep the faith or take the initiative.

To understand fully the importance of courage in overcoming workplace barriers, we must first understand the true meaning of the word. Courage comes from the Old French word *corage*, meaning "heart and spirit," which tells us that courage is really about the center of *your* being— who you are at the most fundamental level. In other words, living courageously is not so much about what you are *doing* as who you are *being!* Only by delving beneath our shallow thought patterns and melodramas can any of us discover our true identity, thereby nurturing our courage and empowering ourselves to integrate courage into our work lives. Whether your entrepreneurial spirit is stuck in self-doubt or your management proficiency is stuck beneath a glass ceiling, your relationship to your innate courage affects how you view challenges as well as your ability to meet them. Courage lies within each of us, and as we learn to employ the tools of courage, we learn to face and overcome barriers that once seemed overwhelming.

What Does Your Work Attitude Reveal?

Your attitude toward your work reveals much about what prevents you from achieving career fulfillment. Do you cherish your job? Very few people do, but I have yet to meet a single person who does not wish to be happy at work. A Gallup poll found that job satisfaction steadily declined from nearly sixty percent in 1995 to just fifty percent in 2004. In 2009, The Happy Planet Index surveyed 143 countries. "The United States snagged the 114th spot .... The United States was greener and happier 20 years ago than it is today."[1] With workers at every income level facing lay-offs, tight job markets and diminishing opportunities for advancement, workplace obstacles seem larger than ever. No wonder the workplace spirit is diminished—most of us don't go to work feeling happy. We forgot what Confucius said, "Choose a job you love, and you will never work a day in your life."

FACE IT! is not about how to get a job, and it is not a theory, but a methodology about learning to use courage techniques to overcome work-related barriers to self-fulfillment—things like uncertainty, intimidation, denial, apathy and self-doubt. Stop for a moment and reflect. If you could choose, what job would you love to have more than any other? A recent *Parade* magazine poll showed 61% of people responded "no" to this question: "If you could do it all over again, would you choose the same career?"[2]

Overcoming difficulties at work begins with learning to stop and reflect on key questions. Reflection invites stillness. Stillness connects your conscious mind with your "heart and spirit" so that you live from your courageous true Self, the internal source of your passion and joy. As you reconnect with the courageous core of your being, you empower yourself to overcome the twelve biggest obstacles that hold you back at work:

1.	Inertia	2.	Defeat
3.	Denial	4.	Self-Neglect
5.	Blame	6.	Self-Doubt
7.	Uncertainty	8.	Apathy
9.	Intimidation	10.	Manipulation
11.	Invisibility	12.	Ambiguity

Each of these obstacles mirrors a specific response called a "courage action" that enables you to transcend the limitations imposed by that obstacle. By practicing these courage actions, you will tap into the hidden power of your innate courage, enabling yourself to prevail over situations that once seemed impossible.

Levels of Consciousness

The profound consciousness research of David R. Hawkins, M.D., Ph.D. provides crucial insights into the dilemmas that stall our careers. In over twenty years of research, Dr. Hawkins has delineated levels of consciousness ranging from "shame" (the least conscious level) to "enlightenment" at the level of complete consciousness. Hawkins' research confirms that a critical shift occurs at the level of *courage* consciousness. All of the lower consciousness levels on his "Map of Consciousness" ("shame, guilt, apathy, grief, fear, desire, anger, pride") describe an existence dominated by levels of force and falsehood, violence and deceit.[3] Courage not only represents the crucial first step into an empowering, truth-based existence, it also opens the door to higher levels of consciousness and personal empowerment.

When we respond to problems from the lower levels of consciousness, we invariably are unable to face the situation. Even if we manage to face our problems, we find ourselves repeating the same patterns and repeatedly stalling at the same obstacles (like a bad version of the movie *Groundhog Day*) until we respond from a higher level of consciousness. Simply put, eliminating StuckThinking™ requires the power of "heart and spirit" courage. Regardless of your unique circumstances, courage elevates your consciousness into the realm of truth, empowering you to advance your life's work.

Contemplate these questions:

- How do you handle problems at work?
- How frequently do you step out of your comfort zone?
- Do you have the backbone for inviting change?
- When was the last time you offered a new idea?
- How engaged are you at work? (One hundred percent? Eighty percent?)

Answering these questions is your first step toward the courage consciousness that empowers you to conquer the unique set of challenges on your career path!

To apply courage to the obstacles that hold you back on the job requires self-realization. Self-realization is nurtured in reflection and contemplation which is very different from self-help. You *cannot* slip sweetly into your true Self by attending a two-day conference. While a conference may be a good start, it will not change the habitual thought of the behaviors reflected in the mirror much less the attitudes that chain us stuck in dead-end jobs or unfulfilling careers. Wherever your habit of attention goes your energy follows. *FACE IT!* requires that you sharpen your intention and allow the power of your innate, heart-and-spirit courage to shape your experiences at work. Empowered by courage, you will not only obliterate the obstacles to your success, you will manifest the wholeness, happiness and the self-confidence of courage-centered leadership. Courage-centered leaders achieve unexpected results at work and in their lives because they consistently choose this forgotten virtue.

May the energy of everyday courage illuminate your mysteries and elevate your possibilities! And remember:

> *Love is the most difficult and dangerous form of courage.*
> *Courage is the most desperate, admirable, and noble kind of love.*[4]

Introduction
Assessing Your Personal Assets at Work

The rung of a ladder was never meant to rest upon, but only to hold a man's foot long enough to enable him to put the other somewhat higher.

— Thomas Henry Huxley

> ➤ Brenda loved her job as an executive with a successful corporation, but she found herself stuck in denial. Her boss delivered toxic tirades and insults on a regular basis, but Brenda chided herself, "I should be able to handle this!" Seven years of looking the other way and twenty-five unflattering pounds later, she found the courage to take the matter to Human Resources (Chapter 2).

> ➤ Steve hated being a lawyer from day one, but self-doubt kept him stuck for nearly eleven years. Holding his young son one evening, he caught himself talking angrily about events of the day to his wife. Suddenly, he asked himself, "How is my three-year-old son internalizing my voice?" That triggered his courage to step up to a more fulfilling and rewarding career (Chapter 8).

> ➤ Karla is an attractive "thirty-something" stuck in uncertainty that creates a downward spiral of unnecessary suffering. Her husband skipped town when their daughter started preschool. Her marketing job as a brand manager is her dream job, but she drives herself harder and harder as her boss's demands continue to grow. The harder she drives herself, the less time she has for her daughter and the guiltier she feels (Chapter 4).

Brenda, Steve and Karla knew exactly when they were not being true to themselves and eventually realized that their lives no longer worked. They realized that traditional job skills were insufficient for conquering the obstacles that stalled their careers. They all had to reach inside to find the innate skills that enabled them to achieve rewarding careers.

Do you feel frustrated, stagnated, unappreciated or unfulfilled in your job? If you answered "Yes," you need to know one thing:

You have the power within YOU to create YOUR best career path!

This is the power of courage—a quality so important that it qualifies as one of the four cardinal virtues (prudence, justice, temperance and courage) and "virtue" in Latin means "energy." All of the real skills needed to overcome obstacles at work stem from this virtuous energy. By recognizing, developing and wielding the power of everyday courage at work, anyone can

- Overcome the obstacles to job satisfaction,
- Earn more rapid advancement at work,
- Develop stronger interpersonal skills, and
- Experience personal fulfillment at work on a level most people fail to imagine.

Regardless of age, background or job description, you will discover if you are energetically "stuck in a rut" you can discover how to be more fulfilled and satisfied in your true profession by applying everyday courage to the situations in which you become stuck! Are you willing to discover your personal courage and face the obstacles you encounter? Are you willing to overcome your own obstacles to self-knowledge? With self-knowledge, you discover personal, "heart and spirit" assets that allow you to design your own destiny. Are you willing to design a life that enables you to become your full potential? Think about the implications of this in your life at this very moment. If you continually commit to activities and people who fail to bring you fulfillment, how happy will you be when you wake up? How fulfilling will your work be over the years? Your relationships? What will ultimately be the meaning of your life? Once you act from your courageous will, you will step up to higher levels of success and fulfillment.

Stepping up in courage is like climbing a stepladder. The first step on the ladder is low and wide. It does take a certain amount of courage to take that first step up, but that first step is the easiest—wide and close to the ground. As each consecutive step is higher and narrower, each step requires more courage than the last, and the ascent can get quite shaky near the top. Nonetheless, according to Dr. Hawkins, "In Courage we see that change for the better is feasible. We stop blaming, hating, and fearing and lift ourselves out of victimhood, weakness, and apathy and strive to make the world better. We give up self-blame and self-pity and affirm the power within us."[5] The first step toward courageous living is to declare your courageous intention—i.e., your conviction to "give up self-blame and self-pity and affirm the power within [you]," the power of everyday courage.

The Skills to Overcome Obstacles

Learning and teaching others about courage is my passion. For over fourteen years, I have conducted extensive research to identify and understand the twelve basic "courage actions." These actions manifest your courage and empower you to overcome the challenges that stall you at work. Using our ladder analogy (not to be confused with climbing the corporate ladder), each rung of the courage ladder represents one of the twelve courage actions that surmounts one of the twelve obstacles that hold us back on the job.

Each person's ladder is unique because different people face obstacles in different sequences—i.e., at different steps up the ladder. With that in mind, I have designed each of the ensuing chapters to stand on its own, making it easy to focus on the obstacle you face right now and the corresponding action that empowers you to overcome that obstacle. ("The Courage Wheel" on the following page provides an overview of the twelve obstacles and their corresponding courage actions.)

Each chapter features an introductory sketch of a historical person who exemplified a specific courage action while overcoming a variety of obstacles. These people experienced defining moments of self-realization that enabled them to recognize how StuckThinking™ stifled the growth of their spirits. Each confronted obstacles masked by other obstacles, requiring them to search for answers and pursue new ideas. They responded with uncanny fortitude, keen vision, undaunted faith and centered self-esteem. Distinct in their careers, interests, achievements and eras, these individuals demonstrated a definite mettle that links their identities to their hearts and spirits.

"When we lose our spirit, we die—we *ex*pire from lack of that which *in*spires."[6] Does your day-to-day work inspire you? If not, what prevents you from making a purposeful move to a fulfilling, meaningful career? What real skills do you need to develop in order to make that move? Whatever the specifics of your situation, our human tendency is to stay stuck in old patterns far too long. Eckhart Tolle (one of Oprah Winfrey's favorite spiritual teachers) recognizes the limitations of this tendency: "Old patterns of thought, emotion, behavior, reaction and desire are acted out in endless repeat performances, a script in your mind that gives you an identity of sorts."[7] This false identity distorts reality and actually creates the most difficult obstacles that we face. Using the personal assets of everyday courage, you can break free from these internal obstacles—outdated emotional patterns, mental "scripts" and false identities—just as others have. You can learn from these courageous individuals and know that you too possess the courage to overcome any obstacle.

The Courage Wheel

12 Courage Actions to Overcome StuckThinking™

Sandra Ford Walston
The Courage Expert

Stuck in a B-Movie

Before we can begin to climb our personal courage ladder, we need to find solid ground to support it. True courage comes from within, not from education, titles, credentials or reputation; nor does it come from mental aptitudes, intellectual prowess or charisma. True courage springs from our deepest values, motivations and attitudes—what many teachers refer to as the authentic Self. The word "authentic" is derived from Greek *authentikos*, meaning "original." In this book, I refer to it as the true Self.

Physicist Danah Zohar's research refers to this type (or level) of courage as Spiritual Intelligence (SQ) or wisdom. "To have high SQ is to be able to use the spiritual to bring greater context and meaning to living a richer and more meaningful life, to achieve a sense of personal wholeness, purpose and direction."[8] Ironically, in order to step up in our careers, we must first delve deeper into our true Self to find a solid foundation that supports living a courageous life.

The real challenge, however, is to rediscover your true Self and act on the insights only such self-realization will bring. In other words, there is no "one size fits all" formula for conquering StuckThinking™. Only by journeying inward, to a deeper level of self-study, can we each identify the appropriate courage action that will advance our lives and careers beyond the challenges we face at any given moment. "Our denial, or unwillingness to look deeply at our own issues," notes Marianne Williamson, "reflects a naïve hope that if we don't look at our wounds, they'll go away by themselves. It takes 'emotional courage' to look deeply into ourselves and face what's there."[9]

Denial can be a huge obstacle, especially when it becomes a way of life, but "Denial has an interesting and insidious side effect. For all the peace of mind deniers think they get by saying it isn't so … the denying person knows the truth on some level, and it causes a constant low-grade anxiety. Millions of people suffer from anxiety, and denial keeps them from taking action that could reduce the risks (and the worry)."[10] The cure for all this denial is simply the courage to know ourselves at a deeper level. The greater the depth of self-realization, the more familiar we become with the transformative power of courage.

Once you begin the journey toward self-knowledge, ask yourself, "What is my real work?" Your true work revolves around being authentic in all you do—being genuine, real. By combining true, "heart and spirit" courage with authenticity, you get the spirit in *you*, your *true essence*! When you live in this awareness, you begin to recognize the scripts that have defined your identity but that limit your perceptions of your true Self. It is as if you discover that the person you thought you were is simply a character in a "B movie." Once you begin to recognize the B-movie script as an obstacle, the inner power of courage enables you to step out of the scripted roles that limit your opportunities.

As the inner conflict between your true Self and your B-movie persona recedes, the energy it once consumed becomes available, allowing you to begin to realize your full potential. As you stop playing the roles of the B-movie script, you not only free up wasted energy, you also generate more positive energy that feeds and strengthens your heart and spirit, your courage.

A Different Model

Our fast-paced culture encourages us to identify ourselves with what we do. *Doing* generally involves a list of things to accomplish—earning another certification, landing a new account, securing another promotion—and the sooner the better. Unfortunately, *doing* can become a career trap with the tools of the modern office serving as a high-tech hamster wheel. This incessant multi-tasking not only leads to unfocused, error-prone work, it also narrows the possibility to perceive your true Self beneath the scripted layers of ego personality. "Our problem is that we get wrapped up in what we are doing and why we are doing it—analyzing it, planning, worrying about it— so that we lose the joy that is always available."[11]

By contrast, *being* comes from a peaceful inner space that reveals our deepest, most genuine identity, "the depths of our being, where we come face to face with ourselves, our weaknesses, and with ultimate mystery."[12] Unfortunately, "The collective disease of humanity is that people are so engrossed in what happens, so hypnotized by the world of fluctuating forms, so absorbed in the content of their lives, they have forgotten the essence, that which is beyond content, beyond form, beyond thought."[13] "Just do it," just does not cut it. Rediscovering our heart and spirit essence requires the stillness of being. Once a state of being is achieved, the necessary actions flow naturally, efficiently and without effort.

Being requires some type of contemplative practice, a discipline that forces us to unplug and slow down so that we can discern the way beyond the limited scripts of doing to the deeper levels of our true identities. Living more deeply, we begin to diminish setbacks and to recognize the B-movie obstacles that undermine your ability to follow a vibrant, rewarding career path. "To know yourself as the Being underneath the thinker, the stillness underneath the mental noise, the love and joy underneath the pain, is freedom, salvation, enlightenment.... You can know it only when the mind is still. When you are present, when your attention is fully and intensely in the Now, Being can be felt, but it can never be understood mentally."[14]

Because this place of being defies mental understanding, each person must experience it in his or her own way. By adopting a contemplative practice, we stop, both physically and mentally, and focus our attention internally, opening ourselves to the deeper levels of our being. We diminish StuckThinking™ in exchange for a new state of consciousness; hence, a new identity. Psychologists have known for a long time that habitual thinking causes suffering. "Compulsive thinking has become a collective disease. Your whole sense of who you are is then derived from mind activity.... The one thing that truly matters is then missing from your life: awareness of your deeper Self."[15] How do you respond to your suffering? In being, you identify with your deeper Self and claim the courage that empowers you to confront others' limiting perceptions; paradoxically, it also allows you to let go of your attachment to those perceptions and move beyond them.

To allow your true Self to manifest your best possible work situation requires your mind to be still and present (i.e., instead of replaying past moments or projecting future events). "You are cut off from Being as long as your mind takes up all your attention."[16] As your introspective practice quiets your mind, you can begin to manifest fulfillment and satisfaction at work by eliminating the old scripts, the obstacles that shape and limit your perceptions about your life. Stillness offers you the opportunity to recognize and transcend your limiting perceptions.

One woman I interviewed labeled her day-to-day experiences "surviving," but as Eckhart Tolle teaches, survival mode represents one of the most limited levels of consciousness. "As soon as you rise above mere survival, the question of meaning and purpose becomes of paramount importance in your life.... There is no substitute for finding true purpose. But the true or primary purpose of your life ... does not concern what you do but what you are—that is to say, your state of consciousness.... Inner purpose concerns Being and is primary. Outer purpose concerns doing and is secondary.... Your inner purpose is to awaken. It is as simple as that."[17] When you awaken to the deep levels of your true, heart and spirit identity, you empower yourself to overcome all obstacles. "In truth, all the knowledge, creativity, love, joy, and peace we are looking for are right within us, the very essence of our beings."[18]

Our work culture does not value slowing down to lead a contemplative life, but that is exactly what we must do to rediscover joy in the workplace. Paradoxically, slowing down enables you to accomplish more at work because you are more focused; hence, you work more effectively. And slowing down could be the single most effective action to initiate your courage: it allows you to live from the center of your being, from your heart and spirit. What would happen if you stopped for ten minutes right now?

Obstacles as Defining Moments

Career-defining moments represent crucial points along your career path, places where you contemplate the virtues that compose your character and choose to step up to the next rung on the ladder or, lacking sufficient courage, slip back down. Every obstacle you face at work represents a potential career-defining moment. By simply recognizing these workplace obstacles as defining moments (things like failing to get an overdue promotion, or enduring verbal intimidation) you begin to rely on your personal, courage-based assets.

Unfortunately, many people miss the opportunities inherent in workplace obstacles, and their responses reflect an underlying sense of self-defeat (Chapter 7). They may perceive these potentially defining moments as just "part of the job," or they may feel that in some way they deserve unfair treatment. If they take on the role of martyr or victim in order to "keep the peace," their true heart-and-spirit Self is further stifled. Frequently questioning your status quo moves you from the dominant "mind-will" that produces StuckThinking™ to the heartfelt will of everyday courage. Heartfelt will expresses itself by confronting uncomfortable truths where mind-will rationalizes in order to avoid confrontations (Chapter 12).

If you have difficulty recognizing the defining moments in your own workday, ask yourself which events make you upset, angry, conflicted, uncomfortable, embarrassed or acquiescent. Identifying these events will point you to the obstacles upon which you will want to focus your emerging courage energy. W. Edwards Deming said, "Nothing happens without personal transformation." By realizing which specific obstacles challenge your effectiveness at work and then acknowledging the scripted pattern that keeps you stuck, you are well on your way to conquering StuckThinking™ and reclaiming your everyday courage.

Agony of Regret

Courage is not something we stumble upon as we round the corner of the cubicle at the office, but a practical internal resource—a portfolio of personal assets that can bolster your position in defining moments. A woman I will call Emily, an art gallery owner, repeatedly relied on courage in her work. She moved from Colorado to California and back again in her quest for professional satisfaction. Recognizing the potential for failure, she remained true to her essence and refused to settle for less. Emily wielded courage action skills to forge her niche in the art world *in spite of* significant obstacles. She placed her commitment to the work she loved at the very center of her being.

Courage dictates that you love your work or you change it. This is what moves you through the mirage of mirrors. "It is impossible to have a great life unless it is a meaningful life. And it is very difficult to have a meaningful life without meaningful work."[19] Emily lives a meaningful life because she has claimed the courage necessary to pursue meaningful work in spite of dis*courage*ing impediments. As you learn to find courage in ordinary life, figure out what triggers the habitual behaviors of your old scripts and look for a matching regret. Identifying the underlying regret empowers you to choose a new response that leads to a more meaningful, fulfilling life. Mary Oliver says in her poem "When Death Comes," "I don't want to end up simply having visited this world."[20]

Are you a participant in your life or just an actor in a minor role? Are you tortured by regrets? "We change the world not by what we say or do but as a consequence of what we have become. Thus, every spiritual aspirant serves the world."[21]

As Within, So Without

Co-author of the bestseller *Megatrend 2000*, futurist Patricia Aburdene writes in *Megatrend 2010*, "The quest for spirituality is the greatest megatrend of our era."[22] To embody the spiritual process of self-realization in your professional identity, challenge yourself to extend your imagination beyond the solutions that worked in the past. Applying spirituality to sustain their inner energy, courageous men and women understand that courageous action leads to illumination and illumination supports courageous action. In *The Eye of the I*, Dr. Hawkins writes, "Illumination refers to those spiritual states where sufficient barriers have been dropped, either deliberately or unconsciously, so that a greater context suddenly presents itself, and in so doing, illuminates, clarifies, and reveals an expanded field of consciousness actually experienced as inner light. This is the light of awareness, the radiance of the self, which emanates as a profound lovingness."[23]

How do you drop the barriers to illumination—the mental and emotional scripts that trap you in a B-movie melodrama? Make a list of your perceived opposites or polarized concepts, such as love/hate, original/copycat, expensive/cheap, body/spirit, victory/defeat, contentment/resentment, survive/change, volume/value, ascend/dwell, and so on. As perceptions of limited ego-based consciousness, these dualities keep us stalled in a vicious cycle of superficial motivations. How do you move beyond them? "To successfully transcend the seeming 'opposites,'" writes Dr. Hawkins, "it is only necessary to see that what appear to be two different or opposing concepts are actually just gradations of possibilities that change quality as they progress along a single base line of perception."[24]

The ego places dualistic judgments on our sensory perceptions, creating a subjective "reality" in the very act of perceiving it. "As soon as something is perceived, it is named, interpreted, compared with something else, liked, disliked, or called good or bad by the phantom self, the ego.... You do not awaken spiritually until the compulsive and unconscious naming ceases, or at least you become aware of it and thus are able to observe it as it happens. It is through this constant naming that the ego remains in place as the unobserved mind."[25]

Invested in Illusions

As Dr. David R. Hawkins writes, "Although the human mind likes to believe that it is 'of course' dedicated to truth, in reality, what it really seeks is confirmation of what it already believes. The ego is innately prideful and does not welcome the revelation that much of its beliefs are merely perceptual illusions."[26] On your journey of self-realization, it is tough to accept that most beliefs are illusions or to grasp the idea that your identity is "a psychological construct of whatever you say you are"[27]—i.e., the false self. Eckhart Tolle reflects, "Some people get angry when they hear me say that problems are illusions. I am threatening to take away their sense of who they are. They have invested much time in a false sense of self."[28] We have all invested much time in a false identity, and in order to live in everyday courage—from our heart and spirit, our true Self—we must invite some form of stopping. And just because we do not invite it willingly does not mean we can avoid it.

Most of us have to go through painful, drawn-out experiences to slough off all aspects of the ego and arrive at the true Self. "Unfortunately, in seeing ourselves as we truly are, not all that we see is beautiful and attractive. This is undoubtedly part of the reason we flee silence. We do not want to be confronted with our hypocrisy, our phoniness.... It is a harrowing journey, a death to self—the false self—and no one wants to die. But it is the only path to life, to freedom, to peace, to love. And it begins with silence."[29] As you establish your contemplative practice, reflect in silence on a time when you felt proud of an outcome. Remember the people, the places and the goals that helped you flourish. Reflect on the times you were the "real" you. Your courage resides in these places—where you shared an open heart, or experienced something truly pivotal.

Once you have made note of those positive work experiences, identify the personal assets you need to employ and the specific actions you need to take to replicate those experiences. Record these on the "Declaration of Courageous Intention," or DCI, at the end of this chapter, or print a copy from my website, www.SandraWalston.com. Sign and date your DCI and post it in a prominent location. Review it frequently and update your intentions so that you continually remind yourself of your commitment to yourself.

Courage development is a process, not an event. If you want to multiply your value at work, increase your effectiveness and enhance your sense of purpose and fulfillment, the DCI will start you on the *your* path. Soon, you will have a record of your own courage development and the challenges you have overcome, and you have found the courage to do what you love. Remember:

Courage is the gift that lifts your spirit.

Automatic Behaviors

The following table, "Five Levels of Courage Consciousness," can help you determine your own level of consciousness. Then, armed with self-knowledge, you can conquer the behaviors that prevent you from achieving a more rewarding work life.

After reviewing the chart, ponder these questions:

- Do you identify with or use any of the statements on the chart?
- Did it motivate you to reflect on your own courage awareness?
- How do you deal with work challenges?

The Five Levels of Courage Consciousness

Classic Comments	Levels	Confront Obstacles
"I don't stay very long anymore in situations that don't make me happy. Life is too short and denial causes me unnecessary suffering." "Absolutely, I have courage. Every time I follow my heart, I am being true to myself. When I die I don't want to be filled with regrets."	**5** **Aware**	Recognize when you get stuck, draw from your acknowledged reservoir of courage and take ownership. Hold yourself 100% accountable and edit your actions. Dismantle old behaviors (scripts). Invite new possibilities; embrace a simpler life. Find joy in the present (not living in the past). Model courage; en*courage* others.
"I failed to speak up at that last staff meeting, but I won't do that again." "I never thought of myself having courage, but I recognize it in other people. Maybe I have been courageous." "I notice when I fall back into my old ways."	**4** **Observant**	Embrace the nuances of courage; dig deeper. Take action to confront oneself and declare a courageous intention. Feel dispirited but saying "Enough!" Begin to awaken your courage and identify your actions as imperative to your destiny. Allow yourself to claim your courage and accept that your life will change.
"I know I've been complaining a long time about this matter, but I'm busy." "I will step up and face this situation as soon as I...." "I tend to get comfortable and have a hard time with change."	**3** **Unavailable**	Rely on a suitcase of reasons to avoid taking action (until forced to by illness, job loss, etc.). Put reality on hold and hide out. Place more importance on your job than your own life. Face your life and sense the times you sold your soul.
"I know I am unhappy, but I am the breadwinner. I do what I have to do." "It's hard to change, but I know I should. I keep trying."	**2** **Excusing**	Stay stuck in pre-scripted dramas. Identify with the attachments to your scripts. Recognize the same repetitive stories but stay stuck on the same obstacles. Be unwilling to embrace discipline.
"I never think of myself as courageous, nor would I describe myself as such." "I'm no 'hero'!" "I don't give much thought to the word."	**1** **Unaware**	Live in denial and/or blame (denial is saying "no" to courage). Feel that you've never done anything courageous. Fail to associate with this virtue (it's a BIG word!). Avoid unpleasant truths.

Once you recognize your level of courage consciousness, begin integrating each level into your life as you step up to higher levels of awareness, a process that engages the complete individual—mind, emotions, heart and spirit. When this happens you will experience spiritual intelligence (SQ as opposed to IQ) in the workplace. Physicist Danah Zohar wrote in *SQ: Spiritual Intelligence the Ultimate Intelligence*, "We use SQ to deal with existential problems—problems where we feel personally stuck, trapped in our own past habits or neuroses or problems with illness and grief."[30]

Business consultant Lee Livermore knows the value of courage consciousness, so he employed "The Five Levels of Courage Consciousness" chart with a group of teachers to help resolve conflict and remove barriers to communication: "I asked the group to review the sheet and give a self assessment.... Then, I asked them to share their thoughts about the chart as a tool. While the feedback was positive, they realized they did not consider themselves in terms of courage.... Courage is a character element that needs to be nurtured so it becomes more a part of people's identities and awareness." Using this chart helps people recognize and take ownership of their unconscious behavior patterns. As they begin to step out of their automatic behaviors, they elevate their consciousness and begin to respond to difficult situations from a more courageous level.

Declaration of Courageous Intention (DCI)
Claiming Your Courage

Facing the obstacles that hold you back on your job takes courage. Committing to your courageous intention will expand your success at work. Be prepared to welcome the true you!

Starting today, I give myself permission to claim and apply my courage. Ask yourself, "In claiming my everyday courage; what do I need to do?"

As you read the book, write the specific courage actions featured in each of the twelve chapters that you need to practice to live a fulfilled work life. The declaration evolves as your courage grows and clarifies.

Signature_____ Date _____

1.

2.

3.

4.

5.

6.

7.

8.

9.

10.

11.

12.

Chapter 1
Give Yourself Permission—
Moving Out of Inertia

Real courage is when you know you're licked before you begin,
but you begin anyway and see it through no matter what.

— Harper Lee

> ➤ Do you feel stalled at work unwilling to face the facts?
> ➤ Have seemingly insurmountable obstacles taught you to be complacent?
> ➤ Are you stuck in a dead-end job?
> ➤ Has a stagnated work life infected your heart?
> ➤ Does work siphon your lifeblood and sap your energy?
> ➤ Do you share the same old story (about why you aren't advancing) with the same old clique?

If you answered "yes" to any of these questions, face it, you are stuck! Jim realized he was stuck after five years at a job that he "couldn't quit" because he needed the family medical benefits. When he realized that his thankless job was killing his spirit, he finally gave himself permission to act with courage and broke free from the inertia that kept him stuck.

Inertia is the first and most critical obstacle that holds us back on the job—the obstacle that prevents us from initiating everyday courage and moving forward. In inertia, life becomes unfulfilling and insipid. In the "The Happiness Paradox," Marshall Goldsmith wrote, "Our default response in life is to experience inertia. Breaking the cycle of inertia doesn't mean exerting heroic willpower. All that is required is the use of a simple discipline... most people fall prey to inertia."[31] The discipline required to overcome this insidious obstacle requires you to

Give yourself permission to claim your courage.

Unless you give yourself permission, you will never fully embrace your courage and achieve the level of success and satisfaction that you desire.

Most people are reluctant to give themselves permission because it means facing change. Change takes us out of familiar territory, and the inertia that keeps us stuck in unfulfilling jobs feels safe by comparison. Fortunately, the misgivings that come with change will quickly give way to greater success in life and on the job.

I invite you to claim your courage now. Are you willing to face the inertia that keeps you stuck? Giving yourself permission to claim your courage obliterates the inertia that prevents you from achieving a successful, gratifying work life, regardless of your job, career or profession. Will you accept the invitation? The choice is yours.

Mother of All Virtues

Can you name the first woman to run for president of the United States? Very few people can, but this nineteenth-century woman embodied a variety of courage behaviors, especially the crucial first courage action. By giving herself permission to be courageous, she journeyed through life as a spiritual seeker, individualist and social activist. Misunderstood, ridiculed and rejected, Victoria Claflin Woodhull utilized her talents to become "the first woman stockbroker on Wall Street, the first woman to produce her own newspaper … a fearless lobbyist, businesswoman, writer and investor who advocated for women's equal status in the workplace, political arena, church and family."[32] Regardless of society's criticisms, Victoria rejected mediocrity and ignored the prejudices that informed her shortsighted critics. She fought for change on virtually every important social, political and economic issue of her time. *You can tap into that same courageous spirit for the strength you need to overcome every obstacle in the workplace.*

Receptive to new views and concepts such as birth control and equal rights for women, Victoria "saw no reason why she or other gifted people should be held back by society's rules and strictures. Clearly, these rules were in place to keep one group of people in a more powerful position than others. She believed in a society based on talent and ability—not sex and class."[33] Working with her sister as a spiritualist, "Victoria could earn a living in a field that was one of the few to give women a voice—because the voice was not her own."[34]

Commodore Cornelius Vanderbilt recognized the sisters' gifts and became their business mentor in the stock market. In 1870, he helped the two sisters establish the first women-owned stock brokerage on Wall Street. Challenging Victorian hypocrisies was not an easy mission, but Victoria never succumbed to apathy. Recognizing the power of the media, she bought a newspaper that became her vehicle for exposing hypocrisies, injustices, stock swindles, insurance frauds, women's issues and human rights. For Victoria, hypocrisy ran rampant through society and represented a key leadership issue. She delivered an honest, insightful message for a better life, but a patriarchal society found it threatening.

During the women's suffrage movement, many movers and shakers sought financial, religious or political reform. But when Victoria attempted to broaden the scope of topics such as education for daughters at the

National Woman's Suffrage Association forum, she was ostracized by the likes of Susan B. Anthony. Phyllis Chesler writes, "Most women are emotionally needy and are therefore emotionally greedy. Like girls, women remain reluctant to stop a group from scapegoating or excluding an individual woman because they are afraid the group might turn on them next."[35] Scandalous headlines about Victoria rarely contained more than a hint of truth, and Harriet Beecher Stowe's written attacks on Victoria demonstrated the classic behaviors described by Chesler (*see definition of "female indirect aggression" at the end of the chapter). Nonetheless, while other women tiptoed towards equal rights, Victoria's courage enabled her to storm the gates of inequality.

Even after major setbacks, Victoria refused to fade into the background. She soon headed a new group of women activists who believed in equality for all people; and in 1872, at the age of thirty-two, she became the first woman ever to run for the U.S. presidency as the candidate of the Equal Rights Party. Victoria had funded the cause of women's suffrage, but when the century's worst recession set in, she found herself broke. Friends turned against her, and she was repeatedly denied residence. Publicly ostracized and slandered, Victoria also faced betrayal at home when she learned that her husband had taken a mistress.

Never apathetic, Victoria persevered and received an unexpected blessing following the death of her longtime friend, Cornelius Vanderbilt. He died the richest man in the country and left most of his inheritance to his son William. The other siblings sued, claiming that their father was not in his right mind. William decided the brouhaha surrounding Victoria and her sister were a liability to his case, so he chose to offer the sisters money to leave the country. In 1877, Victoria, her two children, her sister and her mother settled outside London, where Victoria continued to live her convictions away from the public spotlight. Before she died at the age of eighty-eight, President Wilson signed the bill granting voting privileges to women, and Congress voted in favor of the 19th Amendment. By giving herself permission to claim her courage, Victoria conquered obstacles on a scale that most of us can hardly imagine.

As Victoria experienced, confronting obstacles can result in a smeared reputation. Still today, long after her death, Victoria's life was "a little too flamboyant" for "herstory" to be a part of mainstream history. "She was written out of history [and] censored by historians of the women's movement…. Victoria was arguably the boldest voice for women's rights in the nineteenth century, and she was taken very seriously by her contemporaries and by the media, in spite of her unconventional lifestyle."[36] Victoria never allowed herself to get stuck, no matter how large or seemingly immovable, she had the courage to face the obstacle. Are you tired of being stuck? Are you willing to fulfill your destiny? Are you willing to give yourself permission to be courageous? By giving yourself permission, you allow yourself to uncover and recognize your innate courage; and, like Victoria Woodhull, you empower yourself to overcome inertia and initiate positive change in your life.

Once you have given yourself permission, one simple practice will reveal your innate courage—silence. In *Meditations on Silence*, Sister Wendy Beckett writes, "Silence is a paradox, intensely there and, with equal intensity, not there. The passivity of silence is hard to explain, since in one respect it is intensely active. We hold ourselves in a condition of surrender. We choose not to initiate, nor to cooperate with our mental processes. Yet from this passivity arises creativity."[37] Your life will change if you can simply give yourself permission to be true to the courageous spirit within you. Allowing silence to reveal the depths of your courage will empower you to overcome any obstacle.

Choosing to Choose

Jill Tietjen grew up with parents preaching, "Never follow the crowd just because that's the popular thing to do." Jill was solving jigsaw puzzles at the age of two ("too bright"), she was a tomboy ("too boyish") and a Jew living in the "wrong neighborhood" ("too Yankee"). The eldest of four children, her two brothers relentlessly teased her, and she confesses she never dated in high school.

Like many young women, Jill had a "when I grow up" scenario. "After graduating from high school I will go directly to college, graduate at twenty-one, marry two weeks later, start my first engineering job, have children, work for the same company, receive appropriate raises, retire at sixty-five, and then die." One of only six women in her graduating class, Jill thought she was on her way to career advancement and life fulfillment. Nevertheless, her agenda ran headlong into reality. Her first job lasted only five years. Extensive treatments for infertility yielded no results; then, she divorced after eighteen years of marriage. With her mythology of success obliterated, Jill found herself stuck in the paralysis of inertia.

At age thirty-nine, Jill had forgotten that life was full of possibilities, and she was unclear about what was important to her. Stephen Covey's book, *First Things First*, inspired her to *stop* and look at her thoughts instead of allowing them free reign to reinforce inertia through mental paralysis. Seeking new and clear intentions in her life, Jill realized that she had the courage to start her own business. The voices of her depression-era parents had imprinted the belief that a secure and stable job was the best. Through the therapy process, Jill found the voice of her own heart and spirit, and she understands what it means to give herself permission to claim her courage: "Live your life being true to yourself and making choices that are right for you."

For over eight years, Jill has been a successful entrepreneur. Recognizing the value of conscious choice prompted her to write, "I've learned that not making a choice is in fact making a choice not to change." Put another way, "The choice not to choose is the choice to remain unconscious."[38] In other words, inertia is an obstacle that anyone can choose to overcome. Now Jill chooses what seems right for her personal journey rather than letting someone else's agenda sidetrack her vision. Giving herself permission to claim the power of her courage, Jill stepped out of inertia and conquered the obstacles to her life's entrepreneurial adventure. Jill has learned that courage is acquired by conscious design and that you strengthen it, step by step, choice by choice. The choices you make each day in your life have repercussions in how you advance your career. "When our choice is strong and clear, without indecision or ambiguity, our whole being is strong and clear."[39]

As Jill learned, stopping to reflect in silence pulls us away from the busyness of our culture, the tendency to value only complicated projects instead of life's simple truths. Do you understand simplicity? The person who lives from the heart understands simplicity. This is the gift of reflection. Learning to balance life between action-oriented steps and some type of meditative discipline, you move out of counterproductive habitual patterns (obstacles) and begin to exert your "courageous will." Applying your will, you begin to direct your own destiny just as Jill did. Career adjustments do not come with a set of instructions. The only way to negotiate your unique set of obstacles is to accept the responsibility to act with determination and resolve. If you are willing to give yourself permission to claim your courage, then write on your DCI: *Give myself permission to be courageous.*

Hell in the Hallway

"When one door closes, another door opens." How many of us have heard that statement when facing a particularly difficult obstacle? If you are in the midst of losing your job, changing industries, or confronting pregnancy discrimination, that goodwill statement probably does not help much. After all, the real issue is not about whether the door is opening or closing, but how you deal with the place in between, what I call "hell in the hallway"!

Some doors close in a positive way—a six-month severance package, a transfer or a recertification, for example. More commonly, the closed door represents a negative event—a layoff notice, a lack of promotion, a new boss with his own team or even a bully. During these times, we often find ourselves unconsciously forcing the next door open. If we are alert, our use of force will tell us that this "opportunity" is probably not the right choice.

Hell in the hallway, despite the frustration and sense of loss, provides an opportunity for the introspection needed to shed light on your true (heart and spirit) intentions. The professional and social pressure to achieve insists that we push on the door. The paradox is that by simply allowing the light of our personal courage to radiate—slowing down to examine our professional path and understand where it is taking us—we can develop a sort of Zen fitness, a calming, enlightening transitional space rather than the hallway from hell.

Author Parker Palmer shares his own understanding of the closed-door experience. "As often happens on the spiritual journey, we have arrived at the heart of paradoxes: each time a door closes, the rest of the world opens up. All we need to do is stop pounding on the door that just closed, turn around—which puts the door behind us—and welcome the largeness of life that now lies open to our souls. The door that closed kept us from entering a room, but what now lies before us is the rest of reality."[40]

A courageously observant person re-evaluates their identity to discover what is true and vital then summons their courage to step up. "What identifies the core of the narcissistic ego," writes Dr. David R. Hawkins, "is its inability and refusal to accept personal responsibility, and any such request is vociferously rejected as being oppressive. It feeds off the false sense of empowerment of being the 'victim' and distorts reality in order to be seen as the victim."[41] By avoiding the victim mentality and holding yourself accountable for your choices, you will begin to see how they reverberate throughout your life!

Recall and list some of the times you found yourself in the hallway wondering where the next door would open. Are you stuck in the hallway now? If so, what is going on? Are you anxiously trying to force your way out, or have you given yourself permission to be courageous, centering yourself in courage consciousness? Sometimes a door opens right away, but my clients share that most growth in courage consciousness comes in the lonely hallway. Reflecting, reassessing our goals, delving deeper into our values—this is the place where many of us discover our inner calling.

Most people do not have a clue about their calling. Think about a time when you felt animated or excited. Animation is an energy that makes you come alive in your core—in your heart. Victoria Woodhull felt alive when she was awakening people to hypocrisy and human equality. There is a good chance that you have experienced this positive energy at some point in your life. Perhaps you have all but forgotten it, but if you look closer, you might see that this experience revealed your inner essence. To awaken from the poppy field of inertia and make that essence come alive requires your courage! Giving yourself permission to claim and apply your courage empowers you and invites new challenges. It is a perfect starting place if you want to multiply your talents and effectiveness, define with clarity what is vital in your life and escalate your success at work. Clarity is a cousin to courage.

Underscore Your Footprints

Courage is a joyful essence that supports your true Self, thereby empowering you to embrace new dilemmas, overcome reluctance and rise above ambivalence. In other words, the course of your work life is up to you, even during times of uncertainty. As you begin to embrace the truths revealed by courage consciousness, remember: overcoming obstacles requires intention.

Smart, courageous and innovative, Linda Paralez holds a Ph.D. and is the president of her own company. With twenty-five years of leadership experience across a broad spectrum of industries, Linda radiates success. Each fall, Linda challenges herself. She takes a "self-exploration" vacation to Wyoming. There, surrounded by the Grand Teton Mountains, she ponders a new agenda for that year. One year she decided to explore a series of questions: "What would I do differently if I had unlimited time? Unlimited money? Unlimited market share? Unlimited knowledge?" Her answers to these questions were less than satisfying, since she realized in most ways she had achieved unlimited time, unlimited money and unlimited market share. None of these presented obstacles to her satisfaction. These were the wrong questions.

Near the last day of her vacation, while walking around the pristine waters of Jenny Lake, Linda came up with a better question: "What if I had unlimited courage?" This turned out to be the right question. Linda said, "What makes that question powerful, hopeful and confidence-inspiring for me is that I am a person who has access to courage. When I tell that story to people who do not have much access to courage, their reaction is often 'Yeah, but, you can't just be reckless,' meaning that the reflection of courage in their eyes is something not confidence-inspiring or hopeful, but critical and reckless." What Linda learned later is that we all have ready access that allows us to tap into our courage.

With her wonderful insight, Linda resumed her regular workaday routine and immediately began to apply the new question in all aspects of her life. Soon, she began to notice a greater satisfaction with her work and relationships and more inner peace as she applied her courage to daily problems. She fully believes that the hardest thing to do in life is find the right questions to ask … far harder than answering them.

In retrospect, Linda's insight seems inspired. Three months later, she found herself facing breast cancer, and she needed her newly activated courage more than ever. Linda now says, "Courage is a part of my 'success toolbox.'" Linda's courage enabled her to invite this new unknown into her life, accepting it in courage instead of allowing the ego's innate fears to paralyze her in a state of inertia. "We are all destined to come up against the unknown—above all, the unknown within ourselves. Are we prepared to accept what we do not know? Or do we stop short at the edge of the mystery, only feeling at ease with ready-made explanations that are anathema to true understanding? Indeed, making friends with the unknown is a prerequisite in any transpersonal search."[42] How comfortable are you with the mysteries of your own life?

Every fall Linda becomes a spiritual seeker, using consciousness "as an instrument of exploration and will toward making awareness as transparent as possible, releasing it from false assumptions, passions, and attachments. In this manner, consciousness is refined, clarified, and freed from envy and shame, regrets and fantasies."[43] Challenging ourselves to overcome inertia requires us to ask daunting questions: How am I holding myself back from accomplishing my goals? How am I disguising my courage? Ask questions. Ask more questions. Then, ask another question. Do not seek the *right* answer.

Be patient toward all that is unsolved in your heart and try to love the questions themselves. Do not now seek the answers, which cannot be given to you because you would not be able to live them. And the point is, to live everything. Live the questions now. Perhaps you will then gradually, without noticing it, live along some distant day into the answer.[44]

As psychologist Piero Ferucci observes, "The unsought voice seeks us, comforts and leads us. This happens mainly in supreme moments of choice, or in crisis, when all has been tried again and again, and one feels lost. Then the voice points the way to follow."[45] Linda's motivation for getting away each fall is intentionally to stop, be silent, look inside, wait for the voice and be open to the direction. "I try really hard to pay attention to my motivations, to what I really want, to what I've been doing, to what I like and don't, to what makes me tick and to what I do to and with people. I have a firm belief that I must do an extra special job of paying attention to how I behave. Usually, I'm glad I do."

Not all of us can manage an annual vacation in Wyoming, but we can "choose to set aside time and a place to enter into spiritual quietness. (Those who never do this, or who shrink from it, run a very grave risk of remaining only half fulfilled as humans.)"[46] Whether facing a bully box, medical crisis or unemployment, it's time to ask: "How can my work life bring joy and happiness when external obstacles limit or eliminate my options?" The mental attitudes that shape our perceptions of our external situation reflect the inner reality of our true Self. With the right work, we are able to manifest and fulfill the aspirations of our hearts, and we are happy. "For us to be habitually happy, nobody has to change except ourselves."[47]

There is a Catch

Roberto Assagioli, born in Venice in 1888, was an Italian psychiatrist and founder of pyschosynthesis (based upon the existence of a transpersonal Self as the Center of our being and source of our most beautiful and meaningful experiences[48]). He studied people who had experienced peak moments or who had shown exceptional capacities and "periods of greatest happiness— the states of grace they felt to be supremely significant and beautiful."[49] A creatively inspired pioneer in the vein of Carl Jung and Evelyn Underhill, he, along with Abraham H. Maslow, studied human wholeness. Maslow said,

What is necessary to change a person is to change his awareness of himself.[50]

To change your awareness of yourself means that you actually become another person (Obstacle 10). Piero Ferrucci (Assagioli's protégé) offers a psychosynthesis exercise to incite change in the everyday person. Try it!

Visualize an old and wise person, then having a dialogue with him or her and asking for advice. Help often comes, because, if the exercise is done correctly, the wise old person represents Self and speaks its voice. Inner listening, like inner seeing or visualization, is a function one can call upon for guidance and inspiration.[51]

Linda innately applied this "wise person exercise." She understood that, paradoxically, the invitation to a spiritual journey can frequently feel disturbing, beginning with "emptiness and dissatisfaction. Before the first intimations of a spiritual awakening take place, an individual tends to blindly accept the values of personality."[52] Linda took time to stop, quiet her mind and look inward to reflect back on her life's journey; then, she challenged her spirit to advance according to her vocation.

The spiritual journey is about self-discovery and awakening the deepest, most authentic Self. "To insulate themselves against the pain of living, many people ... develop 'homemade' selves where they feel protected."[53] Unfortunately, these protective identities represent the false self that operates in the lower levels of consciousness and denies the deeper truth of the Self. If you take an explicit role as a seeker of your own fully developed humanity, your true Self, you may be surprised to discover that the journey is clear-cut and personal. Piero Ferrucci offers these suggestions:

- "Do something extremely slowly.
- Eliminate something superfluous from your life.
- Do something you have never done before.
- Break a habit.

- Do something that makes you feel insecure."[54]

Didi Firman is the Director of the Synthesis Center in Amherst, Massachusetts, a non-profit organization dedicated to psychosynthesis research and teachings. She is also a professor at Union Institute and University. "Courage," she said,

> is about the long haul. The long haul, though, requires courage that awakens every day. It is showing up for the little things, the hard things, the easy things, the things that promise huge rewards and the things that promise nothing. The real courage is to stay at it (whatever your life offers, whatever you create) for all the years of your life. This is where the will—which, in psychosynthesis terms, is composed of the good will, the skillful will and the strong will—is a must. And just noticing the qualities of the will, it's easy to see why we need all of them to courageously move through the days (and nights) of our lives.

But there is a catch. When your life operates at today's frantic pace, how do you find the time to identify the courageous will and ask better questions? How do you challenge the status quo when corporate America views slowness as nonproductive? Paul Scott Gilbertson uses his courage to make a difference in the nonprofit world helping children. He defines courage as "being confident in knowing yourself to the extent that you are never satisfied with the status quo and you are always striving to improve and make a difference in the world around you." He believes that the biggest obstacle for people to display courage is procrastination—a specific type of mental inertia re-enforced by the inability to step out of one's comfort zone. When we get caught up in inertia, whatever its form, we settle for less, we fail to live up to our potential, and we miss out on the joy and abundance available to every courageous human being.

Redemption Is in Your Courage

History affords us the opportunity to study the lives of those who passed before us and underscore the courageous steps that enabled them to overcome huge impediments. But the real source of power lies in the noble and courageous voice of the ordinary, everyday person like you and me! Our culture may not celebrate the courage that guides you through the obstacles of daily life, but realize that you make a difference. Look around and you will observe a courageous person—the person who confronted a bully on behalf of a peer or the person who spoke up for the truth. As Parker Palmer sees it, "They decide no longer to act on the outside in a way that contradicts some truth about themselves that they hold deeply on the inside. They decide to claim authentic selfhood and act it out."[55]

The practice of a meditative discipline reveals your deeply held inner truths, enabling you to claim authentic selfhood. In other words, redemption lives in your courage to stand for your truth! How do you begin to incorporate courage into your work life? Learning to claim your courage involves a learning curve and requires a conscious effort. Perhaps your approach is to research the options, review the tasks and then commit to the progression. For example, if you want to learn how to relax, you may decide to practice a type of yoga, which includes various forms of meditation. Wayne Teasdale writes, "They are called yogas because they are ways of union or integration with the divine reality.... Raja yoga is similar, in some respects, to contemplation."[56] Each path touches a different level of *yoga* (union with the divine), such as physical postures, selfless service to others, centering the consciousness or path of wisdom. You pick the techniques that work for you. These options keep you from getting stuck in old and unwanted behavior patterns.

Regardless of your relationship to your personal courage, you will find that your heart and spirit contain a wide range of courage: spiritual courage, emotional courage, leadership courage, ethical courage, physical courage, political courage, social courage and personal courage. As you appraise your current attitude about your work, try to notice the following elements to see if you can identify the qualities with which you are familiar and the ones you need to develop.

Spiritual courage. The spiritual journey requires being in the present. It is a trust in faith that propels you to continue growing. You become a "witness" to your attachments to results and learn to self-correct. You surrender your ego to a higher level of consciousness (review how you rated yourself on "The Five Levels of Courage Consciousness" chart in the Introduction), and you begin to exist in a place "where courage meets grace" (Chapter 12). As all this happens, humility steps in to replace arrogance and righteousness. The sacred within awakens, informing us with Spiritual Intelligence (SQ).

Emotional courage. Similar to spiritual courage, this involves "knowing thyself" (Socrates). It is your "Declaration of Courageous Intention." A path committed to contemplation ("not only prayer but action … and not only prayer and action, but the gift of one's inmost being and all that one is"[57]) is required to release the "false self." (The false self is the self-image developed to cope with the emotional trauma of early childhood which seeks happiness in satisfying the instinctual needs of survival/security, affection/esteem, and power/control, and which bases its self-worth on cultural or group identification.[58])

Leadership courage (individual and organization). The courageous culture of an organization honors and uplifts the human spirit (the opposite of authoritarianism or coercion). The collective intent of a courageous organization is to join hearts and minds in order to achieve inspired results. It means the organization (and its people) will "fall on their swords" to honor their collective personal courage. Courage leadership knows the difference between pride and arrogance versus humility and grace.

Individual leadership courage. Rooted in truth, we live from our inner essence and speak it appropriately. Being able to distinguish truth from falsehood has taken on a new perspective.

Ethical/Moral courage. This courage is activated by the attitude of willingness to choose differently *in spite of* personal hardship. The objective is a higher level of integrity than required for the easy alternative. Moral courage is like a compass. Over a long period of time, if you are one degree off-course, you will eventually discover yourself hundreds of miles off course.

Physical courage. Facing a physical limitation that challenges the human body, utilizing the body to achieve athletic challenges, facing physical dangers or overcoming serious health problems—these are the best understood forms of courage today. Practicing a contemplative life (stopping and "being") or being centered in mind, body and spirit are other less-known physical examples.

Personal courage. The way of one's heart might be the easiest way to understand this form of courage. It is a blending of heart and essence combined with the commitment to hold ourselves one hundred percent accountable for our actions. Applying courage consciousness, we must recognize that our spirit is the author of our fate.

Political courage. Unwillingness to sell one's soul is the key feature, represented by whether one stands as a politician (self-serving) or a statesmen (serving others), in other words, the intention to do what is right by placing society's needs ahead of political aspiration. Political courage is characterized by humility, not egotism. It is a willingness to risk political favor for the sake of expressing an uncomfortable truth. "To see one's predicament clearly is a first step toward going beyond it." [59]

Social courage. Social courage exhibits congenial behavior in public, regardless of the circumstance. With discipline and grace, you reveal a courage paradox: you do not insult others, nor do you suffer an offense in silence. Your image plays a key role, expressing the contradictory qualities of social grace with a rebellion against society's limitations.

Are you a product of courage, or are you so far removed from this virtue that it has lost its human quality? Take a moment to determine if you can claim one or more of these forms of courage; then, begin to develop the missing qualities.

The people featured in this chapter exhibited courage consciousness behaviors that can help you claim your own path. And just as these people encouraged others to claim their courage, your ability to overcome obstacles can encourage the people around you. Therapist Shane Holst believes this type of encouragement is invaluable in helping people claim their courage and overcome inertia. "I believe that when I encourage another I wish to fill the other with courage. And my courage is demonstrated even though I encourage another who may outshine me. I still persist and commit altruistically to the other. Indeed, I celebrate the achievements of another regardless of me, my ego, my needs—that is deep courage; deep integrity; deep truth and a bona fide humility and wisdom." Simply by giving ourselves permission to claim our personal courage, we encourage those around us, making courage contagious and transforming the workplace!

*"Female indirect aggression can be very painful psychologically, socially, and economically. Such aggression is both verbal and nonverbal and includes reputation-wrecking gossip and shunning, which may lead to social 'death' and, in some cultures, to real death as well."[60]

Courage Development Questions to Ponder
- How receptive are you to new challenges?
- Are you willing to embrace a slowing, contemplative process?
- When the inner core of your strength is saying, "I know I can do this," how do you overcome inertia? What process do you use to rekindle your spirit?
- Take time (like 30 days) to reflect on this exercise: Write down detailed descriptions of your passions. Then, ask yourself what you would do if you if you had unlimited courage?

Chapter 2
Remove Yourself from Bad Situations—
Recognizing Denial

It is useless to waste your life on one path, especially if that path has no heart.
Before you embark on a path, you ask the question: Does this path have heart?
A path without heart is never enjoyable. You have to work hard even to take it.
On the other hand, a path with heart is easy; it does not make you work at liking it.

— Carlos Castaneda, The Teachings of Don Juan

Imagine projecting a positive life message through a body racked with constant pain. Imagine having the talent and ambition to become a doctor but having to shelve that goal forever. Imagine coping with physical disabilities. Compound this situation with an abusive husband and the emotional pain of repeated miscarriages. Denial probably would have been the easiest way to deal with so much hardship; instead, Frida Kahlo imparted a deep love for life and demonstrated the enduring depth of true courage. Throughout her short life, this talented artist from Mexico exemplified the courage needed to

Remove yourself from bad situations.

Youthful Traumas

Frida contracted polio at age seven. The disease withered one of her legs, and Frida's father encouraged her to strengthen the leg by playing sports like soccer and boxing, which earned her the label of "tomboy." One of only thirty-five girls in a high school of two thousand, Frida wore the label proudly and incorporated its verve into her style.

But at seventeen, Frida survived a horrific bus accident that broke her pelvis, leg, foot and spine. Encased in a body cast, Frida spent a month in the hospital and two years at home in bed. Without a doubt, Frida stepped into the depths of her heart and spirit during the long days of her quiet confinement; and in those depths—in the core of her being—she found the strength to rise above not only the trauma of a broken body but also the temptation to sink into denial.

Drawing from the inner strength of her courage, Frida chose to transmute her pain into something beautiful and began painting. When she finally shed her plaster cocoon and walked again, Frida needed a cane to support herself, but her indomitable courage empowered her to let go of her dream to become a doctor and continue developing her artistic skills.

Famed artist Diego Rivera entered Frida's life when the Mexican government commissioned him to paint a mural at her school. Known as an egotistical womanizer, Diego lacked nothing in the way of loquaciousness, yet his goggle eyes, obese frame and peculiar nature made him the object of ridicule. Nonetheless, Frida married Diego in 1929. Obsessed with fame, he would become her advocate and art teacher but also her abuser. As Diego became more volatile, Frida opted out of denial and removed herself from a bad situation by moving out.

In 1950, after learning her leg would have to be amputated, Frida again met her obstacle with courage, producing a world-renowned self-portrait that reflected the depths of her pain, depression and passion for life. Three years later, Frida was the first woman artist in Mexico to have her own opening. Since she was too weak even to use a wheelchair, her friends carried her in on a stretcher and placed her in her own bed in the middle of the room at her show. Drawing on the energy of her unquenchable courage, she dominated the party with her joy for life. Frida never succumbed to denial. And because her courage would not allow her to quit, she became Mexico's best-known woman painter and one of the world's greatest artists.

Wisdom Amidst Pain

While most of us cannot imagine a life like Frida's, people in all job descriptions frequently find themselves working in difficult, abusive situations. Abuse at work can come in many forms—bullying, controlling, undermining, belittling, victimizing, gossiping, passive-aggressive behavior and so on. Frida triumphed over abusive situations by refusing to stay stuck in denial.

In *The Mystic Heart*, Wayne Teasdale writes, "Mature self-knowledge happens when we move beyond denial—denial of our faults and limitations, our buried motives or hidden agendas—and beyond judgment of others, beyond projection on others our own need for inner work. The more we see ourselves as we really are, rather than as our ideal self-image dictates, the more we are on the road to the fullness of the spiritual life and the ultimate actualization and realization of our potential."[61]

As Karlfried Graf von Durckheim writes,

The woman or man who, being really on the Way, falls upon hard times in the world will not, as a consequence, turn to that friend who offers her refuge and comfort and encourages her old self to survive. Rather, she will seek out someone who will faithfully and inexorably help her to risk herself, so that she may endure the suffering and pass courageously through it, thus making of it a 'raft that leads to the far shore....

The first necessity is that we should have the courage to face life and to encounter all that is most perilous in the world. When this is possible, meditation (being with life) becomes the means by which we accept and welcome the demons which arise from the unconscious.[62]

What is important is how you define yourself. Do you perceive the steps in your life as courageous, or does your ego's perception of life as survival define your existence? To change this perception requires you to stop, embrace the present and seek the support of others who refuse to encourage your old behaviors. With self-actualization and spiritual courage comes a quieting and shifting of desires.

Do you have a childhood "survival story" that you hold onto for dear life? Having claimed your personal courage, now is the time to let go of that story if you want to remove yourself from bad situations. Such stories are ego-created scripts that block your path to growth, but they can be overcome by adopting a personal meditative practice, which helps to uncover motivations obscured by the controlling tendencies of ego.

A meditative discipline introduces us to a deeper level of courage consciousness that reinforces our ability to live more consistently in the "yes mode" of the true Self (rather than the ego's "yes/no" of survival). We become less reactive, less identified with ego and less externally focused. Eckhart Tolle admonishes us, "Say 'yes' to life—and see how life suddenly starts to work *for* you rather than against you.... By watching the mechanics of the mind, you step out of its resistance patterns, and you can then *allow the present moment to be.*"[63]

Soon, the old ego-scripts, the false self-stories, release their hold. Freed from the past, we no longer replay the old scripts that keep us stuck in denial. "The voice in the head has a life of its own. Most people are at the mercy of that voice; they are possessed by thought, by the mind. And since the mind is conditioned by the past, you are then forced to re-enact the past again and again."[64] As the ego's mental control scripts begin to fade, however, something unexpected happens. The internal space once dominated by the voice in your head begins to fill with joy, "the emotional expression of the courageous Yes to one's own true being."[65] Are you willing to face it? Controller Leonard "Sherm" Sherman defines courage this way: "To face and resolve what every fiber of your body tells you to flee and ignore."

Most of us seem to recognize that denial tendencies probably started when we grew up in dysfunctional families. At times, we even recognize how the dysfunctional scripts continue to show up in our lives. We all need to banish these stale scripts (about physical/emotional abuse, alcohol/drug abuse, winning at all costs, job titles, keeping up with the Joneses, hoarding and so on). We all have emotional, spiritual or physical scarring, but what matters is making the choice to use your courage to make a change, to escape the self-deception of denial.

The Undercurrent of Old Scripts

The pilgrimage out of denial requires us to stretch ourselves—to challenge ourselves. Through meditative practice, deep learning occurs. The simple reflective process reveals the scripts that prevent us from claiming and sensing our courage, thereby enabling us to rewrite our scripts and re-create our identities. Created by the ego, these B-movie scripts define our beliefs about ourselves, others and the world. "Too much risk involved, let's blame someone" and "I'm just trying to survive this job" are scripts that perpetuate denial.

To overcome obstacles rooted in denial, start with letting go of spoken scripts, your automatic verbal responses, along with the unspoken scripts that fill your head. For example, the ego loves for us to go home from work and worry all evening. Worrying about undesirable possibilities keeps the ego in control by focusing attention on the good/bad duality that defines the ego's existence. This ego-scripted control prevents us from experiencing the joy of living, the "courageous Yes" to our true being.

Think of scripts as an undercurrent eroding the fertile soil of your true Self. Each human spirit with whom you work brings to the forefront a particular worldview based on personality and environment. These fundamental influences merge with work experiences, and the perception-based worldview becomes "the truth" based upon a predetermined script (e.g., "Whatever we do it must be fair to everyone," "I'm getting too old for this," etc.). Many of these "truths" avoid everyday courage in favor of denial. Below are four tips to redesigning old scripts.

(1) See through the anguish that comes with transitions. Psychologists suggest it takes three weeks to start breaking old habits. Mental habits control our lives and steer us off course. "Most of us are accustomed to addictions that keep us looking outside of ourselves for fulfillment. We are caught up in *doing* rather than *being*, in *action* rather than *awareness*. It is hard for us to picture a state of complete calmness and repose in which thoughts and feelings cease to dance in perpetual motion. Yet it is through such a state of quietude that we can touch a level of joy and understanding impossible to achieve otherwise."[66] Becoming an observer of our own scripts requires effort. Slipping into a perpetual state of denial is easier than turning the spotlight on ourselves and recognizing our habitual mental patterns. But by identifying these patterns, we "own" them and can pinpoint how they affect others.

(2) Take action to implement the new design. Scripts we learned a long time ago become mental patterns that dictate thinking and behavior. For example, you might discover that your mindsets reveal how you tend to avoid certain people or circumstances in the hope that they will simply go away. Ask yourself, "How do I recognize bad situations, and how long does it take for me to get out?" An act of "courageous will" instigates change. In other words, make a conscious decision to live your life by staying focused. Simply observe yourself so that you recognize and sustain positive emotional energies—joy, happiness, love—and exit quickly from the influence of negative thoughts and emotions. "Emotions are the body's reaction to what the voice in the head is saying."[67]

(3) Find someone you trust to share in a dialogue. To step away from a cycle rooted in denial can be difficult, and people sometimes feel alone on the journey. Finding someone with whom to share progress helps sustain intentions and provides accountability and support. Wayne Teasdale writes, "To assent to the spiritual journey is to say 'yes' to our own ultimate growth as well as that of others. There is no greater gift we can give to others than to assist them on their way, to be there for them in their questions, their darkness, and their triumphs."[68]

(4) Invite stillness into your being. Courage requires you to step up and take action (not become busy or overcommitted!). Action needs a purpose. Purpose is found in self-awareness. Self-awareness comes in silence. In other words, outwardly manifesting our courage to overcome obstacles requires the paradoxical action of taking a step inward—deeper into our identities—to become increasingly self-aware. Only through self-knowledge, really knowing ourselves, can we begin to live fulfilled lives.

Staying in the Question

Denise is a human resource manager who has dealt with plenty of subtle abuse in the corporate environment: "When I first worked as a buyer at General Motors, I was the only woman in a department of approximately twelve men. I made a suggestion in a meeting one day. The men acted as though they didn't hear me. Then, a male colleague made the same suggestion, and everyone thought it was great. I was fed up, so I slammed my notebook on the table and said, 'I just made that suggestion and you all ignored me.' Speaking up made the difference!"

In Denise's situation, simply speaking the truth represented a real threat to her job security and required real courage. Knowing when to take the risk and when to *remove yourself from a bad situation* is supported through quieting the mind. You too can develop the courage to slow down, breathe deeply and surrender your ego-tinted version of truth. "Surrender refreshes and regenerates. Failure to surrender strains and wearies. Behind every genuine surrender lives a faith fulfilled; behind every failure to surrender lies confidence betrayed, a wound that will never be forgotten."[69] Are you consistent in quieting the ego-mind to achieve courage-centeredness? Consistency is a cousin to courage. Remember the old adage: slow and steady wins the race.

Reflect on a situation at work that causes tension (or worse) in your life. As you examine the situation, begin to notice your "default" courage settings. Then,

- suspend assumptions,
- detach from opinions and certainty about what you think is true,
- stay in the question rather than having the answer and
- take responsibility for your courage consciousness development.

By contrast, Donna Cameron described her first job after college. "It was a grand lesson in what not to do. The president of the company was a despot who continually berated employees and rarely, if ever, complimented or even acknowledged accomplishments. I worked in an office 3,000 miles from headquarters, yet everyone quaked at the prospect of arousing his ire. Neither creativity nor individuality was encouraged. When I hear the phrase 'toxic workplace,' this is what I picture."

Drawing on the insightful writings of her favorite poet, Donna averted denial by applying Rainer Maria Rilke's concept of staying in the question: "Staying in the question allows plenty of space for growth. One of the most useful pieces of advice I ever got is that you don't have to know everything before you act. Staying in the question means moving forward as soon as I feel I know enough to start something. It also means that I must begin with the faith that the knowledge, resources or whatever I need to succeed will manifest; and they always do. I love the concept of staying in the question or "living the question" because it allows for mystery and for the unknown, and that's where discovery takes place. As I invite more mystery and unknown in, my life seems to become wider and deeper, providing ever more mystery, hence, more discovery."

Establishing a status quo provides a sense of safety for the ego but eliminates mystery and the creative discovery it engenders. More importantly, status quo fosters denial by silencing courageous ideas and stymieing courage behaviors. Lawrence Diggs, an author and speaker believes it takes courage to question the status quo, "to admit a mistake when it will cost you your job, to befriend an unknown or unpopular person or group or risk rejection and public ridicule to support an unpopular position." On the opposite side of the coin, the positive action generated by courage creates a different type of safety – personal loyalties and a corporate ethic that honors courage and truth.

Do You Fear the Mysterious?

Experiencing abuse one time was simply enough for Donna. It really is very simple—you must remove yourself from bad situations quickly. Her experience provided rich insights about averting denial in order to design exit strategies: "Sometimes, the most courageous thing we can do is leave a toxic workplace or stand up and say, 'this is who I am, and if that isn't what you want here, let's get that out in the open right now.' If one has plenty of other prospects, or no financial worries, that is probably much easier to do than if one desperately needs that paycheck to make the mortgage payment and buy groceries. There's a quote that speaks to me of reaching the point where one must claim one's courage":

And the day came when the risk to remain tight in a bud
was more painful than the risk it took to blossom.[70]

In order to overcome denial, our perceptions about our personal courage play a key role. "Perception reduces reality to what is accessible to us through the small range of our senses: what we can see, hear, smell, taste, and touch.... Every thought implies a perspective, and every perspective, by its very nature, implies limitation, which ultimately means that it is not true, at least not absolutely. Only the whole is true, but the whole cannot be spoken or thought."[71] Do you base your reality on the limited perceptual range of your senses?

Donna expanded her thoughts about how perception slices and limits courage. "Many people perceive courage as something extraordinary. They think courage is what you summon when tragedy strikes. Equally important is the everyday courage, the quiet courage that is with us when we go to work or spend time with friends and family. Courage is more often in the little things—revealing our vulnerability, saying what needs to be said or keeping silent when itching to say something hurtful."

Is Donna's type of courage consciousness familiar to you? If not, practice letting go of attachments to outcomes. As you succeed in letting go, unhealthy desires and emotions will begin to diminish. "We tend to adjust our view of reality to serve our desires.... Contemplation allows us to acquire a clearer perspective, free of distortions created when we see reality through the lens of our desires. This subtle rationalization is actually self-deception."[72] The intention of contemplation is become our true Self. In other words, allowing your desires and attachments to shade your view of reality is a subtle form of denial.

The rampant state of denial perpetuates itself in many forms, all of which can easily be overcome simply by simplifying your life. One of the easiest, most effective examples is trading your television time for some form of spirituality (stopping, meditating, reading sacred texts, praying, etc.). As Albert Einstein once said,

Out of clutter, find simplicity. From discord, find harmony.
In the middle of difficulty lies opportunity.[73]

Doing No-thing

As you practice "doing no-thing," you will find that ideas grow and life turns into a daily expedition into the beauty and mystery of life and happiness. Thomas Keating said, "No-thing means no fixed point of reference within yourself." As the saying goes,

Happiness is not having what you want. It is wanting what you have.[74]

What helps you to stop thinking? What slows you down? To embark on the inner journey and awaken your spiritual courage requires this process of fulfillment. "It is important to be self-directed: We must decide where our life is going, what direction it will take and why. That kind of decisiveness requires courage and perspective; it means that we must cut ourselves free from our cultural conditioning."[75]

Blanche Napoleon left a toxic company to become president of a small entrepreneurial company. No longer traveling 155,000 miles a year gave her time to cultivate a new perspective: "I am so excited to be part of something so small and fresh, plus I was given equity in the company. We are having so much fun already!"

Slowing down allows you to eliminate the state of denial that perpetuates self-inflicted abuse and become more civil and loving to yourself and others. Many people learn how to let go and trust that they don't have to be the ultimate workaholic or political gamesman to succeed at work. As Eckhart Tolle espouses, "The ego knows nothing of Being but believes you will eventually be saved by doing. If you are in the grip of the ego, you believe that by doing more and more you will eventually accumulate enough 'doings' to make yourself feel complete at some point in the future. You won't. You will only lose yourself in doing...."[76]

In the first chapter we explored "doing versus being." One of the ways to accomplish a shift from "doing to being" is to let go of thoughts related to attachments, expectations, justifications, judgments, etc. (more on this in Chapter 4). Tolle again: "'*This, too, will pass.*' What is it about these simple words that makes them so powerful? ... Nonresistance, nonjudgment, and nonattachment are the three aspects of true freedom and enlightened living."[77] Balancing body, mind and spirit is important, but most people who find this balance must pass through an agonizing decision-making process.

As Tolle affirms, some people "find themselves" when they finally step away from "an insane work environment or living situation. So before you discover what is right for you on the external level … you may have to find out what is not right, what no longer works, what is incompatible with your inner purpose."[78] This is where you discover your courage and design your style. Suddenly, "You realize that all along there was something tremendous within you, and you did not know it."[79]

Outside the Flock

Bec's "courage style" won her several good project manager and engineering jobs and contracts, but it also lost her at least one or two lucrative job opportunities. While working at an aerospace corporation, Bec experienced the stress and worry of making a tough decision: whether or not to file formal gender discrimination charges against her company.

Setting denial aside, she said, "I spoke out gracefully and wrote professionally via the formal corporate channels. I exercised the 'Just Say No' attitude to injustice, gender discrimination and retaliation against me and other women at that company. For taking that strong stand in my truth, I was fired. Following the rules of the legal system, I stood in my courage. I stood by my true being—strong and direct."

Bec's courageous actions may have cost her a job, but they also represent a significant step up. Refusing to act could have initiated a slide into complete denial. On the other hand, "Action is the inexorably sincere measure of our abilities. We may make grandiose promises with our words, but actions cannot lie."[80]

Meet Brenda (fictitious name), a senior vice president for a media company. For over seven years, she lived in denial to endure the tyrannical abuse of her toxic boss. One awful day, she glanced down at her body and shook her head at the twenty-five pounds she had put on. Her anguish about his rude behavior and her self-inflicted abuse was squeezing the joy from her life. Brenda had the conventional justifications that keep a woman stuck in denial: she was the breadwinner, and their only child was about to start college. She pondered giving notice, but in a weak economy, she was unable to see past her paycheck or her corner office.

Finally, Brenda found the courage to inform the human resources director about her situation. She said, "As soon as my boss was appropriately confronted, he stopped delivering the abusive comments. Just like that!" While intimidating bosses are typically stubborn and resistant to feedback, uncomfortable with showing vulnerability and rarely self-reflective, you cannot let them get away with diminishing your spirit.

Brenda forgot to pause and reflect. Out of touch with her body, she had forgotten the tools to balance her professional and personal life, and she fell asleep to her Being. "Body awareness not only anchors you in the present moment, it is a doorway out of the prison that is the ego. It also strengthens the immune system and the body's ability to heal itself."[81]. The difference between Bec and Brenda's stories is that Bec knew her "courage style." She was able to summon it quickly, face the facts and remove herself from a bad situation. How quickly do you size up bad situations and take a stand?

Shel Horowitz, green marketing consultant believes people do not display their courage at work for "fear of being ignored, shouted down or faced with hostile behavior." But he asks himself, "What's the worst that can happen?"

"Yes," he continues, "you might lose your job—it's happened to me. I complained about the ethics of how things were set up and I was let go. But, if it's a job where your courage is not appreciated, you'd be happier elsewhere anyway. Getting out of a bad situation is the first step to creating a better situation. My advice is to not let that fear hold you back. The reward for having the courage to do the right thing far outweighs the risk." In spite of her best intentions, Brenda allowed herself to become a victim, "a very common role," writes Tolle. "The form of attention it seeks is sympathy or pity or others' interest in *my* problems, 'me and my story.' Seeing oneself as a victim is an element in many egoic patterns, such as complaining, being offended, outraged, and so on.... The ego does not want an end to its 'problems' because they are part of its identity."[82] Consequently, denial is essentially written into the ego's psychological programming, and a meditative practice is the only proven method to switch off that programming.

The Bully Boss

Drs. Gary and Ruth Namie started The Workplace Bullying Institute years ago in 1998 when Ruth experienced bullying firsthand (at the hands of a woman supervisor) prompting their research and a desire to pass laws to curtail workplace abuses. In a phone conversation with Gary, he shared with me some facts from the *2007 WBI-Zogby US Workplace Bullying Survey*. "More perpetrators are men, sixty percent, than are women forty percent, but when women are bullies, they choose women as targets seventy-one percent of the time. Sadly, when the bully finds his or her target, the target pays with his or her job."

In other words, if the target has the courage to confront the bully, the target will usually lose his or her job. Gary observes, "Over one in three American workers suffer bullying while another 12% witness it. That's 71.5 million Americans who know full well what bullying is." What do you witness today? At work, do you see courageous leadership behaviors or insidious bureaucrats behaving like schoolyard bullies?

"If the bully's a woman, she can pick on women all she wants."[83] The Namies write, "Chronic bullies end careers and shatter the emotional lives of their targets.... We know that eighty-nine percent of bullies are bosses ... workplace politicians. Their goal is simple—to control people they target. To do this, they engage in a variety of tactics.... They all serve to shame, humiliate, and treat the Target like a powerless person."[84] A glance at Dr. Hawkins' "Map of Consciousness" reveals that shame, guilt, apathy, grief, fear, anger—all of the negative emotions felt by the bully's target—are below 200. Have you experienced any of the tactics of bullies? Do you perpetuate these actions in yourself or in others?

The problem will lessen only when we begin to see past our own denial and recognize the self-truths that most of us would prefer to avoid at all cost. Overall, Dr. Gary Namie's findings reveal that "It [bullying] is an 'undiscussable' topic at work because of its career-jeopardizing potential."[85] Overall, Dr. Namie says that seventy-two percent of bullies are bosses and fifty-five percent of those bullied are rank-and-file workers who choose not to sue much less file a complaint; in other words, denial is the real issue! Like domestic violence victims, "Observers stayed in denial because of fear."[86]

The Choice is Always Yours

If you are thinking that the people and their struggles presented in this chapter have nothing to do with you, do not be fooled. None of them saved someone's life or won an award for heroism. They simply learned to remove themselves from bad situations, sometimes just by letting go. They learned to focus on unknown possibilities in the present instead of projecting their happiness into some future longing. Do you refuse to accept unhappiness?

"Coming into the clarity and truth of self-awareness, self-understanding, free of illusions and delusions, we know a continual joy, a fullness of bliss that will never pass away."[87] What can you do? Begin by seeking what joyfully motivates you at work as well as what causes the most stress. To diminish stress, embrace the spiritual journey—one day at a time—and consciously observe the withering ego. Through the practice of increasing Spiritual Intelligence (SQ) at work, your courage awareness grows and expands. Escaping denial, you self-actualize your full potential at work. Your life lights up when your actions become consistently inspired by your everyday courage.

Courage Development Questions to Ponder

- What is one automatic tendency or behavior that you can identify in your life that keeps you stuck in denial?

- When you truly observe yourself, what do you begin to see behind your automatic behavior?
- When was the last time you removed yourself from a bad situation? How long did it take?

Chapter 3
Work Without Regrets—
Eliminating Blame

*People are always blaming circumstances for what they are. I don't
believe in circumstances. The people who get on in this world are those
with the courage to get up and look for the circumstances they want and
if they can't find them, they have the courage to make them.*

— George Bernard Shaw

Many historical incidents illustrate the struggles between the developing
United States with its land-hungry settlers and the various American
Indian tribes. At different times all the Indian habitants knew that the life
they had created, enjoyed and endured for centuries was coming to an end.
Sacagawea—the well-known guide to Lewis and Clark's Corps of Discovery—
might have escaped the history books altogether had her reputation not been
resurrected by the suffragists in the early 1900s. Fortunately, we know quite a lot
about this woman whose courage left an indelible mark upon the path of a
young nation called the United States of America.

When Sacagawea was only about ten years old, Minnetaree Indians
attacked her Hidatsa family and took her hostage. As her abductors
transported her 600 miles through the mountains of Montana and into
North Dakota, Sacagawea faced very real dangers and feared she would
never see her family again. The girl whose name means "Bird Woman" had
ample opportunity to blame others for her hard life; instead, she drew on
the energy of her courage to face the challenge of merging with a new
family and culture. Sacagawea did not choose her situation, but as she
entered her teen years, she chose the responsibilities of womanhood over
blame and victimization.

Sacagawea ended up as the wife and property of French trapper
Toussaint Charbonneau, who wasted no time getting her pregnant. Subjected
to such emotional trauma, Sacagawea must have come to understand the
truth in Gary Zukav's words: "Within each experience of pain or negativity
is the opportunity to challenge the perception that lies behind it, the fear that
lies behind it, and to choose to learn with wisdom. The fear will not vanish
immediately, but it will disintegrate as you work with courage. When fear
ceases to scare you, it cannot stay."[88]

47

When Charbonneau heard about the Corps of Discovery expedition led by captains Lewis and Clark, he convinced the captains that he and Sacagawea could serve as interpreters. On April 7, 1805, Lewis and Clark led their band of explorers—which now included Charbonneau, Sacagawea and their newborn son—up the Missouri in six small canoes and two boats. Immersed in the expedition for 863 days and 8,000 miles, she proved invaluable as an interpreter, cook and guide. Exemplifying everyday courage, Sacagawea refused the easy path of blaming others and stepped up too.

Work without regrets.

During their trek, they met the Nez Perce tribe in what is now northeastern Oregon. Their chief at the time, Joseph the Elder, had as a young boy converted to Christianity and learned English. The explorers, exhausted and weak from a brutal winter conditions in the Bitterroot Mountains, needed food, supplies and horses. The Nez Perce rekindled their bodies and minds, supplying all their needs.

After a miserable stay on the Pacific Coast the Corps of Discovery began the return journey and once again stayed with the Nez Perce while waiting for the snow to melt on the Bitterroots. But, it would not take long for the good intentions of the Nez Perce to be forgotten by a land-hungry United States. Like Sacagawea, the Nez Perce tribe would face their fear—the fear of losing their homes where they had lived in harmony with the land for centuries. Like Sacagawea, Nez Perce Chief Joseph (1840-1904) also worked without regrets, demonstrating remarkable courage.

As the U.S. government tried to take over the tribe's ancestral land, Chief Joseph worked to maintain peace and keep his people in their homeland. Before the elder Joseph died, the tribe had actively supported peace with the United States. But in 1855 the U.S. government reneged on a treaty that allowed the Nez Perce to remain on their land. After several failed treaties, Joseph the Younger succeeded his father as chief, and things drastically changed. The new Chief Joseph tried every possible appeal to the federal authorities to keep the tribe on the land of his ancestors. Before his death, the Elder Joseph had said, "My son, never forget my dying words. This country holds your father's body. Never sell the bones of your father and mother."[89] Unwilling to ignore his father's dying words, Chief Joseph joined with other war leaders to resist the U.S. Army.

In 1877 under threat of attack from the U.S. Army, Chief Joseph decided to lead his people to the safety of Canada, 1,400 miles away. Led by Joseph's younger brother, Olikut, the Nez Perce warriors fought without regrets. Fewer than 200 warriors, outnumbered ten to one, fought and died to protect their families and friends attempting to reach Canada. When Chief Joseph formally surrendered on October 5, it was Chief Joseph's courageous leadership, exemplified in his surrender speech that left its mark on history. Rather than assign blame, "He became a hero not for his battle planning and prowess as a fighter but for his diplomacy and his example as a man of humanity, respect for people of all backgrounds, and most of all, unfailing love of freedom and homeland."[90] Chief Joseph lived out his days exemplifying "heart and spirit" courage, speaking eloquently on behalf of his people against U.S. injustice.

Tripped Up

People repeatedly tell me, "I wish I had acted sooner," a comment that exemplifies regret. "The desire to undo the past is understandable but futile and blinds one to the opportunities of the present. A limitation in one area of life is simultaneously the opening of opportunities and options in other areas."[91] The only remedy for regret is to live with courage from your heart and spirit, which includes not allowing the false self to design a life of blame.

"The false self is a monumental illusion, a load of habitual thinking patterns and emotional routines that are stored in the brain and nervous system. Like programs in a computer, they tend to reactivate every time a particular life situation pushes the appropriate button."[92] Chief Joseph and Sacagawea, empowered by nothing more than courage, chose not to allow those mental and emotional programs to run their lives, and so can you.

Our culture has a tendency to highlight fearful, sensational, amazing, tragic, miraculous or scandalous events—infidelity, extreme whistle-blowing, postal shootings, greed, corruption, etc. The underlying message? If your story is not a headline, it is not valuable. Obviously, this is not true, but this message from the media plays on our fears and helps lock us into the ego's survival mode—the default mode of the false self.

To escape this trap, you must claim the courage to learn what represents *your* truth, not the media's truth, not your best friend's truth—*your* truth. What represents your level of Spiritual Intelligence (SQ) at work? "To follow a path with spiritual intelligence, or a path with heart, is to be deeply committed and dedicated."[93] And ask yourself this question: What percentage of my life, right now, is filled with regrets? Regrets represent lost courage.

Recognizing your past regrets, you learn to *work without regrets*. The task, then, is to cultivate courage and trust that going for it is better than dying without it. This is the difference between heart and mind. An art director, Jeff Davis had experienced this distinction more than once.

> The biggest obstacle I have faced came when my division was surplused after 9/11. I had the choice to take a dream job on Madison Avenue or stay home and be Mr. Mom

for my two-year-old son and newborn daughter. I had many fears; fear of a loss of my skills after being out of the race for the next 5 or 6 years, fear of losing out on professional development and fear that being a "stay-at-home dad" really wasn't the "man-as-provider" way to go. After much soul-searching, my wife and I decided that my children would benefit more from my being at home than they would from the increased salary I would have received. The obstacle, as always, was my own fear. Once I had faced it and understood it, the rest was merely details. I chose to stay at home. As my children grew, I began to volunteer, first as a member of the board of directors at the nursery school they would attend then as a member of the parent organization of their elementary school, where I put my design skills to work. The exposure my work received as a volunteer led to a few lucrative contracts in my community, and I now enjoy a thriving entrepreneur career as an independent designer and filmmaker. I had chosen what was right over what would have calmed my fears, and have never regretted it for a moment.

Jeff said that he knows that, at the end of the day, he will be the face he sees in the mirror.

Learning to stay present may not banish your personality's fear and the blame that it spawns, but you will at least begin to diminish the tendencies (especially blame) that keep you stuck in fear. Fear blocks and paralyzes the heart; therefore, fear blocks courage. Rennie Davis writes,

> Blame is the choice to make yourself victim. Instead of blame and victim, you take responsibility for everything that happens to you. You create your own world. Ending blame is like ending a chronic addiction. One of the great steps in the journey of self-awareness is the day a person sees the subtleties of blame cascading through their thoughts and learns to unlock the prison created by the need to blame. In previous generations, replacing blame with unconditional love was achieved by a handful of people. Future generations honored them as saints in diverse religions and stories. Their lives suggested that any human being in any time or place has the innate capacity to change themselves and thereby re-script their own life experience.[94]

In your spiritual truth you will find courage. Is some aspect of your personality constantly tripping you up, repeatedly causing regret and then placing the blame elsewhere? As Marianne Williamson observes, "The ego would have us believe that, as soon as we place the blame on someone else, we'll feel better. But that's just a temporary delusion—something the ego specializes in. Once we get over the temporary high of having cast the blame away from us, it will come back to us a hundredfold,"[95] not a good tactic for working without regret.

Eckhart Tolle helps us understand how regrets pile up: "The psychological condition of fear is divorced from any concrete and true immediate danger. It comes in many forms: unease, worry, anxiety, nervousness, tension, dread, phobia and so on. This kind of psychological fear is always of something that *might* happen, not of something that is happening now. *You* are in the here and now, while your mind is in the future."[96] The mind functions like a beehive with its incessant chatter. "The brain chatter of thinking is a form of fixation. Awareness is not what you think but what you don't think.... Expanding awareness comes down to just two words: let go."[97] How do you quiet that type of mental busyness? First, ask yourself what obstacles keep you from slowing down and letting go. Inertia? Intimidation? Denial? Blame? Once you identify your obstacles, what are you to do?

To start the process of slowing down your busyness, begin to eliminate the barrage of useless thoughts, particularly the old monologues that find blame or make excuses. "So how can the rest of us access "slow thinking," especially in a world that prizes speed and action? The first step is to relax— put aside impatience, stop struggling and learn to accept uncertainty and inaction. Wait for the ideas to incubate below the radar rather than striving to brainstorm them to the surface. Let the mind be quiet and still.... 'Don't just do something; sit there.'"[98]

In this process, you are highlighting your inner nature—the true Self that lies beneath your ordinary awareness. The way to enable this shift in the mind's capacity is to be present. Paradoxically, it is in sitting still, turning inward and being quiet that you find this divine place of energy, liberation and courage. A pensive journey gradually releases your fear. Contemplate what you fear, and you will begin to dissolve it. How do you do this? Begin to notice the emotional triggers that set you off at work or that seduce you because they are only a response to a thought. Thomas Keating writes, "One of the biggest impediments to spiritual growth is that we do not perceive our own hidden motivations."[99]

This can keep you from finding your inner light and fulfilling your unique calling. Have you even identified your calling? If not, ask yourself what you love to do and what you do well. Marianne Williamson writes,

"There is a 'ring of fear' around the light within us, through which the ego seeks to block our entrance into the heaven within."[100] Spiritual transformation may mean that things at work get worse before they get better. At times, you may feel like you are a coward before you recognize courage consciousness and put it into practice. Gandhi "viewed courage as an essential vitamin for each individual's spiritual growth—in contrast to cowardice, which reduces a person's sense of value and self-respect. Without courage, love and the search for truth are impossible."[101]

The process of slowing down puts us in touch with reality—our own everyday issues instead of the sensationalism of the media culture. This astonishing yet simple process releases us from the tyranny of old habits and scripts, uncovering a deep set of self-actuating principles. "We are lifted from weak to strong; we are lifted from lack to abundance; we are lifted from pain to peace; we are lifted from fear to love. None of this happens in an instant, but over time, through the daily process of living."[102] Many contemplative practices can help initiate this transformative process—sacred reading, chanting, Tai Chi, hiking, a silent retreat, any practice that moves you beyond words and thoughts into the inner silence of the heart where the ego's fears dissipate.

"Real fear," writes Gavin de Becker in *The Gift of Fear*, "is a signal intended to be very brief, a mere servant of intuition. But though few would argue that extended, unanswered fear is destructive, millions choose to stay there. They may have forgotten or never learned that fear is not an emotion like sadness or happiness, either of which might last a long while.... True fear is a survival signal that sounds only in the presence of danger; yet unwarranted fear has assumed a power over us that it holds over no other creature on earth."[103] What counts is how you deal with it. If you can observe your own mental chatter, you will be able to monitor fearful feelings and let go of them as soon as they arise.

Elusive Predicament

Jocelyne Gray's approach to her work life reinforced her unconscious choice to live in the mode of the victim.

> When I was seven years old, I fell four feet from a playground toy. This accident began my phobias, especially heights. Falling flat on my face, I had to have gravel dug out of my gums. To this day, I freak at the fourth step of a ladder. Panic consumes me. I get nauseous when looking out a second story window. Over the years, my fears have developed and moved into my work life. These fears are so strong I will stay in a mediocre job just because it's familiar, secure, and I know

my place (at the bottom). Why risk losing the guaranteed income, easy projects and people who accept me for my dream career?

Jocelyne was a civil engineer with an Engineer-in-Training certificate. Based on her fears and self-blame, she was accomplished at going through all the worst-case scenarios. I met her while presenting a program called "Courage: The Untapped Reservoir." She later confided,

> After that program, I recognized and summoned my courage to face the truth about my current position in my hometown and my fears about relocating. I had lost interest in my projects, and despite reassurances that our jobs were secure, the rumors were flying about work slowing down. I became depressed and began manifesting physical ailments like nausea and headaches. I worried that, if I left, my mother would feel betrayed; but I stepped up, sent my resume out and accepted interviews.
>
> When I received two job offers, I had to conquer my fear of disloyalty. My fears speculated what my supervisors would think when I told them I had decided to leave. First, I visualized my boss losing his temper and throwing me off the premises; then, I flipped the image to a positive one, of "congratulations" and "thank you" for the three years I had worked there. Reality is rarely extreme. What I actually received was a pleasant "best of luck" and "we'll miss you."
>
> Before I accepted the job, I was shaky, nauseous and anxious about moving to a new town where I knew few people. I hate being alone, especially at night. Would I let my fears of the unknown paralyze me, or would I accept the job of a lifetime? My mind started in with all the normal worst-case scenarios: Would I be able to relate to the other employees, was I competent enough for the new job since my responsibilities increased exponentially, and was this really the right company for me? Then, I stopped to review the courageous events in my life, and I prayed.

Hopefully, you notice Jocelyne's progression in discovering her personal courage and then manifesting that courage in her work life. For over two years, Jocelyne had been at her new home, new job and new life. She and her husband were amazed with the experience and their incredible new sense of freedom. "The move required us to prioritize our lives and simplify. By venturing into the unknown, I have found a growing company that is family friendly, provides challenging projects and opportunities for advancement. I am able to participate more in the Society of Women Engineers. With my courage still flowing through my veins, I am able to accept additional responsibilities within the company and SWE."

A few years later, Jocelyne told me,

> My new work is exciting, the responsibility is growing, and I am being groomed for a management promotion. After that, there is only the possibility of becoming CEO. It's better than being at the bottom of the food chain waiting for old fish to die. I also aspire to be SWE president, own my own consulting firm, be a mother and earn my master's degree before I am fifty-years old. Many of my fears have diminished, and I am able to say "Yes" to leadership opportunities. Some is due to maturity (I am twenty-eight years old), some is from the SWE support, and part is from your presentation and newsletters.

Facing circumstances allows you to keep carrying on. Carrying on is a cousin to courage.

As your courage consciousness matures at work, you will notice huge shifts in your perspective about fear, blame and how to achieve fulfillment in your work life, validating the choice of courage consciousness over attachments that trigger life's emotional dramas. Fear seems more powerful in times of doubt, tempting us to resort to blame as a defense mechanism, but as Jocelyne developed her courage consciousness, she became more cognizant of the mental chatter that triggers her fears and the subtle cascades of blame that pollute our thoughts. Real estate developer Troy G. Smith concurs, "There is only one thing that thwarts people's ability to display courage, and that is fear. Cowardice is fear, jealousy is fear, anger is fear, self-doubt is fear, lack of faith is fear, narrow-mindedness is fear, racism is fear, hate is fear. Fear is the antithesis of courage no matter what form it takes."

Blame, though generally unspoken, is plentiful. Begin to notice the triggers in your own work life. What do you dread? What makes you anxious? What do you fear? When something triggers your fears, do you look for an excuse or someone to blame? After a bad experience, do you tend to blame yourself? Like denial, blame can be a huge obstacle that can keep you stuck in a state of fear. What if you moved from the blame cycle to a no-fault decision-making process?

Walk on the Edge

Trust is a big issue when facing fears. Do you trust the Universe constantly or infrequently? French poet and philosopher Guillaume Apollinaire said,

> *"Come to the edge."*
> *"We can't. We're afraid."*
> *"Come to the edge."*
> *"We can't. We will fall!"*
> *"Come to the edge."*
> *And they came.*
> *And he pushed them.*
> *And they flew.*[104]

"Try looking at life as a beautifully well-organized dynamic. Trust the Universe. Trusting means that the circumstance you are in is working toward your best and most appropriate end. There is no when to that. There is no if to that. It is."[105] This is very different from being enthusiastic or optimistic about the future. Dawn Josephson is the owner and founder of Cameo Publications. Her personal courage is adeptly bundled with fear, guts and happiness. How does she combine such diverse elements? "One week after graduating college, I sold all my material possessions and headed north on I-95 from Melbourne, Florida. My friends and family thought I had totally lost my mind. But I knew in my heart that I had to leave, and I trusted my judgment. As I drove north, I remember feeling a sense of excitement, an air of freedom and a healthy dose of unrelenting fear. I thought about turning back home at many exits, but that's when my courage kicked in and I had the mental resolve to keep driving."

With no particular destination in mind, Dawn knew she would end up somewhere where she could take the next step along her career path.

> I stopped at various places along the way to check out the job and housing markets including a stop in Pennsylvania. I ended up landing a technical writing job, so I settled in Hershey. It didn't take long to learn that writing software manuals was not for me, so I quit after only six months. Everyone told me I was crazy, but I trusted that I would be okay. In a matter of days, I landed a job with a national business journal. Thanks to my courage, I eventually worked my way up to editor-in-chief.
>
> One time, the publisher challenged me to develop new editorial content for the magazine. To expand my skills, I attended seminars. I had to pay with my own money and

attend on my own time, but it made me more valuable in the end. When the office manager wanted feedback, I gave my opinions honestly and tactfully. I received some criticism, but that was okay because I knew that in the long run I would come out on top.

Working without regrets, Dawn left no room in her heart for blame, which is why, in spite of her fears, Dawn pursued a fulfilling career. Deep down, Dawn always felt that she would one day be her own boss. "Every day during my lunch break, I would take a walk to a nearby park. During my walks, I visualized myself working from home." Dawn committed to consciously stop and create her life. She continued, "I used each day and each challenge as a learning experience. About three years after starting that magazine job, I began doing freelance work on the side. Again, I listened to my gut, my intuition, and I knew when it was time to quit and devote myself to my freelance endeavors."

Gavin de Becker affirms Dawn's approach. "Trusting intuition is the exact opposite of living in fear. In fact, the role of fear in your life lessens as your mind and body come to know that you will listen to the quiet wind chime, and have no need for Klaxons."[106] Dawn continued to stand in her courage and design her life. "I wasn't yet earning enough money to replace my full-time salary, but I was confident that the money would come. When I handed in my notice, the publisher criticized my decision, assuring me that I would fail and never make anything of myself. Ironically, instead of making me doubt my decision, his criticisms made me more confident. If I hadn't had the courage to believe in myself, his words could have easily been the death of my freelance career," not to mention an easy target for Dawn to blame had she failed to step up in courage.

Celebrating ten years as a successful business owner, Dawn said, "I tap into my courage daily. I can't second-guess myself, and I have to trust my judgment that I'm doing what is right and fair for me and my clients." Was Dawn scared through each phase of her journey? "Yes," she said, "I was terrified, actually. But that's when I called upon my inner courage to guide me and help me see the true direction I was to take. Without that level of self-trust, I doubt I would have been able to make such monumental changes in my life or create a career that I love."

Dawn talks about her "Courageous Decision Process." So I asked her if she could pinpoint the specific steps in her process. After giving the matter a great deal of thought, she replied.

As I was making the decision to move my home-based business, I realized that I didn't focus my energies on what could go wrong. Here are a few of the steps that I employed.

1. Believe that you are capable of anything.
2. Acknowledge the risks, but don't dwell on them. Focus your energy on the positive outcomes you envision so you can stay on track. When those negatives pop into your mind, it's the positives that will keep you committed to your decision.
3. Disregard "contingency plans" and "alternate approaches" (if the first attempt fails, then put another approach in place).

I strongly believe that our thoughts and our internal vision of ourselves determine where we go in life. So I choose to keep the "best-case scenarios" running in my head. In my gut, I feel the fear. In my head, I see the success, and the stronger my feeling of fear gets, the more vivid the positive image in my head gets. It's a balance between the two.

The important point here is that Dawn chose a courageous response to her fear instead of transferring the source of that fear onto someone else through blame. Dawn's advice to working women is worth noting here: "Realize that challenges are learning opportunities. When you confront the challenge, you are actually learning a vital life lesson. I know this is easier said than done. I've had coworkers gossip about me; I've had bosses undermine my efforts; I've had clients reject me. I've had to stand up to male bosses and colleagues despite childhood sexual abuse; I've had to keep up my professional obligations while grieving the death of my son.... While those are all trying times, I look at them as opportunities to glean wisdom, strengthen my resolve and learn things about my character."

How do you learn to trust your intuition and stop blaming and making excuses? Dawn had the courage to bet her career on her intuition. "The root of the word intuition, *tuere*, means 'to guard, to protect.'"[107] Do you trust your intuition? Are you able to size up a situation and recognize the best course of action? "Intuition is really a matter of learning how to see—of looking for cues or patterns that ultimately show you what to do.... Experienced decision-makers see a different world than novices do.... If they discover unintended consequences that could get them into trouble, they discard that solution and look for another one.... They don't need the best solution. They just need the one that works"[108] With each step, Dawn applied her intuitive vision, and that is what separates the good leaders from the rest of the pack. After all, CEOs do not have time to analyze all the quantifiable data. They must develop their intuitive vision to find the solutions that work.

Like Dawn, you can develop your intuitive vision through self-studied reflection. Reflection reflects Spiritual Intelligence (SQ) at work. The natural progression towards higher SQ leads from reflection, through understanding, to wisdom. The way to solve any problem, practical or intellectual, in a spiritually intelligent way is to place it in a wider perspective from which it can be seen more clearly. The deepest perspective of all comes from the centre, from the ultimate meaning and value that drives the situation or problem. Gaining this perspective begins with a process of simple **reflection**—going over the day or project, focusing on where there are difficulties, and thinking how these difficulties have arisen. Such reflection is a daily necessity of the spiritually intelligent life. The next step is to think of possible alternatives to the present situation and to reflect on the likely outcomes of pursuing any of these alternative paths. This leads to an understanding of how the situation can be improved, or indeed whether it can be improved at all.[109]

Courage Cradles Your Actions

Fear and courage live in many perspectives. A courageous person at work leans toward reflecting and then acting willingly rather than reacting out of fear. Unwilling to let anyone else design their lives, courageous people have an inner compulsion to conquer fear for its own sake. Judith Lasater writes, "Many times I think that I lack courage because I feel that I must accomplish a difficult task without feeling afraid. The most important thing to know about courage is that it cradles your action even though you are afraid.... You can rest assured that when you act from true courage, the people, the tools, and your own inner knowing ... will be available to you."[110]

Jocelyne and Dawn demonstrated self-awareness, enabling them to recognize the power of courage over fear. "When surrounded by fear, contradiction, betrayal; when the 'fight or flight' alarm bells are going off in your head and everything inside you wants to brace and defend itself, the infallible way to extricate yourself and reclaim your home in that sheltering kingdom is simply to freely release what you are holding onto...."[111] How do you do this? The proper environment, one that breeds and fosters courage can be invaluable. But actually starting this process requires that you learn what Dr. Hawkins calls the "circular journey of the spirit." He writes, "The Presence is silent and conveys a state of peace. It's infinitely gentle and yet like a rock. With it, all fear disappears, and spiritual joy occurs on a quiet level of inexplicable ecstasy."[112]

"Awakened Doing"

I had been working for several years to chip away my own false self. Between studies and Centering Prayer meditation, I began to experience life as a human "being" rather than a "human doer." During this restorative process, regrets crumble and we discover self-forgiveness, peace and centeredness. Eckhart Tolle calls this "awakened doing." He writes, "Awakened doing is the alignment of your outer purpose—what you do—with your inner purpose—awakening and staying awake…. Consciousness flows through you into this world. It flows into your thoughts and inspires them. It flows into what you do and guides and empowers it."[113] Do you experience this alignment, this energy at work? If not, what fears are holding you back?

Bill Hammer is a wealth management professional with extensive credentials. His definition of courage is "acting in the face of fear—doing what I know I should do even though I may think that I cannot do it, doing what is right even though I will not benefit or that it may not be in my best interest, and taking on a difficult or uncomfortable task." Bill shared how his courage has evolved.

When I went into high school I was four feet eleven-and-a-half and weighed about 90 pounds. I liked football but realized that I was too big to be the ball and too small to be a player. I was sure to letter in swimming, but some of the other swimmers said I was good only because I was so small and had no weight to pull.

Then, I considered wrestling. I could see that it took a tremendous amount of skill and ability, and everyone was up against someone his own size. I had no experience in this sport and heard that many kids had been wrestling since grade school. When I finally decided to go out for wrestling, a girl about my size blurted out that even she could beat me! So with the fear of failure and the discouraging words from that girl, I decided to leave my swimming success. I took a step of courage and went out for the wrestling team without any experience. I worked hard and even read some books on wrestling.

My first year, I was the city sophomore champion in my weight class. Eventually I became team captain and earned a college scholarship in wrestling. This experience helped strengthen my courage to try other things in life. I also found that, when I received encouragement and support from other people, I seemed to have more courage and do better at the things I faced.

Today, at fifty-seven years old, Bill's insight into his fears and how he faces courage at work continue.

Just starting my own business was scary. What if I didn't succeed? But I faced that fear and started my business just like I did with my wrestling career. While I have been successful so far, I still face fears. It takes courage to face these things. Facing them and overcoming them helps me take on new challenges.

Now I am facing a new fear by doing something very new to me, but I feel that I can succeed at it because of my past victories. I am trying to develop something that will help me, my kids and my clients. It will require a lot of hard work, but I am willing to face my fears and the challenge of this new project.

Bill shared with me that he thought most people could be more successful than they are if they would just face their fears with courage and work through them. He continued, "Success comes from having the courage to face our fears with whatever we have and to make ourselves better equipped to do what we think we cannot do."

Rise Above It

After being fired from the helm of Hewlett-Packard, Carly Fiorina said she was "at peace." "My soul is intact. The worst thing I could have imagined happened.... I lost my job in the most public way possible, and the press had a field day with it all over the world. And guess what? I'm still here.... The truth is, I'm proud of the life I've lived so far, and though I've made my share of mistakes, I have no regrets.... You can spend a lifetime resenting the tests, angry about the slights and the injustices. Or you can rise above it."[114] I still find it amazing that someone could endure such public humiliation without resorting to blame.

Kay Gilley, an intention expert writes, "When I describe 'intention,' I expressly distinguish it from goal-setting.... The cycle of setting a goal, getting the object, and then needing another goal and object is addictive. It is the way we feed our egos instead of nourishing our souls. Intentions are deeper. They are what the soul is longing for when the ego substitutes with a desire for a new toy, person, experience or pleasure.... Ask the question, 'If I were to have that, what would it give me that would be even more important?' The process stops the addictive cycle."[115]

Without clear intentions, leadership often succumbs to fear and seeks only to maintain the status quo. With a conscious heart, you can overcome fearfulness and begin to uncover the hidden hunger for genuine happiness at work. This starts with simple beginnings that include laughing at yourself. Are you having fun at work? Do you remain deeply consistent with your intentions (not goal-setting)?

Gilley writes, "It is impossible to overestimate the power of our intentions to create what we choose, but we must recognize that we have a choice, make the choice, and act in accordance with the choice we have made.... We must be willing to surrender all ego ... and step up to our full potential."[116] This is the realm of courage consciousness. Tolle teaches us, "The essence of who you are is consciousness. Every thought, every desire or fear, every action or reaction, is then infused with a false sense of self that is incapable of sensing the simple joy of Being and so seeks pleasure, and sometimes even pain, as substitutes for it."[117] As C.S. Lewis has written:

Courage is not simply one of the virtues,
but the form of every virtue at the testing point.[118]

Courage Development Questions to Ponder

- If you let go, who will you blame?
- When you experience fear, do you tend to seek out a target for blame?
- What fear-based belief are you willing to face and leave behind?

Chapter 4
Hold Yourself Accountable—
Renouncing Uncertainty

I believe God filled our young souls with so much courage that,
if we had possessed but half, we would undoubtedly have
carried out our project just the same.

— Saint Teresa of Avila

All the great saints of all traditions taught this secret: You are it! You are already important, and the answers to your questions lie within (a knowingness not to be confused with arrogance)! How did all the enlightened saints know, and how did I not know? Trappist Monk Thomas Merton said we are "to become what we already are." Twelfth-century Persian poet Rumi expressed it another way: "What is the heart? It is not human, and it is not imaginary. I call it you."[119]

New England theologian Jonathan Edwards wrote, "Saints do not see things others do not see. On the contrary. They see just what everyone else sees—but they see it differently."[120] They started out as ordinary people; then, their purpose unfolded. The difference between the saints and most of us is that they listened and trusted the undertones of their hearts (their courage) while the rest of us have allowed our fear-based scripts to keep us wavering in uncertainty.

Uncertainty may seem unavoidable in our age of information overload, and the accumulation of daily frustrations only enhances uncertainty. But we all have a choice, and failing to face uncertainty is essentially choosing not to choose. Too much thinking can actually make uncertainty worse. In fact, overcoming uncertainty is simply a matter of focusing our attention inward and following our hearts. As we follow our hearts, our faith in our courageous true Self grows stronger, and we move forward, confident that we are following our own true path. To do so is to

Hold yourself accountable.

In *The Mystic Heart*, Wayne Teasdale writes, "Everyone is a mystic. At some deep level, we know that we are not mutually alienated from each other and that we do have sufficient being."[121] Through the mystic heart comes a harmony that reveals our higher selves and unites us all. A Spanish mystic, Saint Teresa of Avila (1515-1582) lived at the Carmel of the

Incarnation from the age of twenty-one and remained there for twenty years until failing health forced her to leave.

Europe in the sixteenth century was an age of discovery and expansion and, in particular, an age of growing self-consciousness (not unlike today). As a young child, Teresa was fascinated by the lives of the martyrs. Around 1556, Teresa experienced her spiritual conversion, initiating a life journey of courage that saw her establish St. Joseph's, a reformed convent, in Avila and eventually receive sainthood. "We're always wondering whether we should do this or that when, from the spiritual perspective, what's most important is not what we *do* so much as who we *become*."[122]

During her monastic life, Teresa suffered constant health problems. "Debilitating seizures were such an integral part of her path for so many years that they came to be regarded as one of the hallmarks of her spirituality. Because of them she was diagnosed ... as suffering from 'hysteria.' Teresa regularly entered into nonordinary states of consciousness while in deep prayer...."[123] Critics have called Teresa the "patron saint of hysterics."[124]

As the founder of seventeen convents and two reformed monasteries, Teresa worked hard and *held herself accountable* to fulfill the vision of her faith. Her accomplishments, especially in such a rigidly patriarchal culture, border on the miraculous; but her efforts also invited the wrath of others — particularly those who benefited from maintaining the status quo. Slander brought her plenty of grief, and people within her own order misunderstood her. Life was no cakewalk for Teresa.

Regardless of the future, Teresa remained steadfast in her contemplative life and companionship with God, and she taught the importance of both of these principles. "Teresa's spiritual value is superiorly contemplative.... She was such a many-sided personality that different scholars have studied her from many aspects. Some have seen her intellectual power, others her virtues, her intense mortifications, her energetic character, her clear judgments, her surety of decisions."[125]

Devotion, love, the struggle of spirit and courage have been of supreme interest to all the great mystics. "The spiritually motivated saints of history did indeed uplift mankind, and such was the nature of their missions and the merit of spiritual courage, which often included even the sacrifice of their physical lives. Collectively, these social saints inspire whole nations and cultures and thus, by their public lives, silently serve all mankind for generations."[126]

Teresa's work has stood the test of time. She seemed to know that "Faith is the quiet cousin of Courage. Faith is willing to put its foot out when there is no guarantee that there will be a step to support it."[127] Uncertainty lives in this unseen step. We question it, we doubt ourselves, we refuse to face it!

Uncertainty is the obstacle that gnaws and manipulates us, many times without us knowing it. This unknowing creates a spiraling of unnecessary suffering—suffering that could have been prevented if there had been no attachments to the outcome. Attachment, like the word courage, is old French, *attaché*, meaning "nailed to." If instead we choose an appreciation for the present, we will not be nailed to future "things" that might elude us to think we have control. Besides, every day is a day of uncertainty. Only the ego mistakenly believes that you have a schedule set in stone when you walk out the door to go to work. Why? The ego strives for certainty. Teresa did not live in the future, so controlling the circumstances was the least of her worries. Each day she held herself accountable with her prayer and contemplative living with penance until she died at sixty-five. The first woman to be declared a Doctor of the Church, Teresa was canonized in 1622.

"When the deepest part of you becomes engaged in what you are doing, when your activities and actions become gratifying and purposeful, when what you do serves both yourself and others, when you do not tire within but seek the sweet satisfaction of your life and your work, you are doing what you were meant to be doing."[128] Does your work, like Teresa's, enhance your spiritual growth? Are you beginning to recognize that you are accountable for every choice in every moment?

Holding yourself accountable requires taking personal responsibility for your life experiences. In other words, accountability is not for someone else. Accountability is inescapable. Sales Manager Devin Campbell portrays accountability "by smiling, leading and being proactive. You have to have an attitude that when you feel you are getting chased out of town, you get out front and make it look like a parade! That's what courage is about—rising above opposition, oppression and discouragement, and forging ahead." To overcome uncertainty, you will need to add *"Hold myself accountable,"* to your Declaration of Courageous Intention.

Like so many other trailblazers that capitalized on their spirit to work, St. Teresa stepped up to fulfill her spiritual Truth. Holding herself accountable, she "kept going, cleansed herself of resentment so as not to waste precious energy."[129] Instead, Teresa's enlightened heart reached out to help others see the light within themselves: "Let us remember that within us there is a place of immense magnificence," and "To have courage for whatever comes in life—everything lies in that."[130]

Waking Thoughts

How do you feel about your work life? Are you living in joyful childlike innocence, or are you an overanxious, controlling adult? One easy way to find out is to take advantage of that first slice of stillness just as you awaken. You can ask a question about something, and the truth will reveal itself with a simple "yes or no." The magic of the morning sets the tone and intent for your mood, as Oprah Winfrey affirms. "I awaken to a morning prayer of thanks posted on my bathroom wall from Marianne Williamson's book *Illuminata*. I think about all those who didn't make it to 51 and were claimed to a different calling before they realized the beauty and wonder and majesty of life on earth.... I knew that I was connected to a power greater than myself—that I need only slow down and get still enough to let the flow that is all life carry me to the next level."[131]

While you're getting ready for work each morning, what attitude do you choose? In the evening, you can ask your inmost self-questions. In the morning, monitor your level of innocence and wait for the answers. Then, invite the wonder of your heartfelt courage into your day. A Hindu mystic will tell you, "It is a good idea to keep a mental diary. Before you go to bed each night, sit for a short time and review the day. See what you are becoming. Do you like the trend of your life? If not, change it."[132] Are you willing to make changes now, or are you waiting for the eleventh hour? If so, it is already here!

Jon Kabat-Zinn (Professor Emeritus, University of Massachusetts Medical School) writes, "Too often, our lives cease working because we cease working at life, because we are unwilling to take responsibility for things as they are, and to work with our difficulties.... In other words, you must be willing to let life itself become your teacher."[133] If you truly want to find the joy (or eliminate the drudgery) in your work life, you must open your mind to face the truth about your unhappiness, your judgments or the suffering perpetuated by your own thought patterns.

"Teresa of Avila called the mind 'a clacking mill that goes on grinding.' This is the nature of the mind: to have thoughts. The purpose of silence is a directed stillness, which receives rather than acts."[134] Review your thoughts first thing in the morning and reunite with your childhood innocence—when you were an open and receptive vessel of brightness. "The duties and cares of the day crowd about us when we awake each day—if they have not already dispelled our night's rest. How can everything be accommodated in one day? When will I do this, when that? How will it all be accomplished? Thus agitated, we are tempted to run and rush. And so we must take the reins in hand and remind ourselves, 'Let go of your plans.'"[135]

On his "Map of the Scale of Consciousness," Dr. Hawkins charts St. Teresa at 715. Dr. Hawkins' consciousness map denotes fields of consciousness ranging from twenty to a thousand. Seven hundred and up represents enlightenment (e.g., Jesus and the Buddha). "At the levels below 200, the primary impetus is personal survival.... The critical response point in the scale of consciousness calibrates at level 200, which is associated with courage."[136] A prayer to St. Teresa affirms the importance of courage:

65

> *Give me the courage to persevere in my spiritual practices*
> *even when others think I am foolish and wasting my time. Help me,*
> *Teresa, to find refuge in prayer and devotions, especially when I*
> *feel out of step with the fads and trends that others think are so important.*
> *May I find inspiration in your life and keep my*
> *sense of humor no matter what.*[137]

So just stop! Slow your breathing. Slow your mind. And stop....

Sit a few moments without thinking.... In this courage-centered place without mental chatter, you gain access to the portal of your heart—the divine eternal spring from which flows joy, peace and love ... the power of courage. What identifies your personality at work? A clique? A job description? A script? Regardless of the meditation practice you choose, the divine light of your courage brightens, the events in your life become easier to handle, and your reality starts to change.

"The more Light, literally, the more en-Lightened that you are, the more you will choose different ways."[138] St. Teresa's contemplative life took practice. Consider practicing some form of meditation for twenty minutes twice a day. Even once a day is a good start. Hence, your work life will take on a different meaning and purpose, moving you to complete accountability.

Running to the Future

If you are unemployed, you may operate like Vickie. She always started her day with: "What do I have to do today to get the results I want? The mere action of "doing something" fosters the belief that what you *do* generates results. Vickie was running to the future (and away from the present). Does this sound familiar?

Eventually, Vickie realized that trying to "get somewhere" left her drained emotionally, spiritually and energetically. She finally admitted, "Absolutely nothing resulted! Sometimes the more you chase things, the farther away from you they go." Take a moment to reflect on your thought process about why you do what you do. Here are two examples.

- You send out a marketing letter with the hope you will receive a response that leads to a nice contract. Expected result: the promotion (or visibility) you have been waiting for.

- You mail your resume with a great cover letter, knowing that you are the perfect fit for this opportunity. Expected result: a phone call requesting the interview that lands you the job.

Observe your thoughts in relationship to your actions, then identify the expectations that you bring to those actions. Realizing that expectations saddle our actions with unnecessary emotional and mental baggage, we can begin to free ourselves from all that extra weight. We can still execute what needs to be done, but by not projecting our expectations onto those actions, we free ourselves to accomplish much more while expending less energy.

An expectation, for example, can promote personal gain; other times, there is a sense of fulfilling a genuine need. Perhaps your self-image is to be loving and generous, and you take pride in your sacrifices. These behaviors protect and enhance your self-image, especially when they do seem to achieve the expected results. Yet, excavating your true Self involves discovering the untruths you told yourself a long time ago, untruths that helped to create the false scripts that keep you stuck in unconscious, counterproductive patterns.

"You cannot choose your intentions consciously until you become conscious of each of the different aspects of yourself. If you are not conscious of each part of yourself, you will have the experience of wanting to say, or to intend, one thing, and finding yourself saying or intending something else."[139]

If your anterior motive is to have more money so you can feel safe (scarcity mentality) or to hoard what you have, you base your sense of security on the idea of achieving financial security at some future time. When you live in the now, you do what needs to be done at any given moment, even if that changes abruptly (due to a flat tire on the way to work, for example). In the now, you have no expectations, and you want nothing because you already have what you need to flow through the day.

In whatever form you stop and invite silence, you will begin to detect how you chase the future. As you become more present and awaken to your courageous intentions, you recognize and master the old thoughts. You become more conscious of your conditioning. Here are a few questions to help you identify where to focus your efforts.

1. What areas in your work life do you try to avoid?
2. What thoughts, feelings and behaviors do you rely upon to reduce anxiety?
3. What current security-seeking strategy might you give up? What interpersonal process can you substitute for it that will be more valuable?
4. Where do you have difficulty letting go?
5. Where do you notice emotional swings?
6. What actions reveal where you undermine your true *Self*?
7. How long do you hold onto grievances?

"We eventually have to accept responsibility for our choices, decisions, and their consequences. Every act, thought, and choice adds to a permanent mosaic, our decisions ripple through the universe of consciousness to affect the lives of all."[140] All you have to do is ask: "What is my motive for this action?" This conscious invitation undermines uncertainty and allows you to take full responsibility for your decisions. In other words, you begin to *hold yourself accountable.*

Freelance writer Ryan Holota frames it another way,

> Courage involves acting with certainty, knowing what you want and not being afraid of anything in order to achieve it. For example, in the industry that I recently worked in, production was directly correlated to time. Produce more by working more, with little to no regard for working smarter or even harder. If you put in the hours, you must be working hard, and if you want time off you must be a slacker.
>
> I fought for three years to change this by working with my clients to plan projects better (so they didn't need to be finished on weekends or after hours), by trying to engage my coworkers in discussions about productivity, and trying to set an example of how things could be done. I must have failed because my efforts did not accomplish what I hoped. Instead, I had to hand in my resignation and create a new career for myself, one that embodied the goals that I have. So, I suppose indecision and inaction were the two obstacles that I faced the most. I overcame them with action. Courage enables action.

The Giants Will Crush You
Whatever your work is, put your heart into it.[141]

Different people manifest courageous leadership skills in different ways. One woman I interviewed displayed her leadership skills with a devotional life committed to the human spirit. Her love for God allowed her to be a willing, receptive and open leader; she exemplified grace with dignity. Her leadership disposition radiated "Be renewed in your spirit" (Ephesians 4:23). I met Liz Smith while giving a presentation for the executive women of IBM. Her courage leadership skills flow from personal mastery skills, and she beautifully combines *her* faith's spiritual truths with one hundred percent accountability. She had enjoyed a smooth and upwardly mobile twenty-five-plus years with IBM; but when her boss asked her to accept an assignment in Tokyo, the conversation left her reeling with reservations.

Knowing your desires is a critical signpost on your journey. Liz and her husband, Joe, were clear about their desires: follow God's plan. "We always prayed that God would open the door for us, and if it was what He wanted us to do, we would do it. When it came to my professional career assignments I always rested on the scripture from Jeremiah 'For I know the plans I have for you,' declares the Lord, 'plans to prosper you and not to harm you, plans to give you hope and a future' (29:11). No matter what, I knew the Lord would want what's best for me."

"In prayer, it became abundantly clear to me, He wanted me to take this job in Asia. Joe's prayers were also confirmed about his business. We ventured off to Japan trusting God would make a way for us, no matter what new challenges or circumstances we faced." In spite of huge uncertainties, Liz was secure in her leadership strengths. She knew her market, her customer's market, the industry, the business issues, the opportunities, and the solutions that would make everyone more successful. "In Japan, I had a desire to win, to make change for the better, to establish relationships and to do whatever was needed to make it happen without compromising my values. With my situation in Asia, these behaviors demonstrated that you're credible, you're trustworthy, you trust your team, and you care."

In Japan, contracts are signed and celebrated over drinks, dinner and more drinks. The men who reported to Liz had warned her about this tradition. For Liz, the courage challenge began when the Japanese executive asked what she would like to start the celebration with, beer or sake. Liz said, "I told him I would toast the customer with sake, and then I would be drinking oolong tea. He questioned me again, and I repeated myself. With a shocked look, he said, 'No, the customer expects you to drink.'

I explained that I would toast him, and then drink tea for the rest of the evening. I thanked him for honoring my request and never offered an excuse for my preference. I was this man's manager, so he followed my request, but I could see the sweat on his face." In the face of significant, potentially career-threatening uncertainties, Liz held herself accountable.

Liz continued, "Word got out quickly. No matter where I went for dinner, the one toast was ready and the oolong tea followed. I never asked. In times of defining moments, my courage and my faith are one. No matter what happened, God was in charge and He would protect me. Whatever the outcome, it would be the best for Liz."

Intrigued by Liz's story, I interviewed Joe, her husband. He said, "So many women are their own worst enemy when they display a lack of courage." Many of the men I have interviewed validate this sentiment; however, women tend to express just the opposite when evaluating other women.

"Socio-linguist Deborah Tannen found that women dislike female leaders who employ an authoritarian leadership style: 'Women managers do best if they avoid behaving like 'authority figures.'... Nevertheless, a good manager must be assertive, and sometimes even ruthless. An assertive woman manager might be viewed as bitchy and non-maternal. The fact that she might be trying to do her job well is precisely what other women may hold against her."[142] So how does Liz Smith handle this leadership issue?

At a recent conference, someone asked Liz to share her most important successful leader characteristics. She replied, "Courage, commitment and consistency. *Courage* to lead through challenge and diversity. *Commitment* to your people because their livelihood rests in your hands. *Consistency* requires staying disciplined to ensure that your team knows what's expected."

Do you like your work or are you "just earning a living?" Do you live in the essence of your true Self? Living in gratitude for her many blessings, Liz consistently denounces what she calls "the grasshopper mentality." "The grasshopper mentality is a mindset of mediocrity and having a small view of self. I choose to be a conqueror who celebrates reaching the purpose. A conqueror moves beyond the belief that her present state is more than she can handle. This is where courage becomes a guiding force."

With unwavering faith and a reverence for life, Liz holds herself accountable. She knows that faith does not grow in certainty and there will always be uncertainties, but that she will prevail in the end just as she prevailed in Asia. While her American colleagues had warned her, "A woman can't do business in Japan," and "The 'giants' over there will crush you," Liz's courage energized her faith and empowered her to stand tall in the land of giants. While she was no giant slayer, Liz was no grasshopper either—and no 'giant over there' squashed her!

In *The Wizard of Oz*, Dorothy stumbled along the Yellow Brick Road only to learn at the end of her journey that she had had the power to fulfill her dream all along. Are you stumbling along a career path because of pre-defined expectations? Or have you fallen asleep in the poppy field? Will you take time for self-reflection—to dwell deeply upon what you might stand for and love? Is conscious personal development your endgame?

Stopping prepares a seedbed of silence for the lotus of your courage consciousness to blossom. In Saint Teresa's words, "The important thing is not to think much but to love much; and so do that which best stirs you to love."[143] In essence, you are learning to coach yourself into personal accountability. "This is the joy of Being.... You can only feel it when you get out of your head. Being must be felt. It can't be thought. The ego doesn't know about it because thought is what it consists of."[144] So what thoughts and attitudes keep you from facing the situation at work?

Deadly Attitudes: Distort or Renew?

Karla, a competent, attractive, thirty-something brand manager, faced a lot of uncertainty when her husband skipped town just as their baby started preschool. Her "big break" came when she landed a job in marketing. She tried to balance the demands of her job with the responsibilities of being a parent, but her boss expected her to put in ten to twelve hours a day. The more he demanded, the harder she drove herself (and the guiltier she felt for neglecting her daughter). Karla had all the hard skills to do her job, but the human factors surrounding the position created inhumane working conditions. In holding yourself accountable, you begin to *feel* your own success. In essence, you are learning to coach yourself into personal accountability. "This is the joy of Being.... You can only feel it when you get out of your head. Being must be felt. It can't be thought. The ego doesn't know about it because thought is what it consists of."[145] So what thoughts and attitudes keep you stuck at work?

Late co-founder and faculty member of Contemplative Outreach, Mary Mrozowski developed a list she called "Seven Deadly Attitudes."

- Judgments
- Comparisons
- Anticipation
- Expectations
- Attachments
- Aversions
- Competition

Mary taught that these deadly attitudes are the root cause of suffering and once said, "No thought is worth thinking about."

To accelerate spiritual growth at work, begin to watch how you move in and out of these attitudes, but remember, this is just a brief introduction of understanding how false self, the ego, controls you. Be patient with this learning perspective. Most people require several cycles through the learning process to finally recognize how they constantly compare, expect, anticipate, judge and so on.

The "Seven Deadly Attitudes" create and perpetuate what Dr. Hawkins calls "positionalities."[146] Positionalities keep us trapped in duality (life/death; blessing/curse; good/bad; perception/essence). In Eckhart Tolle's view, "Mind-created duality is the root cause of all unnecessary complexity, of all problems and conflict in your life."[147] As we examine these attitudes, notice the ones to which you relate the most and be actively conscious of their influence at work, particularly during times of uncertainty. When you become an observer of these mental constructs, you will experience how your ego manipulates your perspective to control you (and rob you of your courage and happiness).

➢ Judgments

Our egos constantly make judgments. First impressions are really judgments based on little more than appearance, and the ego's judgments become the basis for inferences—complete fictions created by the ego. "To relinquish judgment does not mean that you do not recognize dysfunction and unconsciousness when you see it. It means 'being the knowing' rather 'being the reaction' and the judge."[148] How you choose to perceive these seven ego constructs will determine if you allow them to continue to distort your life (increase suffering) or use them to reframe your life (accept accountability).

"Perception is a world of judgment. Life has no judgment. Life is the awareness of comprehension. Comprehension sees everything as perfect.... Perception produces judgment ... our need to blame others for what is wrong."[149] So how do we consciously diminish our judgments? First, discover your own judgments. Through meditative practice, you diminish these attitudes to the point of elimination. "The spiritual journey only begins in earnest when we no longer experience the need to judge others, when we begin to take responsibility for our own inner development."[150] By accepting this internal accountability, a space for humility forms in the heart, allowing you to transcend self-interest.

➢ Expectations

"I do not expect anything from others, so their actions cannot be in opposition to wishes of mine."[151] Before I understood the truth of this insight, I would respond to a request for a presenter's packet by promptly mailing it and then lingering in expectations that this would be my big break. When nothing happened, I experienced tremendous disappointment. Eckhart Tolle clarifies this human condition, "When you no longer have such expectations, all self-created suffering comes to an end."[152] With courage, faith and meditation, I learned how my expectations created my distress and prolonged my suffering. I was able to move beyond my expectations only through the sheer commitment of cultivating silence.

People have different *projections* and *aversions* to the concept of silence through meditation, and many people find it difficult. Jon Kabat-Zinn writes, "People say they can't meditate, what they really mean is that they won't make the time for it, or that when they try, they don't like what happens. It isn't what they are looking for or hoping for. It doesn't fulfill their expectations. So maybe they should try again, this time letting go of their expectations and just watching."[153] How do you deal with disappointments at work? Wouldn't you prefer to avoid disappointment altogether?

72

> ## Comparisons

You may feel that it is only natural to compare things: one project to another, the new boss to the old boss. Comparisons are a natural construct of the ego. We make comparisons without thinking—it is automatic, as are all the deadly attitudes. You may catch yourself saying, "Wouldn't this project have been great if this client...." With that thought, the experience at that moment is no longer perfect. "The ego tends to equate having with Being: I have, therefore I am. And the more I have, the more I am. The ego lives through comparisons."[154]

The ego personality refuses to let you just experience something. It immediately formulates distinctions and judgments that become part of the perception. Fortunately, "It doesn't take long in meditation to discover that part of our mind is constantly evaluating our experiences, comparing them with experiences or holding them up against expectations and standards that we create, often out of fear."[155] When you compare yourself to some standard of success that is not you, you are at grave risk of developing false ideas of happiness that are certain to be shattered.

> ## Attachments

"An attachment is a belief that without something you are not going to be happy. Once you get convinced of that—and it gets into our subconscious, it gets stamped into the roots of our being—you are finished."[156]

While you are alive, attachments, whether to material items or social values, may make you feel safe and comfortable, yet they limit your enjoyment of new experiences in the present moment. Tolle reminds us, "Ego-identification with things creates attachment to things, obsession with things, which in turn creates our consumer society and economic structures where the only measure of progress is always *more*. The unchecked striving for more, for endless growth, is a dysfunction and a disease."[157] Do you seek security through an attachment to your home? Your ethnic group? Your religious affiliation? Your job title?

Try two exercises. Try making a list of the things to which you are attached. Review your list and assess where and how these attachments found a home in your psyche. For the second exercise, pick one attachment and determine its advantages and disadvantages. Stopping is the tool to eliminate this draining energy, and learning to become indifferent to the outcome should not be confused with loss of spirit or passion. Spirit and passion remain constant. Saint Teresa discovered that attachments "are an expression of an inner hunger."[158] "Attachment to things drops away by itself when you no longer seek to find yourself in them."[159]

> ## Aversions

Aversions represent an intriguing energy that seems to possess intrinsic value. Or does it? "Aversion is that which rests on sorrowful experiences."[160] For example, I once believed that if I controlled the situation, I would eliminate or diminish the potential for uncertainty. My lack of trust came from growing up with a scarcity mentality. My old scripts created suffering in a variety of ways—migraines, sleepless nights and needless worry. "Aversions are those things that 'push your buttons.'... These attachments and aversions, semi-conscious and mostly cloaked in self-justifications, virtually guarantee that we will enter situations in life with 'hidden values.'"[161]

Your meditative practice will move you to a deeper spiritual awareness and help you cut off the lure of attachment and its corollary, aversion, so that you move out of the suffering perpetuated by the false egoic self, achieving a higher level of personal mastery. It is in this zone, this connection, this moment, that your courage comes into play. You can assess your self-esteem (confidence level), your vision for a new career, the skills needed to reinvent yourself, or your level of faith during times of uncertainty. Then, you are free to respond in the moment.

> ## Anticipation

One of my clients said, "Business is booming, so we need to hire and train new people." I asked what new business was confirmed to prompt this action, and his response was "very little is for sure, I just need to prepare." Certainly, it is a prudent business move to prepare, but anticipation often creates future dismay. "To be identified with your mind is to be trapped in time: the compulsion to live almost exclusively through memory and anticipation. This creates an endless preoccupation with past and future and an unwillingness to honor and acknowledge the present moment and *allow it to be.* The compulsion arises because the past gives you an identity and the future holds the promise of salvation, of fulfillment in whatever form. Both are illusions."[162]

My client anticipates a better future, but if that future does not materialize, he creates unnecessary anxiety. I suggested that he, as a manager, stop to reflect on this automatic response and then trust that he has the required skills to respond when the moment is real. "Moderation is emotional sobriety, bringing a deep and considered awareness of both the pitfalls and the opportunities inherent in any situation. It implies a capacity for reflection, an ability to stay aware and act responsibly no matter what's occurring...."[163]

➢ Competition

Competition drives our market economy, but looking at history's lessons, competitive mindsets have justified genocide and religious hatred. Competition in the workplace borders on a "me/you" mentality. Being ambitious or driven to achieve is not necessarily bad, but cutthroat competition separates us from each other and leads to justifications about how we treat each other. What is important is to notice the level of aggression tied to your intent.?

I asked Curt Stowers, a regional manager for Caterpillar, "How does competition manifest itself in your workplace?"

"Competition plays a unique role in that it provides both the foundation for the creation of the new and better, and it can serve as the destructive force that tears an organization apart. Within the workplace, you have several different types of competition that come into play. The most reprehensible occurs when an individual who looks to win at any cost. At the other extreme is the "win-win" individual who continually focuses on the good of the organization. In my mind, the issue at the heart of the whole topic is one of values."

Reflections in Gratitude

If you choose to hold yourself accountable, you seek to embrace the intention of your heart. You welcome reflection, and you are learning to let go of the idea that you can control tomorrow. An easy step to accountability is to start a list that reflects your daily gratitude. It is the courage behavior that matters, not the ego's need for self-gratification. Founder of the Newfield Network coaching community, Julio Olalla writes,

> Different emotions predispose us to different kinds of actions; what are we predisposed to in the presence of gratitude? When we experience gratitude, we are predisposed to be a gift to others, to the world. We are not asking life to give us anything, we hold life as the most precious gift in itself, we are just in awe of its mystery, its beauty... And there is more: gratitude is the emotion that makes possible accessing higher levels of consciousness. Humankind has been centered in fear, and its main servant greed. The changes that are needed will come with a profound emotional shift that will allow for new levels of consciousness to arise.[164]

Courage Development Questions to Ponder

- Why do I slip into doubt during times of uncertainty?
- What spiritual experience has brought me the most energy?
- How can I bring the energy of courage to bear on an obstacle I am confronting now?

Chapter 5
Tackle the Tough Project—
Standing Up to Intimidation

One cannot discover new oceans until he [she] has
courage to lose sight of the shore.

— Unknown

History frequently glorifies the wrong individuals while overlooking the courageous acts of everyday people. Through intimidation, social, political and religious powerbrokers control perceptions and perpetuate the stories that serve their agendas. Few human beings have ever faced the level of intimidation that Dietrich Bonhoeffer faced in Nazi Germany. A German pastor and theologian, Dietrich was one of the first Germans to oppose Adolf Hitler during his rise to power, and he openly supported the Jews. His life exemplified deep-rooted courage in the face of social, political and religious intimidation, but instead of bowing to threats, he stood virtually alone in calling for church resistance to the persecution of Jews. Firmly centered in his heart and spirit courage, Dietrich was able to

Tackle the tough project.

Born February 4, 1906, Dietrich came from an educated, non-pious and yet, politically active family with seven other children. At the age of fourteen, Dietrich declared to his family that he would become a pastor. Considering that the Bonhoeffer family rarely went to church, his family was quite stunned at this announcement, but the choice secured Dietrich's destiny.

Graduating with honors from the University of Berlin in 1924, the gifted Dietrich went to New York in 1930 on a teaching fellowship where he was influenced by the lightheartedness of the American theological students ("There is no theology here."[165]) and the black gospel churches and singers in Harlem, which made him acutely aware of the injustices experienced by minorities and the Church's ineptness at supporting integration. Hitler became chancellor in January 1933. Two days later, Dietrich delivered a radio address attacking Hitler and warning Germany against slipping into an idolatrous cult of the *Führer* (leader), who could very well turn out to be *Verführer* (mis-leader, or seducer). His speech was cut short mid-sentence.[166]

By September the German Evangelical Church adopted racist Nazi policies, prompting Dietrich to accept an assignment in London. From London he rallied opposition to the German Christian movement and its efforts to incorporate Nazi racism into the Christian gospel. "The struggle was between the national church (which supported Hitler) and the 'confessing' church, called such because it confessed that there could be only one Fuehrer or leader for Christians, and it was not Hitler."[167] Even after the church bishop in charge of foreign affairs traveled to London and warned Dietrich to abstain from any activity not directly authorized by Berlin, the young pastor refused. He tackled the tough project and stood almost alone as the Confessing Church aided the Jews. In 1935, Dietrich received a much-sought opportunity to study under Mahatma Gandhi, but he decided to return to Germany to head an underground seminary for training Confessing Church pastors. As the Nazi suppression of the Confessing Church intensified, Dietrich's authorization to teach was revoked in 1936, but the crescendo of Gestapo threats and intimidation did not stop him from taking risks to voice his courageous convictions.

In 1939 Dietrich sailed back to New York but soon returned to his homeland—on the last ship to set sail before the start of World War II. He also took on another tough project. He became an agent of the Military Intelligence Department and provided information to Allied agents hoping to assassinate Hitler. Dietrich was finally arrested on April 5, 1943, and imprisoned as a spy for nearly two years of torture and brutal interrogation. During his imprisonment, Dietrich befriended prison guards, who brought him books filled with coded communications from his family and fiancé. He also began writing *Ethics*, an eloquent expression of his courageous beliefs. So sympathetic were the prison guards that one even offered to help him escape, but Dietrich chose not to run, knowing his imprisoned family members would suffer Nazi retribution.

By April 1945, Hitler had survived fifteen attempts on his life, Berlin was a total ruin, and the Germans knew they had lost the war. Under orders to kill the resisters, one of Hitler's special commandos in the Flossenburg stripped Dietrich and hanged him in the nude. The courageous pastor was only 39 years old. Three weeks later, Hitler committed suicide, and American forces liberated Flossenburg. After his death, Dietrich's work became increasingly influential as many civil rights and international ecumenical leaders, such as Martin Luther King Jr. and Archbishop Desmond Tutu, followed his work on ethics. Dietrich stood in courageous opposition to intimidation by continually stepping up to tackle the incredibly tough projects.

Climbing the Ladder

Is someone or some situation intimidating you at work? Learning to observe which obstacles have you stuck and applying the appropriate courage actions provides practical training in the internal competencies of courage. Going back to our ladder analogy, the lowest, easiest step on the ladder is overcoming inertia by simply giving yourself permission to claim your courage. Each consecutive step becomes higher and narrower, but each step also takes you closer to your calling and empowers you to create the unique career path that gives *your* life purpose and fulfillment. Near the top of the ladder, the ascent can get a little shaky, but each step prepares you and invites you to take the next step. Soon you learn, "Not *what* you do, but *how* you do what you do determines whether you are fulfilling your destiny. And how you do what you do is determined by your state of consciousness."[168] Are you too intimidated to step up to the next rung?

The founder and director of a prestigious international education program encountered the most intimidating situation she had ever faced. In the year the program was to receive its accreditation recertification, Ms. Hildebrand learned that she would have to perform all of her work on a PC using Windows instead of her accustomed Mac. Precious time sifted through the hourglass as she not only learned the new software, but also converted over 4,000 documents to a new format. Budget cuts meant no clerical or technical help. She was on her own. Feeling overwhelmed and abandoned, Ms. Hildebrand found herself in an unaccustomed position of feeling intimidated by something as simple as a desktop computer.

When facing a challenge, courageous people step up. Ms. Hildebrand accepted her shortcomings yet acted effectively to overcome this impediment: she relied on students to train her and parent volunteers to convert the data. When you are honest about your shortcomings, you earn the understanding and respect of others. Piero Ferrucci writes in *Inevitable Grace*, "We go through life constantly looking for guarantees, endeavoring to control people and circumstances, striving to conform the world to our plans.... What if we fully surrendered? Such an attitude entails courage, generosity, and the truthfulness that enables us to call ourselves into question, risking everything we are."[169] In spite of the obstacles, Ms. Hildebrand took on the tough project and overcame intimidation.

Obstacles will look large or small to you according to whether you are large or small.[170]

George Buckley, an electrical engineer and CEO of 3M Corporation, offered these words when he was interviewed for an article by David Garner: "Of the seven or eight qualities of leadership … I actually think courage is the highest among them because we are always faced by risk and by uncertainty, and you can't always forecast everything.... So courage is necessary for a person to get off the dime and make the right kind of decision, a courageous decision, in order to make a company grow and improve on where it is today."[171]

The King and the Pawn

The courage of a CEO like Buckley may influence a wider realm than the arc of your everyday courage, but courage behaviors are learned in everyday decisions. Just focus on the moment, make courageous adjustments, step up and remember:

Once the game is over, the king and the pawn go back in the same box.[172]

Unwilling to bow to intimidation, courageous people seek out difficult tasks and take risks that force them to perform above their usual skill and knowledge levels. Therapist David Travland co-founded the Caregiver Survival Institute. He defined courage as "the ability and willingness to take risks in the service of a larger goal." In his experience, "The prospect of short-term discomfort would dissuade most people from displaying courage. Courage requires one to take the long view, to look at matters from 30,000 feet and see the long-term implications of their actions.... Most people don't understand 'enlightened self-interest,' the idea that our interests depend on providing something of value to those who control the resources we desire.... You get what you earn."

David has faced intimidation, yet by recognizing his own enlightened self-interest, he has learned to draw from the strength of his courage to overcome intimidating situations. As a clinical psychologist, David could easily have been intimidated when he took on the project of getting his book published or when he decided to go into private practice. "When I opened my first private practice office, I visited and phoned referral sources, mostly physicians, to let them know I was available. It was one of the most difficult things I have ever done because I knew in my heart that, at that moment, they didn't care about me or my existence, but I knew I had no choice. I swallowed hard and made the calls."

A woman who noticed that a high-ranking position would soon be vacated said, "I thought about it and thought about it. So I did the somewhat brazen thing and went over and asked, "Can I have Vicki's job?"[173] What is wrong with asking, and why is it "brazen" to ask? If you are too intimidated to ask, the opportunity to step up vanishes, and perceiving this woman's action as brazen versus courageous demonstrates a need to rework the inner dialogue. If your tendency is to interpret enlightened self-interest as brazen, bold, brash, blatant or forward, you may be allowing intimidation to keep you stuck on the sidelines instead of playing your game in a way that highlights your talents. To overcome StuckThinking™, it helps to delve into your heart and discover what makes it sing. You can start by recognizing the difference between your potential and your experience. For example, if you are considering a career move, try not to match your style or skills to fit a "perfect" checklist. Instead, develop your potential—express your expectations and cultivate new abilities. Like any other ability, we all have the ability to manifest courage to varying degrees, but putting courage into action requires conscious choice.

David has taken on several tough projects in his career, but the most intimidating situation may have been his work with a board of directors. "Boards are very intimidating!" he declared.

I had arranged to facilitate an emergency meeting of the board of directors of a failing bank. I knew next to nothing about banking and not a lot about boards of directors and how they worked, but I agreed to accept the assignment, prepared like crazy, and pulled it off. The board decided to fire its wayward president at that meeting, just before the feds stepped in and pulled the plug. I accepted the assignment, in part, because their situation was so desperate that I couldn't see how I could possibly make it worse. I suppose it takes a certain amount of audacity to plunge into a situation, purporting to be the expert and in control, without having even a tiny amount of evidence that the outcome will be successful. In a way, taking on tough projects is essential to the development of professional courage. The more times these kinds of frightening undertakings are completed successfully, the less intimidating they seem. So it would seem that professional self-confidence absolutely requires one to display artificial courage on the path to genuine courage.

To illustrate, it might have appeared foolhardy to tackle a project with so many unknowns, such as the banking example above, but my consulting work ethic includes the following concept: TTP (Trust The Process). This means that if you can persuade a group of professionals to trust you as a group leader, they will talk openly about their situation. Because I am a quick study, I have always found it relatively easy to identify the main issues and move them into an effective problem-solving mode, leading to practical solutions.

An even more basic issue is the concept of self-employment. Cutting oneself loose from a regular paycheck to fly on the wings of self-sufficiency requires a great deal of courage. In fact, the entrepreneurial experience practically defines what is so unique about America. But however much we admire those who take the plunge, courage is not enough. If it were, the majority of new businesses would not fail within the first few years. While the allure of owning your own business remains one of the last frontiers of adventure in our society, it takes moxie, hard work, an understanding of marketing and a variety of other skills to succeed. Perhaps we as a society fail by not making entrepreneurial training mandatory in high schools.

The shrewd guess, the fertile hypothesis, the courageous leap to a tentative conclusion—these are the most valuable coin of the thinker at work.[174]

"Anybody can go to a job with a high-growth business and do well. That's easy," said Charlene Begley, CEO of GE Transportation Rail, "Go to a really broken business and make your mark. Those are the most rewarding."[175] The size of the project, your position, title or industry does not matter. The tough project could be anything that challenges you to reach out. "True leadership is not easy. That may be why leadership is not widespread. The world in which we live encourages 'boutique' leadership—where we find comfortable niches in which to become involved but rarely take on the tough work that comes with making fundamental and needed change.... Leadership springs from simple and often small acts of courage, where doing the right thing becomes more important than personal security or gain."[176] Security kills inquisitiveness and awe. The mind (ego) will want to undermine (or obliterate) them. After all, how could something so easy work, and be filled with joy?

Rob Gates is a Partner and Director of Marketing Mail Source and Data. Rob believes that there are two types of courage.

> Short-term courage is where an individual places themselves in harms way for a short period of time and does something that takes great bravery. Things like rushing into a burning building to save someone or tossing yourself on a grenade and sacrificing yourself to protect the other men nearby are examples of short-term courage. Like most people, I greatly admire those who show short-term courage. They are the very definition of heroes, but I have even more admiration for those who show long-term or "everyday" courage. The consultant who knows that he will be unemployed every few weeks, the salesperson who doesn't shade the truth even though

they desperately need a sale and the nurse who works in the oncology ward even though they know that they are making friends with people they will have to watch die. These are the people who show courage every single day.

I observe women applying courage at work more often than men. Between the residue of chauvinism and the realities of 21st century families, women are often in weaker positions economically than their male counterparts. That makes any decision that involves a possibility of job loss far more risky on average for women than the same decision is for men.

Happy Conduit

Mihaly Csikszentmihalyi, author of *Flow: The Psychology of Optimal Experience,* observed that "people reported the greatest sense of well-being while pursuing challenging activities, sometimes even at work, and often while immersed in a hobby. In a "flow state," Csikszentmihalyi found, people engage so completely in what they are doing that they lose track of time. Hours pass in minutes. All sense of self recedes. At the same time, they are pushing beyond their limits and developing new abilities. Indeed, the best moments usually occur when a person's body or mind is stretched to capacity.... They become more self-confident, capable, and sensitive."[177]

When was the last time you sought out a difficult task that forced you to perform above your usual skill and knowledge levels? Intimidation, whether from an internal voice or external circumstances, only perpetuates StuckThinking™! To diminish dispiritedness and accentuate the joy of being "in the flow," find the project that will focus your energies and challenge your abilities. Courageous people have found they can overcome intimidation by asking for the tough project—not asking for high levels of stress or even more money but using the energy of everyday courage to combine purpose with self-reflective growth. "Recent research into happiness demonstrates that the happiest people aren't those with the most money but those with a sense of purpose—a sense that they are contributing to something bigger than themselves.... People want to believe they're part of something meaningful."[178] Are you a happy conduit enhancing the flow of success in your company, or has intimidation robbed you of a sense of purpose? Perhaps you need to focus on this obstacle and add *tackle the tough project* to your DCI.

Betsy Bernard left a *Fortune 500* company as the highest-ranking female executive to become President of AT&T Business. Bernard said of the job that put her in position to build and run a *Fortune 500* company: "It was a job no one wanted."[179] Unwilling to be intimidated by a task that reeked of potential failure, Bernard initiated her success when she stepped up to tackle the job nobody wanted. Volunteering for a project that nobody wants could be just the thing to propel your career to the next step, especially if you have a tendency toward self-intimidation.

Remember that the power and arc of your courage expands the higher you climb on your ladder of success. Imagine that, as you step onto the first rung of our metaphorical ladder, you are allowing the light of your courage to shine. As you step higher on the ladder, the glow of your courage grows stronger, and the heights of your success raise the visibility of your courage. This radiance is your life! Find ways to step up and enlighten your environment. Ask to join a more challenging project team, move to another division, or intensify your networking efforts. To feel accomplished or fulfilled, you must consciously do the kind of work that makes you happy, and if you over-identify with your current role, you run the risk of getting stuck in the script.

Rung of the Ladder
Using a stepladder to demonstrate courage creates a simple yet powerful visual when I speak or conduct training. When I climb the ladder, attendees easily recognize which rung they are on and how long they have been precariously perched on that step. Standing on a step with one leg dangling, I ask the members of the audience to think about a challenging situation they are facing (or avoiding). Then I say, "This reminds me of an ancient Chinese proverb:

He who hesitates before each step spends his life on one leg.

Invariably, people know why they are stuck and what it will take to get going again. One moment of courageous clarity can work miracles in your career advancement. What has to happen to motivate you to confront intimidation? In the words of Sir Edmund Hillary: "It is not the mountain we conquer, but ourselves."[180] And the only way to conquer ourselves is through the internal work of a contemplative practice. Connecting with your courageous heart and spirit is the path to your true Self.

Donna Cameron, business owner, mentioned in a previous chapter, knows about courage: "Courage is accepting change in the workplace, whether it's a change in job description or being required to learn something new or simply saying 'yes' when asked to do something that takes you out of your comfort zone [tackling the tough project]. With each change that is incorporated or accepted, your courage increases to tackle the next one. Some people seem to thrive on these kinds of changes, while others put all their energy into resistance." Donna's insights resonate with the teachings of Eckhart Tolle. "Nonresistance is the key to the greatest power in the universe. Through it, consciousness (spirit) is freed from its imprisonment in form.... Resistance makes the world and the things of the world appear more real, more solid, and more lasting than they are, including your own form identity, the ego.... The play of form is then misinterpreted as a struggle for survival, and when that is your perception, it becomes your reality."[181]

As you go along your road in life, you will,
if you aim high enough, also meet resistance ...
but no matter how tough the opposition may seem,
have courage still—and persevere.[182]

Rest assured the true you will prevail despite outside pressures. Simply progressing up the steps one after the other will brighten the light of courage and deepen your internal courage reserves, and overcoming obstacles like intimidation requires you to become more courage-centered and less risk averse. Peter Bernstein writes, "The word 'risk' derives from the early Italian *risicare*, which means 'to dare.'" In this sense, risk is a choice rather than a fate."[183] From this perspective, the courageous actions we dare to take depend on our willingness to live freely in conscious choice. Choosing to apply courageous will and tackle a tough project is not about being foolhardy or defiant but about recognizing the risks and accepting the challenge. What is your courage tolerance level and how comfortable are you with the prospect of *failing*? In *Truth vs Falsehood*, Dr. Hawkins writes,

The steps out of failure, unhappiness, frustration, lack, want, anger, and depression are deceptively simple. Life is a voyage comparable to being out at sea in which a shift of one degree on the ship's compass will determine by the end of the trip whether or not one is hundreds of miles off course. The strongest tool, which already exists within, is the spiritual will itself, which, when firmly set, will face and take on any obstacle. It is the spiritual will that determines the success of the venture.[184]

Everyday people like Rob and Donna display courage-centeredness all the time, even when they appear to be hopelessly stuck. The difference is that they do not make the history books, much less the local newspaper. They are examples of everyday people applying everyday courage at work. Is courage your compass?

Cold Feet

The perception of security can be the proverbial albatross hanging from your neck, making it difficult to take a step anywhere, much less up. "In the long run, security—if we ever think we have it—kills curiosity and wonder. Risk, on the other hand, has a spiritual value.... Only by taking risks can we truly be.... By challenging our most ingrained personality structures, we earn a salutary shake-up. It is impossible to take risks and remain what we were."[185]

Are you willing to bet the farm or is the risk too intimidating? Many entrepreneurs ask, "What do I have to lose?" If you have consciously nurtured your everyday courage throughout your career(s), the transition to entrepreneur is easier. How many old scripts in your head prevent you from taking a risk? When was the last time you felt excited and curious about what was coming next?

Self-improvement separates courage-centered people from the pack. Ask these questions: "Why does it take me so long to make a change?" "How do I use my downtime?" Would I prefer to believe that my company will take care of me? Hindu sage Paramahansa Yogananda says, "Often we continue to suffer without making an effort to change; that is why we don't find lasting peace and contentment. If we would persevere, we would certainly be able to conquer all difficulties. We must make the effort, that we may go from misery to happiness, from despondency to courage."[186]

Changing the direction in which you look for happiness takes enormous courage. Do you wish to control your career or have your ego control it for you? The false self (ego/mind) does not want you to find the limitless joy available through the truth of your own identity; yet, it is deceivingly simple to find! Morris L. West said, "It takes so much to be a full human being that there are very few who have the enlightenment or the courage to pay the price.... One has to abandon altogether the search for security and reach out to the risk of living with both arms. One has to embrace the world like a lover. One has to accept pain as a condition of existence. One has to court doubt and darkness as the cost of knowing. One needs a will stubborn in conflict, but apt always to total acceptance of every consequence of living and dying."[187]

"In a society that seems to value only work, it requires a strong sense of security to stop working and engage other parts of the brain, but the benefits of doing so pay significant dividends."[188] Is it difficult for you to risk your security? Too worried that a risk might backfire, most people wait and wait, caught up in self-intimidating scripts that prevent them from mustering the courage to take the plunge. It is your courage that supports your ability to let go of deadly attitudes, change the way you organize your time, change your relationships and change who and what you are. Marianne Williamson writes, "If we want our lives to change, it does little good to simply move from town to town, job to job, or relationship to relationship. Wherever we go, as they say, we take ourselves with us. We manifest not so much according to geography as according to consciousness.... For our lives to change, we must travel deep."[189]

Ultimately, risk-taking is about the internal processes of the psyche. "It is from inner space, the unconditioned consciousness itself, that true happiness, the joy of Being, emanates."[190] Review your dreams, study the behavioral patterns that keep you stuck, and uncover your voice as it relates to risk-taking, spontaneity and making mistakes. You learn on the job, and you learn from financial success or financial failure. Risk-taking includes making mistakes, but you recover from your mistakes and step up, better prepared after learning from past mistakes.

Composure is a Cousin

Donna's courage learning comes from two perspectives. "I often hear people say that they move forward through their fears by asking, 'What's the worst that could happen?' If this works for them, that's great. But it troubles me, because that's only *half* the question. There's another question to ask: 'what's the *best* that could happen?' That's where we should be focusing our attention. Instead of moving forward through our fears, always conscious of that 'worst' that we want to avoid, we should move forward with our eyes firmly fixed on the 'best' that we want to manifest." Manifesting the "best" requires a certain amount of composure, which is why composure is a cousin to courage

Donna observes on-the-job courage in many ways. "When someone comes to me and admits an error as soon as she realizes it's been made, that takes courage. It's hard to admit mistakes, but there are very few errors that cannot be fixed if brought to light as soon as they are discovered. And often, creative thinking can turn the error into an opportunity." Are you intimidated by the voice in your head that says "errors are bad, therefore I am bad?" Echart Tolle asks, "Can you take the thinking out of the perceiving? Can you look without the voice in your head commenting, drawing conclusions, comparing, or trying to figure something out?"[191]

Taking risks and hurdling intimidation, courageous people choose to forgo immediate satisfaction. When a new challenge requires them to step up, they do! Changing their lives, they realize (and adjust) their truthfulness.

We must have courage to bet on our ideals, to take calculated risk, and act. Everyday living requires courage if life is to be effective and bring happiness.[192]

If you want to change your life, you have to change your stories and face the limitations that prevent you from transcending your false B-movie scripts. "We don't have to conquer our false self; we only have to observe it. And through observing it, by being aware of it, we transcend its grip on us and move toward our own transformation into love and compassion.... It is essentially through contemplation or meditation practice that a salutary self-knowledge dawns in us."[193] Eliminating the false scripts starts with silence, where we learn to stop thinking and start listening. "Thinking without awareness *is* the main dilemma of human existence."[194] Sitting in silence before deciding about any important matter is a good idea and a theme throughout this book.

Overcoming Ourselves

Often, if you are living a hit-and-miss life, you will miss the defining moments. Misses are chances gone by, never to be reclaimed. For Shane Holst, an author and provocateur for psychological and spiritual health,

> The greatest single obstacle is often risking money/security and job. Confronting a breach of ethics or law is tantamount to career ruin. A good example was when I was doing training and coaching for a major company. There was much that was dysfunctional about the organization and in particular the senior management group of eight people. I spent a lot of time working with these people only to discover, in the main, they were good, competent people. After considerable analysis, it was obvious to me that the problem was at the top—the business owners. The three people who owned the organization were unscrupulous and highly Machiavellian in their management style. I was, however, being paid extremely well and had debt and commitments like most people.
>
> I knew that confronting these men over the negative effect of their behavior on morale and productivity would carry considerable risk (in terms of me being paid!), but so would not doing what I knew was right. "Stand for nothing, fall for anything." I knew it was worth the risk and, after quality questionnaires and research, presented them with the facts (and prepared to be marched to my car and told to piss off). It created considerable consternation and conflict but I believe the way I did it helped them not to take it too personally. I continued to work there but felt the gaze of "one mistake and you're out!"

Feeling intimidated by the constant gazes didn't stop Shane from continuing with the tough project, "Some change was effected. It was difficult, but not nearly as difficult as it would have been for me to have suppressed my knowledge, kept working with the management team and kept sneaking off (as it would have felt) with my financial benefits. Using courage pushes past the need to be popular or liked or even safe."

Staying stuck in intimidation is easy, and the risk of letting people know who you are can threaten your image. Keith A. Ferguson, an engineer said,

> Perhaps the most difficult obstacles I have faced come from within myself. Most often it involves a tendency to

regress to an egoic response when threatened or when a problem arises that challenges my status or self-image. An example of the internal obstacles I frequently face was a recent encounter/disagreement with a senior executive who wanted to insert herself into a strategic proposal process. The intention of her involvement was uncertain. Based on my previous experiences with her it was very easy to accuse her of trying to insert herself due to a desire to be in control, attain recognition of her leadership skills and to achieve personal advancement. Instead of recognizing the capable leadership already in place and supporting the team best qualified to assemble to proposal and win the work, she wanted to direct all activities. Under this circumstance it is easier to criticize the individual rather than work toward a win-win solution.

"Living up to an image that you have of yourself or that other people have of you is inauthentic living—another unconscious role the ego plays,"[195] summarizes Tolle. Your courage and authenticity are not "somewhere over the rainbow;" they are merely hidden beneath the scripts and images generated by the false self, waiting for you to step into the deep levels of your true Self—beneath the ego's shallow false identity.

For all the readers who dream about leaving the dog-eat-dog world to pursue their life-long passion, *start now!* Finding the time to craft the almighty business plan or drumming up financial backing, you run the risk of fumbling the passion. So, if you're bored, burned out or frustrated in your day job, dig into your heart and spirit, and you will see that your courage resides there. If intimidation is holding you back, look for a tough project to tackle, but remember this courage paradox: start by stopping! The commitment to reflection will provide a clearer picture of what you need to do to get where you need to be. Then, you won't be a victim of intimidation.

Courage Development Questions to Ponder
- How have I allowed people to intimidate me on the job?
- How have I permitted my own preconceived ideas to intimidate me?
- When was the last time I tackled a project that no one else had the courage to take on?
- What commitment can I make today to align my actions more closely with my highest intentions?

Chapter 6
Showcase Your Talents—
Defying Invisibility

The highest courage is to dare to appear to be what one is.

— John Lancaster Spalding.
19th Century Catholic Bishop

B orn into a happy and prosperous English family, a deeply inspired nineteenth-century Quaker woman shifted her focus from a life of privilege to the invisible lives of the unwanted and despised. With principled persistence, practicality and deep-felt convictions, she followed her heart and changed how underprivileged women were incarcerated in the early 1800s. Elizabeth Gurney Fry (1780–1845) developed her public career at Quaker meetings during a time when society expected women to remain unnoticed behind their husbands (or fathers). Hiding in invisibility might have been the easiest route for Elizabeth's life journey, but she overcame that obstacle and came to exemplify our sixth courage action:

Showcase your talents.

Growing up in the relatively new Quaker Church (Religious Society of Friends), Elizabeth enjoyed a rare opportunity for a girl in those days. She and a boy started a Sunday school that quickly grew to eighty attendees. This early venue helped to define and cultivate her future abilities of organizing and teaching. After an American Quaker came to Britain to lead a meeting, Elizabeth sensed a conviction to serve God but only in a very general sense.

When Joseph Fry, a Quaker merchant from London, proposed to Elizabeth, she reluctantly married in 1800, knowing that marriage would hinder her conviction to utilize her talents. Following the social conventions of the time, she placed her interests on hold. However, after her father's death in 1809, Elizabeth shifted her energy from society's "good life" to society's discarded spirits. Courageously willing to place her personal integrity at risk and using her well-connected Quaker political associations, Elizabeth visited London's Newgate Prison in 1813. She found women and children in the dark stench of prison wards living like neglected barnyard animals. The women were drunk, cramped, filthy and almost naked; newborn babies cried incessantly; lice infested clothes and hair; beds consisted of dirty straw; and prisoners mixed together without regard for level of offence. Death was common. The standard concept for the period was severe punishment as a deterrent to crime.

The immense obstacles required to reform this system did not intimidate Elizabeth or diminish her convictions. Her desires ran deep as she seemed to "know" what was naturally needed to take on this new project. "She looks around and, seeing a child, takes it in her arms and says, 'What shall we do for the children?' This question entirely transforms the atmosphere. Fry has reached at once for the hearts of women who only a moment before showed hardness and cynicism.... The inmates now realize that someone cares enough to meet them in the darkest and most frightening place, and they feel grateful. Fry has seen at once what needed to be done. With her courageous bet, she had made the unhappy women realize that they *counted.*"[196]

This simple act was the first of many Elizabeth would take in doing what was right and, ultimately, using her talents to change her world. "If the contrast between what you consider to be right and what's happening is too large, the best thing is to go for another job. It is difficult to stay in a position where you feel guilty when you get up in the morning."[197] Do you feel that you make a difference at work, or are you invisible? If you err toward invisibility, how long would it take to step up your job-seeking efforts? Hopefully, you are not caged by other obstacles such as blame or denial. Ask yourself: "Are you done with obstacles that hold you back on the job?"

In 1816, Elizabeth took action to change how Newgate's women prisoners were treated. Showcasing her many talents, she organized the Association for the Improvement of Female Prisoners the following year. "Fry's association put the women prisoners to work sewing and knitting under the supervision of monitors. With a prisoner as the instructor, it also organized a school for women (and their children) to teach them to read the Bible. One of Fry's rules for the Newgate women declared 'that there will be no begging, swearing, gaming, card-playing, quarrelling, or immoral conversation.'"[198] Soon the prisoners were able to sell their work for soap and food and, like most human beings, felt a sense of self-fulfillment.

Elizabeth's courage provided the tonic that the distressed women had desperately needed. Her goal was to assuage the women's sufferings (including the women sentenced to exile in Australia), treat them with respect and help them develop work abilities. Even at this elementary level, Elizabeth taught the women how to showcase their talents! This transformation led to many reforms for prisoner treatment. Do you need to add this courage action to your DCI?

Courageous leadership encourages people to learn, face their doubts and then trust. Putting her simple courageous leadership talents to use, Elizabeth was able to diminish the prisoners' sense of invisibility and hopelessness and open them to spiritual attentiveness. The Association's ladies' committees visited prisons all over the country, and they helped improve treatment of the insane, establish shelters for the homeless and initiate hospital reforms. World leaders heard of Elizabeth's talents and sought her out. In 1827, Elizabeth published *Observations on the Visiting, Superintendence and Government of Female Prisoners.*

In 1828, Elizabeth's husband's business went bankrupt, impeding her work and diminishing her prestige. By the mid-1820s, her prison charities lost money, and policies that undermined her work took precedence. But her dedication continued until her health started to fail after a lifelong battle against nervous depression. At times Elizabeth offended the people she wished to influence, but she stood in her convictions and even challenged the Home Secretary to stop a woman's execution. Controversy is a cousin to courage.

The ultimate measure of a man is not where he stands
in moments of comfort and convenience, but where
he stands at times of challenge and controversy.[199]

Regardless of the cost, Elizabeth stood steadfast to define and demonstrate her leadership brand and stand up for what she knew to be right. For Elizabeth, her soothing voice, her accountability, her attire and her compassion showcased her talents that attributed to her leadership brand. Her overall demeanor had a halo affect on the environment. But by 1835, professional wardens and caseworkers had taken over the field to which she had dedicated her life. Professor George C. Simon Jr. can relate to Elizabeth's predicament. "Courage at work," he said "means putting your own growth and job security at risk for a greater good or goal—being willing to say or do that which may not be politically correct or consistent with the norms, much less the conventional wisdom of the organization." Elizabeth and George applied their courage to define, live and project their talents.

Courageously Forthright

Courageously forthright action did not undermine Elizabeth's femininity. It does, however, allow any person to showcase their talents. Jill demonstrated her talents and caught the attention of a city manager. When he phoned Jill to discuss an administrative position, she knew that negotiating the salary would be difficult. "He saw me as someone who could assist him with furthering the organization's vision. Initially, his offers were below my requirements, but I kept asking for more money. He knew I was ready and willing to walk out the door. So he finally caved in." Communicating face-to-face or via telephone can prove effective in helping to overcome invisibility and move into a better venue for maximizing your exposure. Likewise, try to avoid email correspondence, which greatly increases the chances for misunderstanding.

Jill shared that the city manager who hired her turned out to be the best boss she ever had. "He admired me, respected me and believed in me. He gave me room to display my talents and branch out beyond my job description. We are friends to this day." Courage initiates decisive action and accepts nothing less. Jill did not back down but made the essential connection between displaying her talents and advancing her career. Perhaps this process gave her fresh courage to face other obstacles. At the very least, it helped improve her negotiation skills, an important step toward professional and financial success.

Do your talents energize others? How often do you stand alone to *showcase your talents*? Are you comfortable in this potential awkwardness? John DePalma is vice president of a television production company, believes, "Before you can be straight with someone else, you must be straight with yourself. You must face obstacles head-on with all the facts in hand to make the best choices for the organization. You must recognize that these choices sometimes are painful but must be made." He continues,

> There are clearly many leaders who apply courage techniques at work. It is my opinion that, while the opportunity clearly exists to showcase and apply principles of courage, most men do not willingly lead by example. I have never quite been able to fully grasp why men have so many inequities when it comes to showcasing courage in both normal daily life and life on the job. I believe the quest to "get ahead at all costs" still exists rather vividly, and when it's a race, regardless of rules, men tend to vacillate towards those things that come easiest and without much cognizant thought. As a force of habit, we always retreat to those things that do not require hard work and diligence.

John believes that "as a society we do not see a lot of these principles being applied ... talked about yes, but put into action, probably not."

True courage opens the door to spiritual awareness, and in welcoming spiritual awareness, you learn to refine your talents so they become more clearly visible revealing your Spiritual Intelligence (SQ) . This work becomes easier as you begin to diminish the distortions of the false self. The great sage, Jalaluddin Rumi, knew the significance of getting rid of the false self in order to perceive clearly.

If you could get rid of yourself just once,
the secret of secrets would open to you.
The face of the unknown, hidden beyond the universe
would appear on the mirror of your perception.[200]

How are you progressing with your self-analysis? Is your DCI starting to reveal obstacles and the courage actions you need to face them?

"No" to Conformity

Once you evoke your courage, you get the opportunity to see your own vital energy. Do you see a promise of your inner essence? Elizabeth was willing to display her talents, take a risk, face failure, overcome rejection and say "No" to conformity (a courage killer). In other words, she had the courage to put her ideas and spirit into action; hence, she became a better leader. Conformity compresses talent, as Tom Heuerman can attest. A consultant, writer and colleague, Tom walked away from his high-level job.

> I chose to walk away from the corporate world rather than conform to pressures to be less than my best. Eight years later, I continue to make choices that go against expectations, supported by my resolve and passion to live an authentic life. To be courageous and to exercise our freedom fully is difficult. None of us can be authentic completely, as our imperfections and pressures to conform confront us daily. We often limit ourselves to control the anxiety we feel and, in the process, lower our vision and shut down our creativity. Many in the corporate world live marginally, like walking dead. Many choose mediocrity in exchange for the illusion of security, but we can choose to live courage-based lives just as we can choose to be victims, helpless and powerless.[201]

Chemical engineer Cliff Winter expressed the issue of conformity and courageous leadership another way. "I do not believe that courageous leadership was displayed where I used to work. In fact, most people were conformists, and displays of courage were few and far between. Corporate cultures are generally ingrained pretty deeply so nothing changes very quickly." Reflect on your work environment for a moment. Are you respected for your talents? Or are you stuck in conformity? Political activist and author Jim Hightower writes,

The opposite of courage is not cowardice, it is conformity.
Even a dead fish can go with the flow.[202]

Courage is organic. When you seek high standards that showcase your talents, you learn to discriminate and refine your worth. If you dig into Elizabeth's story of individual professional expertise, you will easily identify the talent called "Elizabeth Fry," a "brand name" that continues to influence prison reform. Naomi Klein believes, "The 'Brand Called You' is the ultimate triumph of space being privatized through branding—even that space in our minds. Being a brand teaches you to turn every part of yourself into a marketable product. But ultimately ... you're not a company—you're a member of society.... What I am talking about is the need for more integrity in branding."[203]

Tina Kashlak Nicolai feels that a resume is as comparable to you, as the book jacket is comparable to a best-selling book. "Reveal enough of the plot to stimulate interest without giving away the ending.... Brand authenticity is the basis for identifying who you are at your *core*. It includes your natural leadership strengths, your true talents, your individualized accomplishments and your character in the workplace. Brand authenticity is who you are in winning times and tough times. This is important because it helps recruiters, HR professionals, hiring leaders and CEOs determine YOU as a complete and comprehensive business commodity. If you see yourself as commodity, today's businesses will also see you as a commodity. You will rise to the top of the resume pile if you are seen as a business commodity on paper. The secret of branding oneself authentically begins at the core." Now, more than ever, the ability to identify your "hard" skills versus your "real" skills will support the self-promotion needed to face your career obstacles.

While Naomi's expertise focuses on brands that integrate a respectful message with integrity, these same principles can define your brand of courage conviction. Courage lives in your integrity. Where are you being unrealistic about who you are? Do you live in convictions or hope? When people meet you, do they connect with the Brand Called You or with a false image that keeps the real you hidden in invisibility? Your branding niche should represent your natural abilities. In other words, play to your strengths, represented by your natural drive and inner calling. In this way, you make courage your daily legacy.

Elizabeth recognized that stopping the inner noise is critical if you want to stay centered in your talents and continue to expand them. Thomas Keating writes, "As you experience the reassurance that comes from interior peace, you have more courage to face the dark side of your personality and to accept yourself as you are."[204] Do you work for a company that clearly brands its values and showcases the creative talents of it employees? A company brand is one of an organization's most important assets. People who want to authentically showcase their talents seek out companies that also have a strong and compatible brand message.

Are you still waiting for clients or management to notice your contributions? If so, begin to reveal your talents by branding your performance results. That is what Emilio Navarro, solutions engineering team leader, proposes. "I always use courage at work while making decisions, while talking to people, while interacting with clients. Courage is who you are, and the decisions you make are how you work and think about different aspects of business and life. Martin Luther King Jr. showed what he was made of when he explained his viewpoints in a transparent style." Emilio works for a company that promotes openness, allowing employees to showcase their talents. Emilio said his current employer "is different from other companies I have worked for where courage was measured by your performance, making it hard to be yourself." Emilio offers this suggestion: "Be transparent and to the point with your team."

One of the best tips to help create your talent showcase is to think of two to three key emotional behaviors you want not only to convey but to demonstrate to peers, clients, bosses or interviewers (e.g., courage, accountability, passion, promises, etc.). Once you know their sentiments, you can weave the appropriate messages throughout your presentation, interview meeting and language you use. Use a variety of words, phrases and stories all geared towards evoking a positive emotional connection to the Brand Called You. You may not get the project, job or desired action, but you will overcome the invisibility obstacle. And you will be demonstrating your courage!

Your Energy Signature

Business owner and entrepreneur Greg Giesen believes courage at work requires that he demonstrate unconditional commitment to his beliefs, values and ideals—not an easy commitment to maintain, especially if you are stuck in invisibility. "When I decided to resign from my comfortable job for a large organization and venture out on my own, I would find myself gasping for air and thinking I should reconsider my decision before it was too late. Call it a fear of failure or fear of the unknown, but I guess it was at those exact moments that I surged forward with courage and re-committed to my belief in myself and to my future, despite the self-doubt. My desire to move forward once again outlasted the desire for predictability and comfort." This perspective represents a common theme for the women and men I interviewed who base their courage on convictions that keep their talents in the forefront, even at the cost of challenging the status quo.

Fourteen years of interviews and research have demonstrated that courage starts with the individual human spirit then expands to how you transmit your energy into the Universe. Your "energy signature" uniquely showcases your talents, and "one size fits all" does not apply to courage. Sensing how to dial into the unique energy of your personal courage is a good first step. As you begin to step up the ladder, the learning curve escalates, and you become adept at extracting and honoring the various "courage frequencies" permeating your environment. "The challenge," says Lou Marines, President of Advanced Management Institute, "is to move beyond the sometimes archaic and pedestrian thinking represented by such items as business myths and anecdotal observations that pass for wisdom." The emergence of our courage gifts and leadership talents take place naturally when we allow our actions to spring from the heart instead of relying on the mental schemes that undermine our talents and keep us invisible to ourselves and our peers.

Oprah knows the difference between playing it safe and showcasing her talents. "Will you let other people define you," she asks, "or do you have enough courage to search yourself and act on your own truth?"[205] Letting other people define you at work depletes the spirit. Courage is in the willingness to buck the work trends.

Neale Donald Walsh, author of *Conversations with God,* writes,

> Let me comment more on why can't I do what I really love to do in this world and still make a living? The posture we often take in order to reconcile our outer experience with our inner reality is the rationalization used by every person since time began to justify remaining in a dysfunctional or unhappy situation: we have "lessons to learn" and we must not shy away from learning them…. You know it in your gut when a thing is not true for you. Isn't that amazing? What's even more amazing is how often we fail to listen to this internal guidance system. Many people spend half their lives doing things they can't stomach. Why? Because somehow they think they're supposed to. Perhaps it is time to disabuse ourselves of such notions. When things in business don't seem to turn out the way you asked for them to, what has happened is that you have confused "doingness" with "beingness."[206]

Elizabeth knew her "beingness," and she demonstrated her beingness through her "doingness," producing visible results in her community at large. Wayne Teasdale supports, "The call into life is a call into being, a summons into a deific possibility for us, an opportunity to actualize our potentiality to realize higher levels of consciousness. Such a possibility, however, takes perspective, work, and discipline; it doesn't come easily, nor in most cases does it just happen."[207] A courageous person and a courageous workplace produce a noble legacy.

Butt Heads

To determine whether or not you are showcasing your talents, analyze your level of contribution. Seeing your true value is a critical step toward taking courageous action. Limited stories that keep you stuck—not finishing college, being the breadwinner, not being courageous—become identities. Deeply ingrained in the mind, these false identities destroy life's joys. Immense courage is required in all work, including learning to re-evaluate your long-held beliefs and finding what you love. Finding what you love naturally reveals your talents. This trademark reveals your spirit's purpose.

Your beliefs drive your actions and your behavior within an organization. Organizations know they get the whole person when you give your heart, not just your mind, just as the organization's convictions show people who they are before profits. To love what you stand for provides the balance essential to a healthy lifestyle. When Karla (branding manager and single mom in Chapter 4) finally stood up to her boss and balanced her work with her parental responsibilities, she no longer felt abused or tired in the rat-race life that she had been living. She declared her everyday courage and ceased enabling her own abuse. With her clearly defined value, she stopped being her own worst enemy. This undoubtedly gave her an edge when she interviewed for her next job, and eventually, her peers benefited from her clearly defined branding value.

In Chapter 2, we learned that consistency is a cousin to courage. Consistent reinforcement of your talents at work—the ones that highlight your convictions mean that you are reinforcing the same beliefs and behaviors regardless of the task or pressure of the moment. The benefit? Your self-awareness expands until, eventually, you remain untouched by colleagues' mental and emotional projections. Once again, your commitment to stopping and allowing internal silence supports this transformation.

Shane Holst, Founder and Director of Altruism Australia shares his viewpoint again, "Unless we commit to a deep psychological understanding of ourselves, others and our relationship to all life, we will continue to make the obscene mistakes with each other's hearts, souls and bodies that we presently do.... I simply believe that it starts with each of us as individuals. Until we achieve total self-awareness—facing our greatness, shadows, hurts, dreams, angers, prejudices, meaning, potentials, gifts and delights—our evolution will continue to be embarrassingly slow, even retarded. This is where, I believe, courage is so important—it is one of the most potent tools to self-awareness."

Claiming your moral courage keeps you balanced in your people skills. Breakdowns and disruptions that hinder an organization's advancement rarely have to do with unskilled employees. Marketing company owner

Tracy O'Neill understands the value of "hard" skills as well as personal skills. "I was working at a company where I did not agree fundamentally with the direction in which the company was moving," she told me. "As vice president of planning and distribution, I played a key role in maintaining inventory control. The company was relinquishing those disciplines to pursue sales at any cost. I had a strong conviction that this would hurt the company, but my arguments fell on deaf ears. I could have easily agreed to go along, particularly since it was a well-paying job with a lot of opportunity for growth."

Circumstances like this reveal how, in many cases, talents and convictions merge, offering an opportunity to showcase the depth of your talents. Tracy continued, "I decided to butt heads with management and risk it all for my beliefs and my dignity. Although my arguments were not accepted, I was proud of how I presented my case. Unfortunately, because I was sure of my predictions, I ended up resigning in frustration." Without another job in place, Tracy had the courage to face an uncertain future. Ask yourself: "What is the courageous conversation that I am not having with my boss (partner, spouse, loved one)? What is the courageous conversation I am refusing to have with myself, in my own heart, with regard to my work and the present life threshold on which I find myself?" Tracy clearly defined her many competencies by acting with genuine respect and concern.

Neglecting your courage is as easy as accepting a low salary, knowing all along that you are being undervalued. Why? Mainly because you do not ask. These experiences perpetuate invisibility. How willing are you to promote yourself and your skills? If you champion others, why can't you champion yourself?

> *Whatever you do, you need courage.*
> *Whatever course you decide upon, there is always*
> *someone to tell you you are wrong.*
> *There are always difficulties arising which tempt you*
> *to believe that your critics are right.*[208]

Place at the Table

Elizabeth Fry and Tracy O'Neill did not face setbacks by wallowing in self-pity. Stepping up to their challenges one rung at a time, they organized themselves, developed solutions and spoke up. You, too, can showcase your talents. Your personal courage is smoldering. All you need is the breath of fresh air that fans it back to life—the fresh air of meditative discipline.

Elizabeth's convictions were uplifting to the people around her. Her brand was more than a logo or a corporate identity campaign. Bringing her unique attributes to the prison system, she accomplished great things without waffling. Self-promotion is not a dirty word, but it is different from boasting about something you have not accomplished, which can lead to disappointment and an image of arrogance. Define your leadership qualities with the courage, talents and convictions that make you who you are rather than being invisible or becoming arrogant. In other words, make a place for yourself at the table.

Self-differentiation enables you to be fully yourself (and accept your limitations). People cannot help but notice your good works when you push a project forward with unwavering commitment. Harriet Rubin writes, "I think most men and women would say that courage is the virtue that they would most want to secure for themselves."[209] The driver behind courage is the meaningfulness to *your* life. Will you live a fulfilled and truly satisfied life? Will you discount your courage as elusive? As Dr. Hawkins notes, "Spiritual evolution is a process of unfoldment, emergence, and purification as a consequence of what one has become rather than as a result of what one is doing or has been.... To continue to evolve requires development of courage, determination, and the alignment of priorities as a consequence of intention and, eventually, commitment."[210]

Courage Development Questions to Ponder

- When the opportunity arises to display your talents openly, do you take advantage, or do you remain invisible?
- Describe your distinctive branding characteristics that you display at work—the ones that showcase your leadership prowess.
- What percentage of your life lives in conformity versus courage?

Chapter 7
Manifest Your Vision—
Refusing to Accept Defeat

Courage is one of the scarcest commodities there is.
That's why it's a significant source of competitive advantage.

— David Maister

Born in 1881 in unremarkable circumstances, young "Alec" was the seventh child in a family of eight in southwest Scotland. Alec grew up on a farm with no running water and loved to explore the countryside, where he developed keen observational skills. After his father died, Alec moved to London at the age of thirteen to attend school. Ahead of his class, he completed his schooling early and took a job in a shipping office. A job well below his capabilities, the stint lasted four years, leaving Alec bored and stuck in a dead-end job he despised. But Alec refused to accept defeat; instead, he demonstrated an important courage action skill:

Manifest your vision.

Interestingly, Alec took a step toward manifesting his vision when the Boer War broke out in South Africa. He and his brother Robert joined the London Scottish Rifle Volunteers, and while they never left London, they became expert marksmen. After the war, Alec's uncle died, leaving him money. His brother Tom suggested he use the money to enter medical school, but Alec had to pass the entrance exams and take the required Latin courses. Nonetheless, Alec would not allow himself to be defeated. He enrolled in classes to prepare for the medical exams and hired a tutor to teach him Latin. He passed all the medical tests with the highest marks and chose to attend St. Mary's Hospital Medical School where he became a surgeon and in 1905 achieved the highest honor as a Fellow of the Royal College of Surgeons.

Ready to embrace his new career as a surgeon, Alec instead "fell into" a position in St. Mary's hospital laboratory in order to support the St. Mary's rifle team, which had sought him out because of his reputation as a marksman. Few would have thought a position in the bacteriology laboratory appropriate to a skilled surgeon, but growing microbes became Alec's life work in an important field of medicine. At the time, vaccines that we now take for granted—for diseases like polio, smallpox, measles and typhoid fever—were being researched and developed, and

101

Alexander Fleming was poised to make a contribution to mankind that would span generations.

A defining moment arrived with another war—World War I. When war broke out in 1914, the director of the laboratory at St. Mary's Hospital had Alex assigned to the military hospital and research center he spearheaded in France. Alec was pained to see so many lost lives from infections, and it left an indelible mark. With the end of the war, Alec, now married to an Irish nurse, returned to London and the laboratory at St. Mary's.

The loss of lives he had witnessed in France prompted Alec to research antiseptics and antibacterial substances. As fortune would have it, Alec discovered a chemical in his own teardrop when the tear accidentally fell on a Petri dish where he was growing germs from mucus in his nose caused by a cold. He discovered a natural protein with bacteria-killing properties that he named lysozyome. The discovery helped inspire additional discoveries, but manifesting his vision required hard work and a willingness to make sacrifices.

Sacrifice comes from the Latin root *sacer facere*, to make sacred ... "to rise up vertically in a single act from the profane world of greed and fear, up into the serene, still dimension of the sacred, and to transfigure one's whole life in one moment."[211] Sacrifice does not mean giving up your "heart and spirit" identity or enslaving yourself to a self-destructive "work ethic." Real sacrifice is about giving up the delusions and false pretenses that keep us stuck in defeat so that we can face and manifest our true vision.

As Alec worked in the laboratory growing various samples in Petri dishes, he noticed the staphylococcus bacteria were being dissolved by a mold sample. While researching the antibiotic properties of the mold, Alec lost his brother to pneumonia, motivating him to redouble his efforts. He soon realized that "it was not the mold itself which acted against the bacteria, but a juice given off by the mold. Would the mold juice be harmful to human beings? He added some of the mold juice to a sample of human blood. Minutes, then hours passed, and there was no bad reaction."[212] Alec conducted the normal tests of the time by injecting rabbits and mice, then he tried a test on a laboratory assistant who had a sinus infection and discovered that there were no side affects from the mold juice. This "mold juice" was the *Penicillium* mold, but how could he thoroughly test it?

Alec knew the procedures required and the reports to be written in all the proper journals. Much to his surprise, the response was lackluster at best, even after repeated attempts to promote his research. Feeling defeated, Alec thought maybe it was time to retire. But then he met Oxford University pathologist Sir Howard W. Florey and biochemist Ernst B. Chain, who were also investigating ways to fight bacteria. They had been studying Alec's findings on the enzyme lysozymes and his original report on penicillin. They valued Alec's findings and became his advocates in promoting the "miracle mold."

With World War II starting, Alec went to Oxford to meet the two doctors. By 1941, Florey and Chain developed penicillin into a useful antibiotic. The problem was producing enough of the pure penicillin to treat patients. Concerned about the Germans bombing London, Florey went to the United States to obtain mass production of the penicillin, which became known as a wonder drug, a drug from which we continue to benefit today.

Staying on Target

Alexander Fleming faced each opportunity when it came knocking on his door. As a marksman, Alec easily refocused his vision as new targets presented themselves. Being able to "re-vision" the target is a big part of applying courageous leadership. "A vision is something we reach for, writes physicist Danah Zohar, something we aspire to, something that is the glue of our enterprise, the driving force, the vitality within it. When we are touched by a vision, our deepest values come into play and we have a sense of abiding purpose to our enterprise. In our world today, the thing we are most lacking is leaders who can convey vision."[213]

In any enterprise, creating a vision requires individuals to aim at the same target. Metaphorically speaking, many individuals (and organizations) shoot rifle shots as they try to create a vision. But often, the shots are scattered, rather than orchestrated in the same direction. Why? The "vision" or mission statement is stuck in an intent that has very little heart (caged courage) and sewn in empty words. This was not the angle of vision for Alec. He had witnessed too many people dying needlessly. "In Scotland," says Sandy Simpson, partner in an organizational consulting firm,

> We are very proud of our inventors, philosophers and scientists who have helped change and enhance the world ... none more so than Alexander Fleming. I grew up twenty miles or so from where he was born and educated, so I have known his name and his work for almost as long as I can remember.
>
> A marksman in his private life, Fleming hit the ultimate professional bull's-eye. In my organizational consulting work I'm often struck by the stark difference in outcomes between the firing of single unfocused rifle shots and the execution of integrated, but still targeted, strategic initiatives. What results would Fleming have achieved with the scattered, mixed-messages approach that organizations often send to their people?

Having a vision, ensuring that everything that touches employees is integrated with that vision and with each other, releases focused energy throughout the enterprise and ramps up organizational effectiveness and creativity.

Take a couple of examples from my own consulting experience and guess which is the most successful. One company stated that it is not just what you achieve but how you achieve it; yet, they rewarded a senior sales executive with a promotion despite having the reputation of "leaving bodies in his wake." The other example was when I provided executive coaching support to help an executive with similar issues improve her relationship awareness and competencies. Good strategy badly implemented is bad strategy and results in off target results.

Fleming had a vision to improve medicine and had a relentless focus on doing just that! Was his world-changing breakthrough luck? As golfing great Ben Hogan said, "The more I practice the luckier I get."

Sir Alexander Fleming was knighted in 1944, the year before Fleming, Florey and Chain were awarded the Nobel Prize for Medicine for the discovery of penicillin. Alec was also given an honorary degree by Harvard University and made a Commander of the French Legion of Honor. He continued to work and traveled the world speaking until his death in 1955. Alec never stopped aligning his vision, and he left his mark with a "miracle drug" that has saved millions of lives.

False Images of Success

Do you have a vision—a calling that resonates with your heart and inspires your soul? Or were you once inspired by a vision that now lies obscured by a sense of defeat? Everyone experiences defeat at some point in life, and in spite of how society sets us up for defeat with its ludicrous images of "success," we can overcome this obstacle simply by working to manifest that which inspires us—our personal vision—and it is different for each of us. Buying into someone else's image of success sets us up for defeat, like studying to become a doctor because that is what your parents always wanted.

In *Man's Search for Meaning*, Viktor Frankl wrote, "Don't aim at success—the more you aim at it and make it a target, the more you are going to miss it. For success, like happiness, cannot be pursued: it must ensue, and it only does so as the unintended side-effect of one's dedication to a cause greater than oneself or as the by-produce of one's surrender to a person other than oneself. ...success will follow you precisely because you have *forgotten* to think of it."[214]

Society provides an abundance of false images of success. Hyper-individualized multi-tasking, eighty-hour workweeks, the "more is better" mentality and the virtual world of iPhones and apps are just a few of society's success deceptions. As my yoga teacher said, "'Busy' has become a status symbol." To embrace your heart's true desire and manifest your vision, are you willing to sacrifice your attachment to an idea of success based on society's ploys? What superficial roles are you attached to? Are you stuck in exaggeration? How often do you hit the pause button?

Reviewing where you focus your energy will help you redefine your intention and manifest your own vision, which recognizes success in your everyday life. In "Shattered Vision," Thomas Keating asks us to look at how we create defeat by becoming too attached to the external world, "How does one push on? Is it by giving up the vision? Not exactly. Rather, it is by being *willing* to do so. For that renunciation is the only way to move beyond what one *thinks* is the vision and embrace what really *is* the vision. In other words, you must transcend all your own ideas of how to reach the place of vision in order to get there."[215] Keating suggests that what you push for may require sacrifice, misunderstanding or even vilification. You must have the courage to say, "I know the truth, so I can live with this. I will never lose courage."

Even during times of hesitation, you will feel more secure and less alone because you are working to manifest *your* vision—not your mother's vision, not your employer's vision and certainly not society's vision. Do you know, or have you witnessed, anyone who, in his or her pursuit of career advancement, demonstrated selflessness to achieve fulfillment? Re-read the definition of sacrifice and take a moment to reflect. Do you think the courageous individuals mentioned in previous chapters understood this transformation?

Sir Alexander Fleming chose to follow his passion by taking concrete steps to manifest his vision, a vision that led to new antibiotics such as streptomycin. With vision comes sacrifice. With sacrifice comes personal change. With personal change come stumbles, suffering and, ultimately, gratitude for the light of spiritual splendor.

Vortex of Complexities

What about you? Are you stuck in a vortex of complexities that leave you feeling defeated? Are you afraid of the sacrifices needed to bring your vision into fulfillment? Alexander Fleming once said, "It is the lone worker who makes the first advance in a subject; the details may be worked out by a team, but the prime idea is due to enterprise, thought, and perception of an individual."[216]

Claiming the courage to manifest your vision will lift you out of defeat, empowering you, like Alec, to take the steps necessary to achieve results.

Vision without action is merely a dream.
Action without vision just passes the time.
Vision with action can change the world.[217]

Most people will say that when they are in step with their passion, they feel *joie de vivre*—an unlimited energy that flows from the *heart and spirit*. This energy empowers everyday people to obliterate defeat and achieve amazing results that upend the status quo. Companies stand still in status quo. Unable to match outcomes with actions, status quo perpetuates defeat and becomes an obstacle to people applying everyday courage at work. Wade, a project manager said,

> The culture/structure of the work place keeps people from understanding the value of courage at work. Some workplaces are set up to be so risk averse that they discourage employees from trying anything that goes against the status quo. In those workplaces employees are discouraged from doing anything that could result in failure, regardless of the potential upside from a positive outcome. As a result, people who would normally display courage by using creative and innovative ways to solve problems more effectively are discouraged from doing so.

> Courage works for me in the sense that I am not afraid to take on a challenge that may seem insurmountable at the beginning, whether it is taking on an incredibly challenging new project with a big upside or building a program in a new geographic area. However, it is important that I demonstrate "intelligent courage" in the sense that I approach challenges incrementally and regularly evaluate my progress and likelihood of being successful.

In *The Mystic Heart*, Wayne Teasdale describes people who have overcome the self-inflicted aspects of defeat. "They move beyond emotional swings. They are not victims of their feelings, nor ruled by their desires. They are free, and so are capable of giving to others and their communities. Their actions are consistently animated by compassion and love.... They are able to appreciate interspiritual wisdom because they are inwardly free, with no vested interests to defend."[218]

Clearing the Mind

Balancing a future vision with attainable goals certainly adds heft to your resume; however, be aware that goals can shift your focus away from your vision and onto one of society's deceptions—that success is about attaining something "out there" in the future. Your mind confirms that what you do produces what you get in the future. Herein lies the courage paradox: by staying present (in the now), you will do what is best for you. Clearing the mind invites an indescribably joyful and more relaxed inner experience. "We see that the mind has gotten cluttered over the years, like an attic, with old bags and accumulated junk. Just knowing this is a big step in the right direction."[219]

Manifesting vision at work means focusing daily on the results and staying in the ever-present inner "yes mode." "The only thing one can actually 'do' is to 'be' one's potential to the fullest."[220] By staying present, you can easily respond to unexpected changes, adjusting your vision and aspirations rather than getting stuck in a quagmire of defeat compounded by foolish grit and false determination.

Manifesting your vision combines intention with action, empowering you to deliver what you promise. People earn success by learning. As you learn, you stop repeating mistakes and start moving out of defeat. Armed with courage, forging ahead on your heart's mission means you press through the winning banner that reads, "I did it my way." The power of your spirit illuminates the steps that correlate your success quotient with your courage quotient. Embracing this concept calls for a great deal of courageous will so that you can sacrifice the seductive illusion of the external world to find the truth hidden in your internal world, the source of your vision. This requires focused concentration, which is a cousin to courage.

What You Do Matters!

Faisal Hoque has been at the forefront of business and technology management for many years, but it was not always that way. Faisal called forth genuine nobility of spirit and depth of vision to overcome a myriad of "no's" along his workplace journey. An American entrepreneur, Faisal said that if he summed up his entire life, career and all the decisions that he has made, they would boil down to one word: courage! Faisal said, "I have always taken unconventional paths and it has always been about the 'journey;' therefore, the topic of courage is something I can relate to, and courage is what I have always lived with."

His story transcends defeat:

> Twenty-three years ago, I had just finished my first summer semester at Southern Illinois University Carbondale after arriving from Bangladesh in 1986. I was

17 and a student of the College of Engineering. After paying my tuition for the summer and fall, I had $700.00 left to survive, secure an education and start my life. I didn't quite realize how tight of a situation I was in. It was only after facing thermodynamics and advanced calculus that I realized those classes were a breeze compared to what I was about to face.

I met some local students who became good friends. They suggested I introduce myself to the "art and science" of on-campus "janitorial engineering." So began my expertise in polishing marble floors, cleaning arena bleachers, offices and bathrooms. My friends urged me to request financial assistance going forward. So my "pitching" career began with efforts to set up meetings with the dean, provost and university president. I even gathered the courage to leave hand-written notes on their desks when I cleaned their offices.

It is here in the corridors of Carbondale I experienced rejection when I was told "No" to my request for financial help. The provost began by suggesting I should seriously consider going back home. After much persuasion, the school eventually awarded me a $750 scholarship toward my tuition per semester. Soon after that, I dug deep for the courage to apply to twenty-five universities seeking a full scholarship. With a little help from a friend's introduction, I received a full scholarship to the University of Minnesota in Duluth, where I would get my next "No," but one I would rebuff by building my first software/hardware product, which was commercially sold by a local company.

Not long after, I accepted an offer from Pitney Bowes, even though it was not in the financial industry where I initially envisioned myself. From Pitney, I moved onto Dun and Bradstreet and then quickly realized I now had the courage to build my own company, KnowledgeBase.

Fast-forward: I was asked to join GE to help them launch their first B-to-B e-commerce spinoff as one of their youngest business executives at the age of 24. If there was ever time to have courage! Ten years since my journey here began, I started my next company, EC Cubed. We launched in December 1996 and immediately signed up GE as a customer. Less than two years later, after raising millions of dollars from "expert" venture capital firms, and securing top-tier customers, I was about to hear my next "No."

According to the VCs, the company was not "growing fast enough," and therefore I was fired as CEO. Not only did I lose my company, I also lost rights to the book manuscript I was working on. But what I did not lose was my dream, or the courage to rebuild it. I returned to the drawing board and wrote another book, then prepared for the launch of my next company, BTM Corporation.

In December 1999, my book was published; I closed our first round of financing and signed up our first customer. We officially opened our doors for business. Since then I have heard many "No's," and I am sure there will be more to come. But now, unlike during those days in the corridors of Carbondale, I neither fear nor get frustrated with them. I simply smile because I now know a "Yes" is never far from my grasp.

No one ever lost from having the courage to try.

Billionaire entrepreneur John Sperling holds a Ph.D. from Cambridge University, but he also studied at "the school of hard knocks," from which he learned, "Never set a goal. An English historian once observed, 'He goes farthest who knows not whence he goes.' There's much truth to this. If you have a goal, you're constrained by the goal."[221] Instead of drawing attention to specific goals, declare your courageous intention and confirm that your DCI mirrors the real you. Whom will you see in this collection of mirrors? Because you will see a genuine smile—the truth always smiles and blind spots fade away.

In the present mode, my business becomes a spiritual experience each day. I attempt to trust each day, no longer inserting my desire to control tomorrow. Sure, I may have committed to conduct a webinar, but that will be and this is now. Such an approach "may not mean that you will change what you do, but it may mean that you may want to change how you see it or hold it, and perhaps how you do it. Once the universe is your employer, very interesting things start to happen, even if someone else is cutting your paycheck."[222]

Unless you take time to become still in the present moment, you will remain blind to the immense energy you exert attempting to control the future. Familiarizing yourself with a stopping process expedites this self-awareness. "To let go means to give up coercing, resisting, or struggling, sort of allowing things to be as they are without getting caught up in your attraction to or rejection of them, in the intrinsic stickiness of wanting, of liking and disliking."[223] This consciousness comes from practicing some form of contemplation. Contemplation becomes a support system that keeps you out of the realm of self-defeat and moves you into an unforced unfolding of your essence.

Weird Failure

Remaining present strengthened Sir Alexander Fleming's ability to manifest his vision and prevail in the daily struggles that often leave us feeling defeated. Like Alec, "You will need a vision that is truly your own—one that is deep and tenacious and that lies close to the core of who you believe yourself to be, what you value in your life, and where you see yourself going.... Our vision has to do with our values and with our personal blueprint for what is most important in life."[224] Tim Sosbe understands. He left his job of seven years without another one in place. "It took a ton of courage," he said. "I had a good position and a home to pay for, but I knew something would come along if I had the fortitude to make the leap. I'm happy to say courage does pay off: I've found a better job in the same industry with a company that firmly believes in the productivity potential of work-life balance. On top of all that, I'm working from home! It's really all about visualizing what you want and having the courage to make it happen."

Wouldn't it be great if we received our "calling" in an elusive dream? Unfortunately, many times the calling happens when we are going through "hell in the hallway" (Chapter 1). One of the greatest gifts you can receive is the revelation of *your* calling during a dark night of the soul. "Your calling isn't something you inherently 'know,' some kind of destiny. Far from it. Almost all of the people I interviewed found the calling after great difficulty.... Most of us don't receive epiphanies. We only get a whisper—a faint urge. That's it. That's the call. It's up to you to do the work of discovery, to connect it to an answer. Of course, there's a single right answer.... The funny thing is that most people have good instincts about where they belong but make poor choices and waste productive years on the wrong work."[225]

Are you open to a divine solution even when you think you know what is best? "In finding [contentment] we experience relief; we feel centered. It is a beautiful discovery to which we can frequently return. Who would have thought it could all be so simple?"[226] Is your work life disappointing or bordering on unbearable? Eckhart Tolle reminds us, "It is only by surrendering first that you can break the unconscious resistance pattern that perpetuates that [unbearable] situation."[227] Kabir, the great Indian poet, expressed how difficult it is for individuals to move from defeatist tendencies and accept what they are not:

The truth is you turned away yourself,
and decided to go into the dark alone.
Now you are tangled up in others,
and have forgotten what you once knew,
and that's why everything you do
has some weird failure in it.[228]

Your choices limit or expand your vision. Alec's courage empowered him to choose action rooted in his vision despite the likelihood of setbacks and defeat. To embrace an intentional process that allows self-knowledge to surface requires an evacuation of your dark corners and the prepackaged values that keep you from wholeness—"a complete undoing of all our carefully laid plans, and a lot of letting go of our preconceived ideas.... This letting go into the unknown, this submitting to the unloading process, is an essential step into the mystery of our own unconscious. Hidden there is not only our whole life's history ... but also the positive elements of our potential for growth, faith, hope, and divine love."[229]

Jon Kabat-Zinn continues, "Non-doing has nothing to do with being indolent or passive. Quite the contrary. It takes great courage and energy to cultivate non-doing, both in stillness and in activity.... Non-doing simply means letting things be and allowing them to unfold in their own way.... Meditation is synonymous with the practice of non-doing."[230]

Troy G. Smith, mentioned in a previous chapter, said, "The greatest sin is to waste talent, a day, a moment, anything. I'll take someone with great heart and a modicum of talent over an extremely talented tin man any day! One of my favorite quotes is from the wise old master, Yoda, 'There is no try, either do or do not.' In my line of work, 'courage' is synonymous with 'vision,' and in real estate development 'vision' is the art of seeing something where presently nothing exists."

Your vision produces specific effects in your inner world that instigate bleak times—times to stop and contemplate your next step. Caught in this indeterminate state, defeat may tempt you to give up. Instead, use your DCI as a tool to move you through tentativeness and help you sustain a gradual process that *manifests your vision.* "Your first chance is to surrender each moment to the reality of that moment. Knowing that what *is* cannot be undone—because it already *is*—you say yes to what *is* or accept what isn't. Then you do what you have to do, whatever the situation requires. If you abide in this state of acceptance, you create no more negativity, no more suffering, no more unhappiness. You then live in a state of nonresistance, a state of grace and light lightness, free of struggle."[231] Do you go to work free of struggle?

Goals Are Footprints

Developing your own vision entails identifying the vision and then making the most of opportunities that serve to manifest that vision. What can you do to start the process? Stop to reflect. Move beyond the self-defeating traps of mental noise until you can begin to sense the soft-spoken message of your heart. As you become centered in your heart and spirit, modify your DCI to reflect the truth of your courageous Being.

Success is never final and failure never fatal, it's courage that counts.[232]

In Blanche Napolean's job as a Manhattan executive, she knows firsthand that defeat can reign as queen for the day. But it is never too late to learn something new or to make a career change that supports your vision. For Blanche, "The key to success is to have the courage to do everything differently. There are no shortcuts to gaining courage. It cannot be purchased in a store. Courage comes from within after a seed is planted. Time and experience nurture it.... I am not afraid to fail because my courage will allow me to learn from this experience and store the lesson deep inside."

Courageous people like Faisal and Blanche maintain inspired standards that honor their struggles. Finding a way to prevail, they never succumb to defeat, and they refuse to allow complacency to undermine their vision. Courage illuminates the paths of these successful people and reveals the steps necessary to manifest their vision. "The word 'ambition' shares a root with the word 'ambient'—*ambire*, meaning 'to move around freely.' That word originated in the 14th century, when politicians would travel broadly to get votes and support. Taken literally, to have ambition is to create your life's journey. Ambition is not a single-minded focus, a career obsession or rampant self-promotion at the expense of others.... True ambition is this: after you do something amazing, you do something ordinary—and you discover the importance in it."[233] If you did not know the root of ambition, you might mistake true ambition for a form of passion or enthusiasm that feeds the defeatist delusions of the ego instead of manifesting your vision.

Courage Development Questions to Ponder

- How do you strive to manifest your vision on a daily basis?
- What have you sacrificed in order to manifest your vision?
- When you feel discouraged or defeated, what helps you renew your commitment to your vision?

Chapter 8
Motivate Yourself from Within—
Exposing Self-Neglect

It takes a lot of courage to release the familiar and seemingly secure,
to embrace the new. But there is no real security in what is no longer meaningful.
There is more security in the adventurous and exciting, for in
movement there is life, and in change there is power.

— Alan Cohen

The man who exemplifies the next courage action was born in France on June 11, 1910. A frail child who was told never to exert himself, Jacques refused to wither in self-neglect. In spite of significant physical limitations, he learned to swim and became an inventor at eleven years old. He went on to become a naval officer, innovator, underwater explorer, author, filmmaker, photographer, environmentalist and marine conservationist.

The legendary Jacques-Yves Cousteau was not only "small and skinny and anemic, he seemed to catch every illness that came along. His parents took him to doctor after doctor, to no avail."[234] Defying the advice of the doctors his father's employer said that exercise would be the best medicine for the eight-year-old boy. Swimming became a passion and slowly, this type of exercise did make Jacques stronger.

In 1930, hungry to see the world, Jacques entered the prestigious French Naval Academy. In his third year at the academy, he embarked on an around-the-world cruise, during which he saw pearl divers in the South Seas using goggles. Back home on leave, Jacques broke his right arm in a terrible car wreck. When Jacques awoke from being unconscious he learned that the doctors wanted to amputate his arm. He refused and dove back into swimming to rehabilitate his arm. The arm would remain crooked for the rest of his life, but Jacques did not allow himself to fall into self-neglect.

While off duty from the navy, "He was given a pair of underwater goggles, the kind used by [pearl] divers. Cousteau was so impressed with what he saw beneath the sea that he immediately set about designing a device that would allow humans to breathe underwater."[235] With swimming buddies Philippe and Didi, Jacques, now a tall skinny young man, started using "aviator goggles" to thwart the saltwater sting in his eyes. This experience changed his life and became the three men's journey—to design

113

variations of underwater equipment that would allow them to breathe underwater and go deeper and deeper.

Like Dietrich Bonhoeffer, Jacques, a member of the French Resistance, faced tremendous challenges during World War II. After the war, Jacques returned to the French Navy until 1957, when he resigned to focus on underwater photography and underwater gear. In 1960, he used his growing influence and expertise to help halt French government plans to dump atomic waste into the Mediterranean Sea.

Greg Allgood, director of Procter and Gamble's Children's Safe Drinking Water Program said, "What intrigued me the most about Cousteau is that, during World War II, he and a few naval colleagues invented the Aqualung. They were banished to a small island in the Mediterranean to diffuse bombs and took the opportunity to invent the Aqualung along with a new sport [called scuba diving]. He then made these experiences famous through his television show, while impressing upon a whole generation the need to protect our oceans and planet from contamination. A courageous man and one of my personal heroes, he had a big influence on my life."

Recognizing his true destiny, Jacques energized his life with classic "heart and spirit" courage, constantly motivating himself from within. Do the challenges you face seem so daunting that you have allowed your unique talents and unlimited potential to wither away? Has self-neglect either in the form of physical decline or spiritual depletion robbed you of the inner strength to act in your own best interests? If you answered "Yes" to either of these questions, you can begin to strengthen your spirit and overcome the obstacle of self-neglect by learning to

Motivate yourself from within.

The courage to act is the mark of wholehearted living—the opposite of self-neglect. Jacques' exceptional self-actualized drive motivated and guided him to the centeredness of his true Self. For more than fifty years aboard his famous ship *Calypso*, Jacques documented the underwater world of the oceans. His television show, *The Undersea World of Jacques Cousteau*, premiered in 1968, captivating viewers with ocean wonders.

As he documented the beauty and mystery of life in the seas, Jacques began to realize that marine animals needed protection and preservation. The courageous power of his innate motivation and love of nature propelled him beyond obstacles like self-neglect. Illnesses never stopped him from helping advance the state of the art for diving gear. Even after the loss of a dear friend in a diving accident, Jacques continued to share the magic of the ocean with the world, taking on more tough projects. In 1973, he and his two sons created the Cousteau Society for the Protection of Ocean Life.

Parker Palmer writes, "How much dissolving and shaking of the ego we must endure before we discover our deep identity—the true self within every human being that is the seed of authentic vocation."[236] Self-examination is hard work but worth the investment, particularly in tough times. Troy G. Smith said, "Have the courage to zealously pursue your passions and you will never work a day in your life!" Do you despise your current vocation, or does your work bring you joy and fulfillment? Throughout the day, how many masks do you wear? When was the last time you shed one false image? Parker continues, "There is a great gulf between the way my ego wants to identify me, with its protective masks and self-serving fictions, and my true self."[237]

Many writers have written about the masks we wear. In "Love and Its Counterfeits," Geoff Olson writes, "The word 'person' is drawn from persona, an ancient Greek word for mask, in the theatrical sense. The root meaning of the word betrays the illusory, playful nature of our surface personalities. In Greek tragedies and comedies, the masks had carved openings through which actors spoke. Who, or what, speaks through us?"[238] What mask are you wearing right now? Does it keep you stuck in self-neglect? Depression? Judgment? Suffering? Blame?

Greg Allgood, Ph.D. has his reasons for identifying Jacques Cousteau as his courageous hero. Greg's definition of courage is "Being willing to face your own limitations and overcome seemingly impossible obstacles." He continues, "Courage gives me the strength to face the challenges between me and success—in work and in my personal life." Greg recalls an obstacle he faced at work and the courage he applied.

> I asked the largest consumer-products company in the world if I could turn a commercial effort that had failed into a not-for-profit effort. I asked for responsibility to run it as a not-for-profit effort even though I had no formal business training. I received approval, and we created a unique and innovative distribution model that is now saving thousands of lives and providing more than a billion liters of clean drinking water every year. The Children's Safe Drinking Water Program has been successful because of the courage to try innovative solutions and take the time to develop new partnerships built on trust and long-term commitment.

> We also had the courage to listen to the beneficiaries and change the program based on what they told us. One of the biggest changes was to focus on helping people with HIV/AIDS. Experience told us that AIDS humanitarian groups would view providing safe drinking water as

competition. But in the field in Africa, we heard women with HIV/AIDS telling us that the safe drinking water provided by our purification packets was saving their lives. One woman came to me to share the impact on her life. On her deathbed she had weighed 70 pounds. Then she started treating her water with our packets, and now she's healthy and helping raise 30 orphans.

An experience in rural Kenya helped me find the courage to start a not-for-profit business. A woman was collecting water from the only source available—a filthy pond that we wouldn't want to walk through barefoot. I demonstrated our purification packets, and she was amazed to see it get clean and clear. As we chatted, a man who was standing to the side came up and stole the bucket of clear water. Clear water is that valuable in this part of the world. Before we left, the woman got on her knees and begged me for the packets.

Influenced by Jacques Cousteau, Greg noted that the famous Frenchman's influence had been passed to his daughter, studying to become a marine biologist.

Illness and Loss of Self

In the context of work, self-neglect leads to two significant conditions: illness and loss of self. Overcoming illness involves listening to your body and taking better care of yourself. Waiting too long to have a needed surgery out of fear you will lose your job is one example of self-neglect leading to illness. Another example is staying in a stressful job like many of the people I have interviewed. One woman told me, "My blood pressure was so high at work from the stress that my colleagues expected to call 911 on any given day. I hated my place of work. I was depressed, and I had stayed way too long." Why did this woman choose self-neglect rather than drawing from her innate courage to motivate herself from within? What type of stress does your work invoke? What is the ratio of stress to joy? The stress and physical illness that stem from self-neglect produce an unhappy work life that spreads misery into all aspects of life. Motivating yourself to initiate a change takes courage, but it could save your life.

The flip side of the self-neglect coin is loss of self, which often accompanies the loss of a job or some other traumatic event that disturbs the ego's sense of identity. Regardless of the immediate circumstances, loss of self requires time and reflection to examine what truly needs mending. Identifying the first small step to motivate yourself quells the anxiety. Focus on something immediate and easily reachable. This narrow focus helps you recognize that courage is an accumulation of small steps up the ladder, and this simple recognition helps you to continue stepping up.

Search in the Dark

When you commit to stop and reflect, it affects your ego's masks and takes you outside the limitations of your false self-story, the source of anger, suffering, apathy, blame and unhappiness. "The greatest achievement of humanity," writes Eckhart Tolle, "is not in works of art, science, or technology, but the recognition of its own dysfunction, its own madness.... To recognize one's own insanity is, of course, the arising of sanity, the beginning of healing and transcendence.... What is it that lies at the root of this insanity? Complete identification with thought and emotion, that is to say, ego."[239] Notice how our culture promotes and even mandates working longer hours, which ultimately keeps us trapped in the ego's false scripts and prevents us from enjoying the real blessings that life offers in every moment.

Life ought to be a struggle toward adventures whose nobility will fertilize the soul.[240]

During life's struggles toward noble adventures, we start to recognize the aspects of our work lives that need to be released, like the manifestations of self-neglect—the things that cause illness and loss of self. In his videos, Eckhart Tolle speaks to the manner in which our society created what he calls "nervous mind energy." Have you experienced the way people gather for the "critical" staff meeting? Most attendees display a nervous "hyperactive" energy, as if this is a key intrusion in their lives because they are so-o-o-o busy.

If you have participated in or observed this craziness, the next time you attend a meeting, suggest that everyone stop for three minutes, breathe deeply and quietly compose themselves. You will notice a shift in the mood as people become focused and centered. A different appreciation for listening will manifest, and the "mood" will shift toward more cooperation and peacefulness. "Cooperation is alien to the ego, except when there is a secondary motive. The ego doesn't know that the more you include others, the more smoothly things flow and the more easily things come to you."[241] My Aunt Marilyn shared with me that "Peace comes in minutes at a time, then hours and finally, most of the time. After you become accustomed to it, you will learn to call it back when you are not at peace."

A culture dominated by "nervous mind energy" promotes self-neglect. It denies the needs of the heart and devalues solitude and inner silence, when in fact, "Mind creates the abyss, the heart crosses it."[242] As Piero Ferrucci observes, "We have become too externalized, perhaps, so that we have grown accustomed to the harsh noises of traffic, television, pneumatic drills, and rock music. And who, amid such a cacophony, is able to hear the subtle voice of the innermost core?"[243]

Strength in Vulnerability

Overcoming the self-neglect that leads to illness and loss of self is not easy. Palmer writes in *Let Your Life Speak*, "It means waiting, watching, listening, suffering, and gathering whatever self-knowledge one can—and then making choices based on that knowledge, no matter how difficult. One begins the slow walk back to health by choosing each day things that enliven one's selfhood and resisting things that do not. The knowledge I am talking about is not intellectual and analytical but integrative and of the heart, and the choices that lead to wholeness are not pragmatic and calculated, intended to achieve some goal, but simply and profoundly expressive of personal truth."[244]

It may sound trite, but your belief system is probably the greatest single determinant of your success at work. Colleen Abdoulah is the CEO and President of a mid-sized telecommunications company. At forty-five, she learned she had breast cancer. "I left the doctor's office and sat in my car. I knew I didn't want to focus on the cancer! Instead, I decided to focus on how I would experience it. So I prayed and asked for three things: to be aware of my interactions with others, to pay attention to the messages I was to receive, and to always be gracious towards others. What I learned after only two chemo sessions was that I desperately needed to learn to be gracious to myself!" Colleen recognized the dangers of self-neglect and refused to let it become an obstacle to her healing.

Colleen also learned how illness at work reveals one's need to be vulnerable. "I sat with my staff and told them about the diagnosis and how I wanted to live as normally as possible. I told them I wanted to stay involved as much as possible. Then, I shared my fear around that desire: fear of losing contact and feeling out of the loop. I also shared my feelings that I might be a 'drain, a burden.' I was very vulnerable. Their response was, of course, wonderfully supportive and genuine, and they truly helped me during the tough times."

Communicating a weakness, such as illness, imperfection or loss builds solidarity at all levels by liberating people and encouraging them to stay in touch with their own issues. Facing a life-threatening disease, Colleen continued to motivate herself from within and projected her courageous spirit's light into her colleagues, who continued to achieve results. Colleen exemplified "courageous will" and confirmed that staying connected generates support from those around you. As Colleen demonstrated, courageous will keeps each of us connected to the true Self; whereas, ego will keeps us stuck in the false self.

Jarring Transitions

During jarring transitions, we tend to experience a loss of self … a depletion of spirit. In other words, we forget how to love ourselves. "If we have not experienced ourselves as unconditional love," writes Thomas Keating, "we have more work to do, because that is who we really are."[245] Self-neglect belies a distinct absence of unconditional love.

In over twenty years in management, Denise experienced the greatest test of her courage during a jarring transition—when a colleague committed suicide.

> As the director of human resources, I took the call from the colleague who discovered the body. I decided that it would be best if the President announced the death of our colleague and summoned the courage to interrupt a senior management meeting. My heart was beating terribly, and my body was shaking as I walked into the room and asked the president to come out into the hall, where I gave him the tragic news.

> Afterwards, I broke down crying, and he just put his arms around me for comfort. I had always held firm that crying was not something you did on the job. I didn't think at the time that my crying was courageous. I now realize it was definitely a form of being authentic, and it always takes courage to be authentic.

"Grief is an important healing mechanism, a way the psyche makes the transition from one situation to another. Our contemporary mania for pulling ourselves up by the bootstraps, getting back to work as soon as possible after a deep loss, and staying active no matter what is not always a perfect antidote to pain."[246] In fact, denying ourselves the opportunity to move through the grieving process not only eliminates authenticity, it also becomes a damaging form of self-neglect that extinguishes the light of our "heart and spirit" courage.

People are like stained glass windows …
their beauty is revealed only if there is a light from within.[247]

Debra Bradley Ruder has been a writer and editor for the past twenty-five years, and like others with whom I spoke, she did not feel her story was worthwhile. I met Debbie at a conference where I was speaking, and I was immediately in awe of her courage! Not only had she survived a brutal assault and abduction at age twenty-one, she had faced cancer shortly before her attack.

Like Jacques, Debbie was determined not to become stuck in self-neglect, so she became a crusader to help others face their illness. "As a survivor of Hodgkin's lymphoma, I was afraid of being around the disease on a daily basis since it might remind me of unpleasant times and of my chances for recurrence. But after joining the Dana-Farber Cancer Institute, I saw that it was a profoundly meaningful move. I've become much more open about discussing my medical past with others; it has even become a source of strength. This has carried over to other parts of my life, and for the first time in twenty years, my encounter with cancer has served as an asset, not a liability."

I was curious how working at Dana-Farber Cancer Institute had allowed Debbie to turn this health stigma into an asset, and she responded with these three elements.

- **Empathy.** Being a cancer survivor helps me carry out my job as a writer and editor. When I interview patients and family members for stories, I can understand what they've gone through and what they are facing.

- **Giving Back.** Working at a cancer center has enabled me to give back to the cancer-research community that helped save my life.

- **Advocacy.** Through my writing and editing for print and online publications, I can help spread the word about the latest cancer treatments and research. I can also help inform our readers about ways to prevent cancer. Lastly, whatever I can do to help cancer survivors understand the long-term effects of their past treatments and live longer and fuller lives is a privilege.

Working at Dana-Farber has helped Debbie grow as a person. "On a daily basis," she said, "I encounter people who demonstrate strength and perseverance, who accept their diagnoses without self-pity and find ways to make a difference, whether by sharing their stories, counseling others or raising funds to support care and research. Call it courage, resilience or generosity, they inspire those around them to appreciate each day." In other words, illness and grief can actually serve to strengthen one's courageous identity as long as they do not become excuses for self-negligence.

Loss of Self

Loss of self in the context of work frequently entails the disruption of the ego identity, especially if the masks we wear at work define that false identity by "glamorizing the superficial."[248] This manifestation of self-neglect produces a "small" view of ourselves or an attachment to a certain image of ourselves.

Becoming aware of this type of self-neglect can also provide an opportunity "for increased intention to reevaluate spiritual principles and put them into actual practice rather than just intellectual appreciation."[249] In other words, learning to motivate yourself means moving away from what prevents you experiencing joy in your work in order to find what you love doing.

Dorie McCubbrey knows about this kind of self-neglect. In high school and college, she excelled in math and science. She entered college as an engineering major at the advice of guidance counselors and family members. She excelled scholastically and earned a doctorate in bioengineering. Despite never feeling any passion for this type of work, she was reluctant to change her career path, and in this state of self-neglect, she developed a severe eating disorder. She said, "My passion finally emerged while I was being treated for my eating disorder. It became clear that my mission was to help others overcome their eating disorders." Turning down a six-figure salary, Dorie returned to college to earn her counseling degree. From her book *How Much Does Your Soul Weigh*, Dorie shared a sentence with me: "The conflict of not being who I really was eventually caused so much pain that I became willing to let go of my fear of change."

Now, as an expert in the treatment of eating disorders, Dr. Dorie notes that approximately half of the patients in her practice have struggled at work with a loss of self. She explains that anorexia, bulimia and binge eating are ways to feel a sense of control over something, in this case, food. "When someone's professional life feels out of control, I recommend three courage steps:

- Be aware of any eating disorder patterns.
- Identify how these patterns relate to and are triggered by specific situations at work.
- Step up and initiate changes in these work situations so that there is no need to control the intake of food as a means of coping."

Marianne Williamson affirms Dr. Dorie's wisdom: "Living in the realm of body identification rather than spirit identification, we are constantly at risk for the experience of loss. We think we lose every time something in the world of form doesn't unfold the way we wish it to…. To the ego, that means the relationship is over; to the spirit, that means the relationship simply changes form."[250] To overcome loss, delve into your heart and spirit to discover the courage to let go of your ego, for "the ego does not become enlightened but instead disappears."[251] When your consciousness shifts toward enlightenment, everyone benefits exponentially from your action.* As a courage model, your courage consciousness moves us all up the ladder because you are designing your life's work, regardless of the circumstances. When you design your life's work, you are motivating yourself from within—you are practicing "human intention made visible and concrete."[252] Are you willing to design your courage at work and manifest your courageous intention?

On One Leg

Remember the Chinese proverb mentioned in Chapter 5:

He who hesitates before each step spends his life on one leg.

Steve worked as a lawyer and never liked it. "I was very frustrated. I came home one evening, and while I was holding my young son, I noticed I was talking angrily to my wife about my day at work. I wondered how my three-year-old son was internalizing my voice, and that was it! After eleven years as an attorney, I quit. With two children and no prospects lined up, it was scary."

I asked Steve when he first became conscious he was unhappy with his law career, and he replied, "On the first day." Stubbornly stuck in self-neglect for eleven years, Steve confirms that unhappiness at work produces a proportionate level of regret. When Steve became conscious of his attitude and noticed how it filtered into his family's spirit, he finally started to motivate himself to look for a career change. After three months, an association hired him as the education director, and in three years he became the CEO. "They took a chance on me because I had no management experience, but I think they saw my litigation-related skills as an asset."

Steve learned the hard skills needed to run the association, such as budgeting and technology, but as a lawyer, he brought the critical "real" skills, such as problem solving, consensus building, creative thinking, advocacy and analytical thinking. Are you still hesitating instead of taking a step out of self-neglect? If so, how many years have you been "standing on one leg?" Are you cognizant of your full range of skills? Are you a "self-neglect profile" in non-courage?

Regardless of your level of education or age, self-neglect can quickly drain years from your life before you realize it. Many people admit that they dislike their careers. If you are one of these people, reconnect to your heart and spirit and rely on your innate courage to motivate you to step up! "Presence is giving one hundred percent of ourselves to a situation without allowing our thoughts to be distracted by the lure of future events, or by the regurgitation of unassimilated experiences. Every act serves to focus the mind on the present reality.... A person who is able to appreciate the value of every situation is free because he or she is using the mind in the most open way."[253]

Stop for a moment to review your DCI and ask yourself: "Did I really commit to giving myself permission to be courageous?" Are you masking your reluctance? Do you believe you can do the work described in this book? Through your chosen form of inner silence, you chip away the false self and reclaim the parts of you that you lost. Basil M. Pennington writes in "Why We Flee,"

> Unfortunately, in seeing ourselves as we truly are, not all that we see is beautiful and attractive. This is undoubtedly part of the reason we flee silence. We do not want to be confronted with our hypocrisy, our phoniness. We see how false and fragile is the false self we project. We have to go through this painful experience to come to our true self. It is a harrowing journey, a death to self—the false self—and no one wants to die. But it is the only path to life, to freedom, to peace, to true love. And it begins with silence. We cannot give ourselves in love if we do not know and possess ourselves.[254]

Diminishment of self to discover true Self is a humbling process. Humiliation usually surfaces on the spiritual journey long before humility arrives. "For some of us at least, go through humiliation, where we are brought low, rendered powerless, stripped of pretenses and defenses, and left feeling fraudulent, empty, and useless—a humiliation that allows us to regrow our lives from the ground up, from the humus of common ground."[255] Purging the false self allows the light of your spirit to become brighter and brighter. "The ultimate best use of talents seems to be to sacrifice them. You may not like to hear this, but I'm afraid that is the truth. It's in letting go and allowing the divinely inspired process of humiliation and growing sense of powerlessness to enter our lives ... the pain of facing one's own interior corruption and the intimate purification that divine love brings about in those who ... have the courage to say an unmitigated 'yes' to whatever happens."[256]

Interior Corruption

The dispirited heart longs for the true Self, and the wisdom that comes with this discovery. This is why learning to stop and eliminate the interior corruption is so critical to finding fulfillment with your work. "It is also well to know in advance that all suffering is not intrinsic to spiritual gain but strictly due to resistance to it. Suffering is due to dragging one's spiritual feet and the ego's insistence on having its own way."[257]

Rennie Davis writes about being stripped of "big time" image. "It took collapse to discover there was beauty in the condition of emptiness. While my personal descent spiraled into economic depression with no income whatsoever, my internal condition blossomed. With time on my hands, I found delight in the simple encounters. Curiosity found a home in me. The more I let go, the more joy I felt."[258] When you choose to let go of an attachment, then you can start to reflect on your spiritual health and make room for authentic growth, especially when that attachment is to an aspect of the ego's false self. As Davis observes, the loss of self creates opportunities to realize the true Self and experience the joy that accompanies this realization.

As we experience the process of self-realization, it is important to notice how we interact with our colleagues. Ask yourself these questions. How do I serve others? Is my service limited by predetermined boundaries? Do I play it on the safe side? When I do reach out, is it constrained somehow? How do we keep each other stuck?

Hospitality has no boundaries. Hospitality is the fragrance of loving grace that reflects a humble, compassionate heart, and compassion is a cousin to courage. Do not confuse compassion with fixing. Efforts to fix things, even out of a sense of compassion, ultimately rest on judgments. Compassion helps us move past the tension and see through the false identities that create the tension.

Illness Combines with Loss—Keep Going
In the words of Winston Churchill,

If you are going through hell ... keep going.[259]

Dr. Lynn Hellerstein has applied her loving mother's teachings at her optometry office for nearly thirty years: "We treat our employees well. I'm sure there are other jobs with better pay and better benefits, but we empower our employees and treat each person as an important member of our work community. We don't micromanage them. We show our appreciation by furnishing treats, saying thank you, acknowledging a job well done and sharing compliments. The bottom line: we give them the courage to be all they can be."

When Lynn asked her employees why they remained with her office for so many years, they responded, "We go home happy. Everyone loves each other." In Lynn's office, love goes full circle in giving. Giving of yourself negates self-neglect and creates a positive spiritual energy that permeates the work environment. Do you work in a place where you talk about and express a loving attitude towards your colleagues?

Lynn's personal growth accelerated when her mom passed away, creating a desire to share her experiences and enlighten others to the fulfillment that comes by allowing love and peace to direct their lives at work. She related this example: "I just had an annual review with a vision therapist in my office. Her performance is excellent, her work ethic is excellent, but she operates from a place of fear, always worrying. She has all the knowledge she needs, yet she has a fear of failure. I reached out to her and shared my own personal story about how I almost gave up my passion for public speaking. I had begun to doubt myself and question whether I was keeping up with the literature. What if someone asked a question that I didn't know the answer to? What would people think?"

To reveal her vulnerability to a staff member took courage, but Lynn says it paid off. "That staff member holds me in high esteem. I've always been very protective of my personal image, always striving to be perfect. My employee couldn't believe that I had such thoughts or weaknesses." Lynn believes that sharing empowers employees with the courage needed to move beyond their concerns. Lynn added, "My fear of looking stupid and the perfectionism issues almost strangled my life."

Striving for excellence motivates you; striving for perfection is demoralizing.[260]

As we have seen, the behaviors of self-neglect come in many forms, including depression, bulimia, obsession with identify and humiliation. In November 2002, Lynn had surgery to remove a tumor from her colon. "The very difficult recovery process from the surgery ended up being a gift from the Universe. Before, I kept myself so busy and distracted with work, kids and accomplishments that I never allowed time for me—to process me. After the surgery, I couldn't work like I used to, which triggered financial concerns. There's a saying about money and courage: 'Money lost, nothing lost. Courage lost, all is lost.'[261] What was most important was my loss of self. I was not only disconnected from my body but also disconnected spiritually."

Realizing that her illness and loss of self both manifested self-neglect, Lynn sought healing that nourished her soul and helped reconnect her mind, body and spirit. Yoga, meditation and Reiki now play important roles in Lynn's life. She has come full circle, from learning her mother's lessons in childhood to becoming a successful professional, losing her mother, growing in spirit, inviting vulnerability, reclaiming her inner Self and re-energizing the love lessons she learned in childhood.

"The paradox is that we can never fully fulfill our role until we are ready to let it go. Whoever we think we are, we are not. We have to find that out, and the best way to do so, or at least the most painless way, is through the process that we call the spiritual journey."[262] What can you do to reflect on your neglected heart and spirit, the source of your courage? Does your ego's self-image create automatic reactions, or have you begun to act from the love in your heart and spirit?

Reflect on the choices you make, for unconscious choices tend to keep you in a state of self-neglect, a condition dominated by false scripts and deceptive illusions. As you recognize your unconscious choices, the ego's deceptions are revealed, and you can move into a more honest, courageous level of consciousness. Your innate motivation provides a direct reflection of your level of courage consciousness.

Courage Development Questions to Ponder
- How has job-related stress affected other aspects of my life? Has this stress affected my personal relationships? Has it affected my health?
- Recall one or two incidents that allowed you to let go of a false pretense.
- If you find you are constantly on the "run," review your inner scripts that impede you from slowing. What childhood pattern no longer works? Did this pattern keep you in indecision?

Power vs Force, Dr. David R. Hawkins: "It's very important to remember that the calibration figures do not represent an arithmetic, but a logarithmic, progression. Thus, the level 300 is not twice the amplitude of 150; it is 10 to the 300th power … An increase of even a few points represents a major advance in power; the rate of increase in power as we move up the scale is enormous."[263]

Chapter 9
Establish Higher Standards—
Working Out Self-Doubt

All of the great leaders have had one characteristic in common.
It was their talent for confronting unequivocally the major anxiety of
their people in their time and giving them the courage to face those anxieties.
This, and not much else, is the essence of leadership.

— John Kenneth Galbraith

When it comes to working out self-doubt, the crucial manifestation of your everyday courage is your ability to

Establish higher standards.

Failing to challenge ourselves to meet high standards keeps us stuck in a place of unrealized potential. In other words, we all have unrealized potential, and if we do not establish personal standards for ourselves, we simply cannot break away from self-defeating doubt that undermines our efforts to manifest that potential. Ask yourself this question: Are you ready to ditch your doubts and take a chance?

Roll Up Your Sleeves

Katherine Meyer grew up in a privileged family and graduated in 1938 from the University of Chicago. Her father had urged her to launch her career in journalism by working for the paper he had purchased five years earlier, *The Washington Post*. Unlike her staunchly conservative parents, Katherine sought diversity and intellectual openness; so instead of accepting her father's job offer, "she moved to San Francisco to work on the *News* as a reporter for twenty-five dollars a week. Seven months later, despite her ambivalent feelings toward her parents, she agreed to her father's offer of a four-dollar-a-week raise to come home to work for the *Post*."[264] Young women of this time rarely contradicted their parents' political viewpoints.

Perhaps Katherine's exposure to the lives of other courageous women informed her opinions. She knew of the hardships and social injustices that Victoria Woodhull endured (Chapter 1), declaring, "I would love to have known Victoria Woodhull.... Everyone interested in the history of women's rights will be fascinated by the story of this little-known pioneer."[265] Katherine's recognition and admiration of Victoria Woodhull's courage

127

affirmed her own courageous spirit, and her willingness to contradict her parents' views revealed her courageous spirit at an early age.

Katherine's sincere reflection regarding the decision to move back produced a defining moment that characterized her core identity and confirmed her courageous leadership. Even in tough situations, Katherine delved into her true Self to establish her standards. In *Transcending the Levels of Consciousness*, Dr. Hawkins writes, "Courage brings inner confidence and a greater sense of personal power because it is not dependent on external factors or results."[266] There is a fine line between being overly confident and having an ego-centered identity, one of many reasons why learning to stop and open oneself to introspection is so important. Reflective self-analysis produces personal progress. How do you know you are making progress? You are happier at work and more fulfilled each day.

Katherine married Philip Graham in 1940, and the couple purchased her father's publishing business in 1948. Stepping to the sidelines, Katherine retired to become a wife, mother and congenial hostess for her husband, now the CEO of the *Post*. Life was good, but in 1963, everything changed with a single gunshot. Katherine heard the gunshot and found her husband's lifeless body. Brilliant but bipolar, Philip Graham had committed suicide.

Philip's suicide negated the couple's well-laid plans and required Katherine's immediate response. She concealed her stunned anguish, rolled up her sleeves and took the helm of the *Post*, which was considered just a regional paper. While the man's world in which she found herself perpetuated the myth that a woman's place was in the home, Katherine had shown that she was an independent thinker. "At first patronized and intimidated by her male employees, as well as painfully shy ... Graham slowly gained self-confidence and executive authority. Her goal was to remake the *Post* into a respected, world-class newspaper."[267]

Katherine had a good sense of who she was, which kept her grounded in her decisions and enabled her to establish higher standards even in the face of her mistakes. "A mistake, she said, is simply another way of doing things."[268] No matter how intimidating or potentially damaging the outcome, Katherine was determined to maintain her standards and get the job done. We all encounter ample opportunities to test our courage, "which includes the capacity to endure inner fears when belief systems are shaken,"[269] but the obstacle of self-doubt can keep us stuck for a lifetime if we fail to respond to these opportunities in courage. Katherine kept asking questions founded in her convictions until she was able to assess the situation, apply the necessary courage and establish higher standards. "Absolute conviction destroys existential doubt and frees the human soul. The Eastern traditions say that doubt is one of the biggest obstacles to the profound discovery of enlightened awareness."[270]

Defining Moments

In 1971, a defining moment presented itself to Katherine in the form of the *Pentagon Papers*, the documents that revealed the government's deception about the War in Vietnam. With the *Post* preparing for a public stock offering, the timing could not have been worse. Katherine courageously chose to follow her heart. Dismissing scripts of self-doubt, she stepped up to the challenge and maintained her standards. In *The Seat of the Soul*, Gary Zukav writes, "When you enter into your decision-making dynamic consciously, you insert your will into the creative cycle through which your soul evolves, and you enter consciously into your own evolution. This requires effort, but is it really more difficult than living through the consequences that follow a decision to act in anger, or selfishness, or fear?"[271]

Katherine and her team at the *Post* stood behind the decision to publish the *Pentagon Papers*, even while the Nixon administration made threats and the company's stock dropped. Revealing the values in which she believed most strongly, Katherine displayed a courageous combination of integrity and high standards. The merit of Katherine's resolute spiritual courage was reflected in her refusal to play it safe, dodge discomfort or hedge her bets. Holding herself accountable for her decisions, she endured the temporary discomfort of outside pressures and the potential for failure. When was the last time you failed? Did you use that failure as a gain? As Robert F. Kennedy once said, "Only those who dare to fail greatly can ever achieve greatly."[272]

Nixon's resignation in 1974 vindicated Katherine and the *Post*. By establishing higher standards, Katherine profoundly elevated the *Post*'s stature. "The great soul is the person who has taken on the task of change. If he or she is able to transcend fear, to act out of courage, the whole of its group will benefit and each one, in his or her own life, will be suddenly more courageous, though they may not see how or why."[273] With no female role model, Katherine was the epitome of "where courage meets grace." Dr. Hawkins writes, "Gracious power patterns acknowledge and support life, and respect and uphold the dignity of others.... [Graciousness] also implies generosity of spirit, such as the willingness to express thanks or acknowledge the importance of others in our lives. Grace is associated with modesty and humility, for power doesn't need to flaunt itself; force always must show off, because it originates in self-doubt."[274]

Katherine made tough decisions based on high standards when self-doubt could have easily undermined her integrity. When you face tough decisions, does self-doubt erode your integrity, or have you established personal standards that allow you to manifest your courage under pressure? Establishing higher standards at work includes things like summoning the courage to tell your boss what you are worth. In other words, to request what you deserve requires courage. When offered a new job, are you able to equate your worth with the top salary tier? Do you step away from situations that do not cultivate your courage?

Most people do not push past certain boundaries, particularly the artificial boundaries of corrupt or unethical workplace standards. Reflecting an absence of courage consciousness, such standards drag us down and create inroads for self-doubt. How do you learn to move beyond artificial boundaries? Do you emulate someone who exemplifies courage, a "courage change agent"? Have you claimed the courage to align your personality with your spirit? Have you begun to the abundance that comes from this internal unity of spirit and personality?

Katherine Graham became a courage change agent and a legendary CEO, probably the most courageous CEO of our time. (In 2000, she was one of only three women who ran Fortune 500 companies.) "If I were forced to pick only one business leader from whom to draw professional learning and personal inspiration," writes Jim Collins, bestselling author of *Good to Great*, "that one leader would very likely be Katherine Graham."[275] Comfortable with her identity as a woman, Katherine balanced the behaviors of courage with high standards. Businesses fall apart when the courage of their leaders lapses, and the remains of these businesses clutter the corporate landscape.

Katherine admits throughout her Pulitzer Prize winning autobiography, *Personal History*, that she experienced self-doubt about her decision to run the Watergate story. The fact that she overcame her doubts but is willing to admit them demonstrates that she understood the value of humility. "Humility is the basis of an honest, mature self-awareness that accepts ourselves as we are, without covering up, making excuses, or blaming others.... When we have humility and simplicity, we are free of hypocrisy."[276] At the age of 84, Katherine died from a fall. Honoring her memory, the editor of *Vogue* wrote, "She saw no reason to slow down with age and always remained true to her principles and enthusiasms."[277] There are many courage styles and no single "better" way—only the action required to establish your higher standards.

Whether you are a first-time manager, CEO or entrepreneur, building your career on the sands of self-doubt will produce a shaky, disaster-prone work life. Have you established the personal standards needed to promote your talents and overcome self-doubt? Whether you are a man or a woman one easy way to emulate Katherine's gracious style of courageous leadership, the source of her high standards, is to offer frequent words of encouragement. Encouragement is oxygen to the heart and goes a long way toward elevating the standards of your colleagues at work. In the *I Ching*, we read:

It is only when we have the courage
To face things exactly as they are,
Without any self-deception or illusion,
That a light will develop out of events,
By which the path to success
May be recognized.[278]

Some might say that self-esteem is the underpinning of courage. Certainly, one could make the case that, if you are prone to speak your mind, display your convictions, stop abuse on the spot and so on, you probably are a confident person. For example, while visiting President Johnson's Texas ranch in 1964,

> *Washington Post* publisher Katherine Graham grew outraged at angry criticism the president directed at the first lady in her presence, and she reminded Johnson that Lady B "got you where you are today."... That episode ... indicated that Graham, who had been verbally and physically abused by her husband, Phillip Graham, had by that time found new courage with men and a new sense of entitlement to stand up for herself and other women in similar circumstances.... She also encountered sex discrimination in the industry organizations to which she belonged and was often the only woman at their gatherings ... a brilliant, strong-willed woman ... who defied the diminished expectations for women of her time and proved to be a courageous, values-driven leader and hard-nosed businesswoman.[279]

Taylore Sinclaire, founder of IlluminEssensce works with women. Taylore said in a phone interview that once a woman "starts to realize she no longer needs to apologize for her viewpoints, or how she feels, she has just been given permission to be herself. Now, she lives her convictions with courage. On the opposite side of the coin, if her natural state of being feels disapproval (whether from herself or an outside source) her self-esteem and courage erode."

No Excuses

Most of the women I meet possess unidentified courage. A woman I will call Beth is talented, well-educated and successful. She wrote to me, "I have been traveling this month. I know you asked me to write about my use of courage at work, but I have to tell you that I truly have not felt very courageous with decisions regarding my career. I still have not taken some of the steps that I should (and could) have." Beth also was not happy, a common sign of low self-esteem (which is quite different from but can be a major source of self-

131

doubt). Why would a bright and well-educated woman not feel competent to meet life's challenges and excel?

Self-esteem diminishes suffering from anxiety, frustration, despair and, of course, self-doubt. Denise, whose management career encompassed over twenty years and numerous reinventions, had this to say: "My mother taught me to have a positive outlook, and she told me I could do anything. She always encouraged me to stand up for myself and to be true to my beliefs. As a black woman, I have faced much criticism and many obstacles—not only outside of my race and gender, but frequently within my race and gender. Blacks thought I was too dark ... and women thought I was arrogant."

Denise's experience points to the feminine double standards that Phyllis Chesler's research has identified. "Strong women don't seem to behave in 'girlish' ways. As a group, women tend to 'protect' weak women and punish 'strong,' expressive, direct, risk-taking or 'original' women."[280] The significance of this double standard cannot be underestimated, for it exacerbates self-doubt and prevents women from acting in courage.

Denise's courage played a central role at work, "Having courage at work has allowed me to advance my career many times. I have started out in jobs that were entry-level positions, but because I displayed my courage through my self-confidence and high standards, I took on more responsibilities. I was determined to get the job done, and I had the courage to express to the right people that, if given an opportunity, I had the ability and skills. I was promoted time and time again." By establishing higher standards, Denise designed her courage. Centered in courage consciousness, her workplace persona provides an honest reflection of her inner being.

"Your self-doubt or self-loathing will sabotage you.... Nobody can talk you into feeling good about yourself—you get the solid good feelings from success. What's going to bring you success that will make you feel good about yourself?"[281] Success is about developing your own identity, your true self, so that you feel fulfilled and happy in each moment. Novelist Jane Rule writes, "My private measure of success is daily. If this were to be the last day of my life, would I be content with it? To live a harmonious balance of commitments and pleasures is what I strive for."[282] Commitment is a cousin to courage.

A therapist will focus on childhood wounds, the residual effects of the bad experiences and the resulting scripts that continue to limit one's potential. Unfortunately, we can use this therapeutic self-knowledge "as an excuse for not making an effort. It's easier to sit in a therapist's office and talk about something that can't be changed than it is to do what needs to be done now. You can blame your parents, spouse, boss, race, social status—there's a whole slew of things you can use to slide out of responsibility for what you're going to do next.... The best you can do is notice what's happening and get on with your life."[283] Taking action is a key component of courage.

Average Joes?

Most of us are "Average Joes" working with the abilities we were given. Many people who started out as Average Joes learned how to "make a difference, as Eleanor Roosevelt did in her campaigns on behalf of the disenfranchised; or as Betty Ford did for forcing people to rethink alcoholism; or as Paul Newman was doing, raising millions for sick kids by selling salad dressing and spaghetti sauce."[284] My finest interviews about courage have been with Average Joes—the everyday man and woman. They just do not make the headlines! What have you done with your gifts? Did you trade them for a cushy job or an incomplete education?

Bill Laughlin is executive vice president for an energy technology company. He defines courage as "the willingness and ability to absorb mental obstructions, abuse or cruelty without depression, discouragement or negativity." Bill's understanding about courage and how to eventually apply courageous leadership blossomed when he was a teenager.

> As a teenager, I felt verbally and mentally abused in several situations. The example that has had the most significant impact on my life was when I was a sophomore member of the high school ski team and several seniors were exceptionally verbally abusive toward me. It was a difficult time as I was searching and hoping for acceptance among my peers.

> I had to have courage to accept and deal with the mental abuse. Rather than withdrawing and entering a shell, I dealt with the matter head-on. I remember vividly being in a hotel room at a ski meet in Jackson, Wyoming. There was a moment that I felt beaten down, terribly alone and abandoned. I looked in the mirror and realized that at the core of my problem was a lack of confidence and self-esteem. I willed myself to be more confident and worked to improve my self-esteem. To me, this was the epitome of "courage." This was a defining moment in my life. I was soon elected captain of the ski team.

> Often I have faced a lack of confidence in my ability to accomplish a task. Each time I've retreated to the loneliness of that Wyoming hotel room and reflected on my finding the courage to move forward in a confident manner. Another defining moment came when I entered

Law School. Because of my absence from school for over two years, I once again needed to summon the confidence to compete in the classroom. With courage (and hard work), I rose to the prestigious position of managing director of the school's law review.

Courage in my business life has always been important and paid huge dividends. One time I was released from a significant position because the company was being liquidated. This was extremely difficult with two small children and no income, but once again I retreated to that experience in the Wyoming hotel room. It took courage (and a lot of patience) to hold my family together while waiting for the "right" position to become available.

Continuing today, I regularly reflect on the need to apply my self-confidence and self-esteem or what I call courage to compete in the business world. I enjoy and appreciate the challenges of business and life, respect those with whom I work and enjoy the "ups and downs" of life in general. Ultimately, I am courageous and I now possess self-esteem in a humble way.

Bill said that he continually asks himself "Am I proud of myself? Have I been the best that I can be?" Working out one's self-doubt is not easy. When people stay in StuckThinking™ they thwart the courage actions that support everyday courage at work.

Me, Worthy?

If your current obstacle is self-doubt, you will find the journey to self-fulfillment extremely difficult. Believing in *you* is critical. Joe Rei, Ph.D., is a director of executive development. Joe shares a story of self-doubt that has riddled his spirit—even today, at 60 years old.

I had a terrible experience one time in Dallas when I was to give a speech. I was 28 at the time and to make a long story very short; I nearly passed-out in front of about 300 people who where there to hear me speak. For months and years I wanted to flee the room when we "went around the table" to introduce ourselves in small gatherings. It was decades before I could stand before a crowd without feeling faint. It is only recently that I have started to cherish the thought of public speaking.

I tried everything to overcome this, but in the final analysis, I had to believe that I actually had something to say. I had to feel confident that I was prepared, that I had

134

"been here before" and that my opinions, thoughts and research were good (not great, just good).

Entrepreneurs know the face of courage. Jason Simms is 25 years old, a freelance writer, PR agent and musician. He said,

> A courageous person is unaffected by the opinions of others, fear of failure or self-doubt. Though a courageous person may take risks, there is nothing reckless about courage. A courageous person is clear-headed enough to weigh the odds and is prepared to bear failure with dignity, but fully expects to succeed. Courage helps me trust myself and my plan. For example, I must constantly fight for my next assignment, client or gig. It's easy to get derailed by someone who is threatened by me and wants me to fail. I have to muster courage to say, "I am good at what I do. If I continue doing what I know how to do, I will have whatever I want." I use a similar strategy when negotiating fees for my work. People who don't want to pay me very much commonly try to convince me that the service I provide is not worth what I am asking. It takes courage to set your price and stand by it.

Fear of Success

The amount of time we spend stalled in unrewarding situations (standing on one leg instead of climbing the ladder) also indicates a lack of personal standards that challenge us to continue manifesting our potential. Steve, mentioned in the previous chapter, stayed stuck for eleven years. On the path that *you* design to manifest *your* vision of success, your courage consciousness expands and reflects who you are.

Deep and concentrated efforts to stop and reflect are required for self-actualization to blossom. "It is not only *what* we think, but also *how* we think—the style, the rhythm, the cogency of our minds—that powerfully determines the patterns of our life."[285] Jason continues,

> The summer after my first year of college was my first summer on my own away from my parents and the first time I had to get a job in a new city. I pounded the pavement for weeks before finally landing a gig at Guitar Center nearly an hour away. I worked for minimum wage. My job was to stand at a desk near the door and stamp receipts on the way out in an effort to keep people from stealing.
>
> My second or third day on the job, a stool appeared behind my desk. I sat down and stamped receipts that

way. A couple of weeks later, my superior told me it was corporate policy that I had to stand. He said the stool was not a negotiable issue, so I stood. Standing is more exhausting than walking around a shop working or even mowing lawns all afternoon like I did in high school. I would get home from my long commute every night exhausted. I didn't have the energy to play music or write or ride my bicycle or be a part of the city.

So after about a week of this, I told my boss I had to either be allowed a stool or leave right then. He let me leave. I think people should have the courage to stand up for their own well-being at work. Just because something is commonplace doesn't mean it's healthy or a good idea. Every time I see an employee standing needlessly at a bank or store, I think about my job at Guitar Center and my heart goes out to them. It's not always possible to quit your job of these types of disagreements, but I think people often lack the courage to stand up for themselves and defend their health.

The DCI is your blueprint, your game plan. If you are currently on the wrong career track, if you have dreamed of starting your life over again, if you have been remiss about how you are going to climb over an imposing obstacle, and if you are open to starting from the ground floor, then follow the guidelines of the people described in this chapter. They were not trapped in self-doubt and a dwindling self-image. They internalized their experiences and drew on the internal energy of courage to step up. Are you trapped by your own self-image? Is success a difficult concept to face?

Many people really do fear success. If your self-evaluation reveals a tendency toward excessive modesty, a need to work faster or a sense of threat from self-confident colleagues, now is the time to work toward a new or refined self-image. We all know that bad stuff impedes or derails a positive self-image, so how do we go about improving it? Your current self-image did not create itself overnight. It developed over time. There is no quick fix or "miracle of the week." The keys to developing a positive self-image are to recognize that you have untapped potential, to realize that you deserve a fulfilling life and to establish and maintain the personal standards that support you in doing both.

Lowly Loathing

Rooted in our self-doubt, we all have a tendency to sell ourselves short. If you loathe your job, establishing higher standards at work requires separating yourself from your job, which requires introspection. Introspection leads to self-knowledge—the most important trait of a courageous person. With reflection and self-knowledge come self-confidence and success. "As soon as you apply yourself to reflection, you will at once feel your senses gather themselves together; they seem like bees which return to the hive and there shut themselves up to work at the making of honey.... At the first call of the will, they come back more and more quickly. At last, after countless exercises of this kind, God disposes them to a state of utter rest and perfect contemplation."[286]

The contemplative state of reflection varies as widely as individual personalities. Jason listened to his inner voice and responded before the downward spiral of self-doubt undermined his self-confidence. The *I Ching* beautifully sums up the issue.

Difficulties and obstructions throw a man back upon himself.
While the inferior man seeks to put the blame on other persons,
bewailing his fate, the superior man seeks the error within himself,
and through the introspection the external obstacle becomes for him an
occasion for inner enrichment and education.[287]

Millions of people go to work every day to do jobs they hate, to work with people they detest or to perform unrewarding tasks. Unable to see past their paychecks and benefits, they often blame the boss, company and culture for their misery. If you hate your job, you should reflect on your level of self-esteem. A person with healthy self-esteem takes steps to direct a change.

Awareness is the first step toward a cure, but if you lack the courage to establish higher personal standards and exemplify them at work, your boss will have no idea how you feel. *Establishing higher standards* at work takes a lot of effort. Apprehension and emotional stress create self-doubt—the opposite of courageous self-confidence. Are you blaming your boss, the company or the corporate culture? If you are tolerating this type of situation, you have not found your beehive and its honey. Look to your heart and spirit, and draw from your personal courage to establish the personal standards that will promote your success.

Courage Development Questions to Ponder

- What do you use to medicate your self-doubt?

- How do you display your courage for others to remember you?

- Do you convey your lofty personal standards on the job or do you simply accept a lowest common denominator of what is just good enough for that work environment?

- How do you remember who you are and what you stand for?

Chapter 10
Install Self-Discipline—
Overcoming Apathy

No one has looked back sadly on a life full of experiences,
but many look back wishing they had had the courage to do more.

— Anonymous

In the Jewish quarters of Kiev, Ukraine, Golda Mabovitch's family heard the screams of discrimination: "Death to Jews!"[288] A religious minority, Jews were hated and segregated in Russia. Feelings of terror and anger brewed in Golda's bitter spirit; yet, with curiosity, she wondered what about her religion made people want to hurt her. This innate inquisitiveness revealed her purpose: one day there would be a safe place for Jews to live, and she would save other Jewish children from this type of terror-stricken life.

Poor to the bone, Golda's family lived with persistent malnutrition in one cold room. Only three of the family's eight children survived the appalling living conditions. Feeling hopeless, Golda's father gave up on the idea that he could find work as a carpenter and decided to immigrate to the United States. Once he settled in Milwaukee, the rest of the Mabovitch family began the long, arduous journey to America in 1906. Golda loved the tall buildings, bright advertisements, cars, ice cream and soda pops. Jewish friends would gather at their apartment to drink tea and discuss their heritage, imagining a homeland that would one day be their true address. These ideals infused her spirit's passion.

When her older sister, Shenya, contracted tuberculosis, the doctors recommended recovery in the dry Colorado climate. This was great news because her sister's boyfriend had immigrated to Denver. Shortly after Shenya moved to Colorado and married, Golda began to be annoyed with her parents. They wanted her to drop out of school and work in their shop, but she loved learning and studying and had the innate self-discipline to excel in academia. When her parents informed her that she would not attend high school because she would be marrying an older man, she became defiant.

Only fourteen years old, Golda snuck out her bedroom window and traveled to Colorado to be with her sister and brother-in-law. Even at fourteen, Golda demonstrated a combination of passion and self-discipline that eliminated any possibility of getting stuck in apathy. I wonder how many of today's teenagers would actually care enough to run away from home in order to continue their education? And at fourteen, how many of us had the self-discipline that Golda demonstrated? Golda's self-discipline proved key to her ability to manifest her passions and her dream. In fact, the courage action necessary to overcome apathy (loss of energy with dulled emotions) obstacle is

|nstill self-discipline.

Though she only stayed a year in Colorado, Golda fell in love with one of her sister's friends, Morris Meyerson, who introduced her to exciting new books and ideas. When Golda returned home, her parents were thrilled that Morris had expressed his desire to marry her, so they conceded in letting her attend school. She graduated from high school in less than two years then attended the Milwaukee Normal School for Teachers.[289] Golda demonstrated her natural genius in high school and college, but genius should not be confused with intelligence quotient (IQ).

As Dr. Hawkins writes, "It would be more helpful to see genius as simply an extraordinarily high degree of insight in a given area of human activity.... Genius can be more accurately identified by perseverance, courage, concentration, enormous drive, and absolute integrity—talent alone is certainly not enough.... One could say that genius is the capacity for an extraordinary degree of mastery in one's calling. A formula followed by all geniuses, prominent or not, is: Do what you like to do best, and do it to the very best of your ability."[290]

Dr. Hawkins' definition of genius leaves no room for apathy, and words like "perseverance" and "concentration" point to the importance of self-discipline. Genius, then, has a lot more to do with finding your passion and developing the self-discipline to follow that passion than with intellectual skills. Have you identified what you like to do best—or has a jaded culture of apathy taught you not to care? "Through apathy ... people sometimes do not want to have anything to do with the Self. The Self is, after all, an uncomfortable subject. It asks us to revolutionize our lives ... it demands hard work and exposes us to danger. Ignoring the whole matter and getting on with our everyday lives may be far easier. This response is the greatest form of betrayal—the denial of what we really are."[291]

Are you satisfied to remain stuck in apathy? Did you once have a passion for something but failed to instill the self-discipline needed to manifest that passion in your work? If we do not develop the self-discipline to face the obstacles within us, we will prolong the suffering of unfulfilled work. Do you need to add *instill self-discipline* to your Declaration of Courageous Intention (DCI)?

Marrying the bookish Morris in 1917, Golda endured ridicule from neighbors. "She was the husband—she worked while he shopped, cleaned, cooked, and even bought her clothes."[292] In *A New Earth*, Eckhart Tolle writes, "Applying negative labels to people, either to their face or more commonly when you speak about them to others or even just think about them, is often part of this pattern [complaining]. Name-calling is the crudest form of such labeling and of the ego's need to be right and triumph over others: 'jerk, bastard, bitch'—all definitive pronouncements that you can't argue with."[293] Constantly dodging the labels thrown her way, Golda's self-discipline and unrelenting courage permitted her to express her beliefs. One belief was that men and women could share duties equally, a belief that continued throughout her life.

After World War I ended, the British announced that Jewish people from around the world would be welcomed in the newly acquired Palestine. Morris did not share Golda's passion, but she could be very persuasive. So they courageously set off to establish themselves in the Jewish homeland, where they soon learned that Golda was pregnant. Eventually, Golda had to face the truth. Her calling did not guide her in the path of the traditional Jewish mother, and she could no longer imitate the life that Morris wanted. Choosing to put her calling first, she accepted a job as secretary of the Women's Labor Council (the Pioneer Women) and moved to Tel Aviv with her son and baby daughter. Her heart's mission remained clear: to build a Jewish nation. Many of us ask ourselves the question, "What will I be when I grow up?" Golda demonstrated what Oriah Mountain Dreamer affirms:

It doesn't interest me what you do for a living. I want to know what you ache for, and if you dare to dream of meeting your heart's longing.[294]

When the world learned the truth about the concentration camps at the end of World War II, Golda hoped the British would let the survivors go to Jewish Palestine. Sadly, the opposite occurred. Sensing that the Jews would have to fight other countries for their borders, Golda headed for the United States to raise money for the new Jewish state.

Golda possessed the courageous self-discipline to reflect on changing situations and then make progressive adjustments to manifest her vision, unlike many visionaries, who lack the self-discipline to put ideas into action. Courage lives in action. Golda also knew "well-behaved women rarely make history."[295] Bob Wendover, generational consultant shared, "... those who succeed in their choice of endeavors work hard at coming up with solutions to the obstacles placed before them. In fact, those who succeed at the highest levels seek out problems to solve rather than waiting for an obstacle to arrive on their doorstep."[296]

Unflagging Devotion

On May 14, 1948, the State of Israel was born in Palestine. Israel won its War of Independence in January 1949, and Golda came home when she was appointed minister of labor following the first Israeli election. Fully embracing her passions, Golda wanted her last name to reflect the country's Jewish heritage, so she changed Meyerson to a Hebrew name, *Meir*, meaning "illuminate."[297] Golda's love for politics provided the perfect outlet for her passions, and for the rest of her professional life, she courageously worked to ensure that there would be a safe place for Jews to live.

With a family to support and a cancer diagnosis to face, Golda accepted the role of Israel's fourth prime minister on March 17, 1969. Applying her forty-five years of political experience, she always maintained her self-discipline and focus. Her cabinet met each Sunday night in her kitchen to discuss the latest terrorist attacks. Golda retired as prime minister on April 10, 1974. *My Life* was published in 1975, and she died in 1978. Some historians say she never achieved her dream of a peaceful country, but one thing was for sure—she confirmed that gender is not the issue!

It is important to recognize that courageous men and women like Golda Meir, Helen Keller, Dietrich Bonhoeffer and Vivien Thomas, the man featured in the next chapter, did not live easy or glamorous lives—they just chose never to be average. They were all, just like you, everyday people who listened to their hearts and spirits to make hard choices rather than choosing apathy—the easy way out. Hopefully, their examples encourage you to find the courage you never knew you had—the courage to live in self-fulfillment, to find what you like to do best and to do it to the best of your ability!

Chris is a divisional sales manager who motivates his team to not fall into the "average" mindset but to instill self-discipline. Chris believes that applying courage "is the only way to create something unique. Doing what everyone else does will give only similar results." Chris shares an example of everyday courage:

> The best way to clearly view courage would be from the perspective of full-commission sales people going through the monthly cycle. I know each of my reps well, and I can tell when they are bumping along the bottom of the cycle. I remind them that being average at what we do takes more than most people bring to their jobs every day. I remind them that any time wasted worrying or

delaying the proven activities that generate revenue costs them money.

It takes courage to do the hard things like prospect and follow up with important deals. There is always fear of rejection, but there is also fear that a piece of pending business is not what you think it is and you do not have enough going on to pay your mortgage. My job is to cut through whatever they see as an obstacle and get them to start doing the hard things that they have been putting off. It takes courage from them to finally pick up the phone.

We all have different courage styles. One style does not fit all. Golda's non-intimidating personal style achieved results, yet her courage style was quite different from the grace of Katherine Graham. Nonetheless, each of these women demonstrated her individualized style of courage, but you don't have to be a famous headline to be courageous. The trailblazers that you have read about thus far carry the bulk of the burden because they are ahead of the innovation curve—creating something unique—making courage their daily legacy by the choices they make.

When was the last time you applied self-discipline to further your own advancement? While your courage style may not resemble Golda's or Chris', it should manifest the kind of devotion to your calling reflected in the following lines.

The bud stands for all things,
even for those things that don't flower,
for everything flowers, from within,
of self-blessing; though sometimes it is
necessary to reteach a thing its loveliness,
to put a hand on its brow
of the flower and retell it in words
and in touch it is lovely until it flowers
again from within, of self-blessing. [298]

Flowering Again and Again

Reset ... refashion ... reappraise ... recast ... reframe ... rethink ... revisit ... rediscover ... rechallenge ... rebuild ... regroup ... regenerate ... reimagine ... repack ... restory ... restructure ... recontextualize ... reconfigure ... reposition ... revision ... reorient ... reteach ... reconsider ... regroom ... reshape ... rebrand ... reconstruct ... regenerate ... recuperate ... recalibrate ... redevelop ... refresh ... revive ... reenchant... restore ... realign ... revisit

... rehabilitate ... reenergize ... redefine ... relabel ... reinforce ... reform ... regather ... recharge ... re-emerge ... repair ... reinvent.

Any aspect of renewing your mind offers you an opportunity to discern your spirit's will. In *Inevitable Grace*, Piero Ferrucci writes, "All we have is our will—the will to believe, to focus on the next step, and to move forward. Make no mistake: The will we are speaking of here is not 'willpower.'"[299] Do you have the courageous will to take the next step to instill self-discipline? Courageous will is not for everyone. Controller Leonard "Sherm" Sherman, mentioned in Chapter 2, shared his opinion about why people don't display courage at work: "The repercussions of stepping outside one of the 'masses' or the trepidation of what leaving the flock might mean. For most [people], I think it is not as important to rattle the cage as it is to live as peaceably as possible in their own spheres of influence."

No one can go back in time and start over, but if you come from a place of renewed passion and discovery, you can begin to undermine the apathy that keeps you from making a new beginning. Some people innately understand how to stay at the forefront of business changes and continuously reinvent themselves to suit changing circumstances. Reinvention starts with asking heartfelt questions. In *The Mystic Heart*, Wayne Teasdale suggests that you ask, "*What* am I?" He writes, "Sometimes, in a fleeting moment, we receive an answer, a glimpse of our true identity. It is real but intangible, indefinable. Although we might attain a momentary peek, the locus of individual identity remains a mystery, a source of reflection for as long as we've been conscious."[300]

Anytime is a good time to review your career to determine if you have allowed apathy to seep into your consciousness and dissipate your passion for your work. Gayle Richardson began her career as an untrained accounting clerk with no degree and no accounting experience. Self-disciplined and willing to make sacrifices, she went to night school, gaining self-confidence as she furthered her learning.

> This newfound confidence helped me redefine myself as a highly skilled accountant. I was promoted into a management role, and with courage, I started to question their traditional managerial behavior. I quickly got on board our corporate initiative, and through my determination, my division eventually emerged with a participative management style. I continued to apply these values and techniques as I changed departments and eventually careers. With my own circle of influence, I redefined myself as a technical and statistical analyst and management consultant. I adopted an attitude that I still

stand by today: "I am willing to be fired for staying true to these core values."

Gayle said that, after so many years with the same employer, she began to pray that she would discover her next journey. Her enthusiasm had been waning for a long time, and when she looked into her heart, she began to recognize the apathy that had taken root. She was honest, admitting, "My heart's no longer in it." Determined to overcome apathy's insidious influences, she committed to finding a career that fed her heart. No one forced her to take a career risk; she considered the consequences and made the choice to act from her "heart and spirit" courage. Fortunately, she possessed sufficient self-discipline to see her decision through. Making a drastic career change requires a process of awakening to live in conscious choice, the opposite of being on "apathetic automatic."

Have you noticed how much of the talent pool in this country is underutilized because apathy has set in? Dr. Hawkins' "Map of the Scale of Consciousness," provides an indication of the significance of apathy, calibrating this obstacle at 50, along with despair (far below courage at 200). Why would those low levels equate with needing courage to make a career change?

Few people have the courage to make a career change as dramatic as Gayle's. Many of us think about it, but few actually pursue a significant career transition. Having the courage to recognize your discontent, to know you have a choice and then to make a change indicates that you are finding your own everyday courage at work. Eckhart Tolle writes, "Your entire life journey consists of the step you are taking at this moment. There is always only this one step, and so you give it your fullest attention. This doesn't mean you don't know where you are going; it just means this step is primary, the destination secondary. And what you encounter at your destination once you get there depends on the quality of this one step. Another way of putting it: What the future holds for you depends on your state of consciousness now."[301] If your next step is informed by courageous self-discipline, you can and will find meaningful work, particularly when courage becomes an underlying theme as it has for Dot Todman, celebrity vocal coach. "Without courage, I would not have made mistakes to learn from or discovered the creative genius within. I would have simply stood still."

A New Face
Are you doing work that keeps you from being happy? Loss of passion strangles the heart. "Passion" originates with the Latin verb, *pati*, meaning "to suffer." As the Latin root indicates, searching for and manifesting your passion can involve some suffering along the way, but the lifelong rewards

are well worth the price. Start by asking yourself what you do well. "People who *deduce* an answer usually end up mistaking intensity with passion. To the heart, they are vastly different. Intensity comes across as pale *busyness,* while passion is meaningful and fulfilling. A simple test: Is your choice something that will stimulate you for a year or something that you can be passionate about for ten years?"[302]

With a predisposition for action, a courageous person instills self-discipline as they reinvent themselves. "There are no shortcuts to discovering the perfect job. There is just a journey.... Can you actually speed up finding the answer to the 'What should I be when I grow up' question? I think you can, but you need to embrace a practice that requires discipline, candor, and a bit of courage."[303] Defining your true talent through your values spurs passion and reveals your calling. Rennie Davis, a member of the infamous sixties group, the Chicago 7, presents workshops on "A Declaration for a New Humanity." At one event he said, "Passion … reveals excitement, curiosity and an unconditional mind.... All you have to do is re-script yourself. How you see yourself is how you see the world. The first way to invite this ardor is to stop blaming."

Most people daydream about making radical career changes, but without the self-discipline to take action, they remain stuck in apathy, perhaps hoping they will win the lottery but never buying a ticket. There is no need to throw the baby out with the bathwater when confronting apathy. Simply focus on each day's effort and the results will follow. Your learning curves never flatten out. You just kept adjusting old skills in new ways. What helps is to let go of what the results may look like. Then, you begin to trust the process with no attachment to the outcome. With no attachment to the outcome, your DCI statements reflect your intention and guide you to awakening your essence.

What a new face courage puts on everything.[304]

Courageous people seek feedback. They want to hear how others perceive them. Just like all workplace competencies, courage can be learned. To integrate a new level of self-discipline, you may need to face a paralyzing fear (Chapter 3) or confront patterns of denial (Chapter 2). Sometimes what you are suited for is not on your radar. Isolating yourself to one career may hide (or hinder) your transferable skills. What is important is to learn how you are going to let the real you shine. Sometimes losing a job is the kick in the butt that motivates us to push apathy away and demand more in our lives. "We therefore live a life far below our psychological and spiritual means. Also, there are ways of discovering—or rediscovering—who we are and of what we are capable. Sometimes this is an easy process that is carried out in an elegant fashion.... At other times it is fraught with trials and errors, doubts and sheer hard work. But it is always worth it."[305]

Connie Evans never thought her work life portrayed courage. "I always thought the things I endured or survived in my life were just 'normal.' I've just always done what was needed to survive. If anything, I felt I was a weakling, insecure and unable to support myself." Eliminating the false script that life is just a struggle to survive, Connie said, "I realized my own courage." Connie's definition of courage at work is to maintain authenticity, be true to yourself and live with purpose. How do you know when you are being true to yourself, being authentic? "Something is true when it resonates with and expresses your innermost Being, when it is in alignment with your inner purpose."[306] "Now that I have come to terms with my courage," Connie said, "I will continue to be successful at fulfilling my dreams. When I keep my faith and believe in myself, I am the most successful." Have you lost sight of your dreams? Perhaps this insightful poem from Joyce Monfort called "Dreams" will help motivate you to rediscover your dreams.

Dreams

Where did my dreams go when I awoke?

Are they forever lost, with the night,

or, is there a place where they still abide,

to help give me courage, to face morning light?

They slip through my mind,

Like sand slips through my fingers.

Are dreams less permanent?

less necessary?

Have you tried to build a life

Without a dream?[307]

Simple Beginnings, New Endings

One of the keys to success is to have the courage to do everything differently. That is probably why organizations are constantly trying to reinvent their leadership models and redefine expectations. Strategy means the ability to re-create daily, not just during the annual budget meeting at corporate headquarters. Entrepreneurs tend to know this naturally. Rarely generalists, they represent portraits of courageous endeavors. They trust their own abilities, define their own careers and demonstrate the self-discipline necessary to create the businesses of their dreams. As a result, they reap intrinsic rewards and achieve the results that lead to long-term success. Often, they sacrifice image and income, but the rewards of fulfilling their dreams make the sacrifices seem inconsequential. Business philosopher Jim Rohn understands:

Success is not to be pursued; it is to be attracted by the person you become.[308]

Instilling her self-discipline, one woman was quite courageous in reinventing herself when she used her own capital to step up in her area of expertise, but she had her share of doubters. Being an entrepreneur gave her the intellectual freedom she had never experienced as an employee. Because most people do not claim courage as one of their primary professional virtues, they mistakenly believe they are not courageous because they do not recognize truly courageous moments (e.g., exploring new ideas, creating an innovative business, transcending rejection or taking initiative).

Even if you are not an entrepreneur, it takes courage to transition through different career paths. If you know your skills, feel confident about your abilities, are skilled at interviewing and are motivated to learn, why can you not progress from education to real estate, banking, corporate training, publishing, writing, speaking and whatever else you *want* to do? Yes, it takes courage to capitalize on opportunities, to reinvent yourself in what Eckhart Tolle calls "flowering consciousness."[309]

Self-disciplined people use their knowledge and skills to restore their spirits with contentment. Contentment is a cousin to courage. Contentment reveals an internal satisfaction versus settling. Below are a few probing questions to contemplate. Use them as a guide to question your existing model.

- What is it that you do really well?
- How do you rediscover your core strengths?
- What do you like to do?
- What do your peers, family or clients' value in you and think you do well?
- How can you sell your strengths in a competitive environment?
- What excellence do you stand for?

Unending Learning
Nothing is more valuable than to deepen the sense of who you are. Regardless of the goal, it takes conscious choice and effective action to dive into your heart and spirit in order to confront the real you. In other words, "Know thy Self." Socrates' counsel still prevails after twenty-five centuries. In *A New Earth*, Eckhart Tolle writes, "What those words imply is this: Before you ask any other question, first ask the most fundamental question of your life: Who am I? Knowing yourself deeply has nothing to do with whatever

ideas are floating around in your mind. Knowing yourself is to be rooted in Being, instead of lost in your mind."[310]

New emotions that surface are inevitable. But these new emotions become the foundation for learning, and the growth that comes with learning feeds new spontaneity. The actions of self-aware leaders are founded on their courage. Danah Zohar's work on Spiritual Intelligence (SQ) says, "Self-awareness is one of the highest criteria of high spiritual intelligence but one of the lowest priorities of our spiritually dumb culture. From the moment we begin school we are trained to look outward rather inward, to focus on facts and practical problems in the external world, to be goal-oriented. Virtually nothing in Western education encourages us to reflect on ourselves, on our inner lives and motives. We are not encouraged to let our imaginations run. ... Developing greater self-awareness is a high priority for raising SQ."[311]

It is never too late to be what you might have been.[312]

As the founder and president of O'Neill Marketing, Tracy O'Neill identifies courage at work as the ability to accept and respond to uncertainty. She said, "I would not differentiate between courage at work and courage in my personal life. In my mind, courage is courage." And Tracy is demonstrating her courage by embarking upon yet another courageous venture: "I've decided to take my painting and photography more seriously, with the ultimate dream of making it my full time occupation. Since December, I've been spending every free moment taking classes, reading, drawing and painting to learn and gain experience. I am absolutely obsessed with it! For now, I am continuing to run my marketing business, but I am being more selective about my clients and how I use my time. Most artists don't know how to promote themselves, or manage their own business. Starting my career on the business side, I have that covered. My issue is getting inventory that people will want to buy."

Significant life changes require self-discipline. Once you have centered yourself in your core being, you can continue with conscious personal development that reflects your intentional design and your choices. Applying courage to each of life's stepping stones leaves a unique footprint, an imprint that reveals a dedication to being your best. Courage is about your personal make-up. It is your fundamental nature. Stepping up to reinvent comes from the courage to restructure your consciousness.

When you fulfill an aspiration, it amplifies what you love, and you know it is perfect. My friend Blanche Napoleon wrote, "Courage is both my friend and my teacher. Without courage, I would be an empty shell. With courage, I am complete and full of love and yearning for life and whatever it brings." Does your work feed your spirit in addition to putting food on your table? "Classic spiritual work, no matter what the religious tradition, is about transcending the ego. It seeks to awaken within a person something that is recognized as 'true self,' or higher Self. This does not necessarily mean eliminating the ego, but rather displacing it as the seat of one's personal identity."[313] In other words, you "die" to your limitations and consent to be transformed into the limitless joy of being your true Self and fulfilling *your* vocation.

Courage Development Questions to Ponder
- What ignites your passion?
- How have you demonstrated the self-discipline needed to follow your passion and manifest the joy of self-fulfillment?
- Do you replay the stories of your past, or are you eager to create a new future?
- What doesn't work anymore?

Chapter 11
Reveal Your Vulnerability—
Defending Against Manipulation

It takes more courage to reveal insecurities than to hide them,
more strength to relate to people than to dominate them, more 'manhood'
to abide by thought-out principles rather than blind reflex.
Toughness is in the soul and spirit, not in muscles and an immature mind.

—Alex Karras

Born into poverty in New Iberia, Louisiana, scientist and inventor Vivien Theodore Thomas refused to resort to manipulation to feed his ego or promote his own agenda. Perhaps he understood that when we manipulate others to achieve our own goals, we have become stuck in uncourageous thinking that perpetuates a false self image. His life certainly demonstrated that he possessed the courage necessary to practice our next courage action:

Reveal your vulnerability.

Revealing vulnerability exposes a person's true nature and undermines the ego tendency to get stuck in self-serving illusions.

One of five children, Vivien graduated from high school with honors. Working summer jobs as a carpenter to help pay for college, Vivien learned valuable leadership lessons. In his autobiography, Vivien recalls the time when his boss told him his carpentry work was unacceptable: "I knew I had already learned the lesson which I still remember and try to adhere to: whatever you do, always do your best; otherwise it might show up to haunt or embarrass you."[314]

Vivien saved every penny he had to manifest his vision—graduating from college and eventually medical school. He enrolled in Tennessee Agricultural and Industrial College as a pre-medical student. But it took only one day for his life's savings to be wiped out as one bank after another failed at the start of the Great Depression. Forced to drop out of his first year of college in 1930, Vivien took a lowly position at Vanderbilt University Medical School laboratory to sweep floors and clean the animal cages. The lab was run by a young doctor named Alfred Blalock who noticed Vivien's interest in the lab and his ability to manage it. Dr. Blalock was looking for someone he could trust and count on, so he hired Vivien as his surgical research lab assistant.

Even though the lab work paid less than the janitor position, Vivien refused to let ego get in the way of the opportunity. At times he worked sixteen-hour days, but he constantly stepped up to support Dr. Blalock's research and make workplace contributions. Vivien also demonstrated calm poise. On one occasion he made a mistake that precipitated screaming and cursing from Dr. Blalock. Unwilling to be manipulated by this type of behavior and refusing to accept the abuse, Vivien faced the situation head on with unflinching courage.

"I said that I had not been brought up to take or use the kind of language he had used across the hall."[315] Dr. Blalock apologized and asked Vivien to come back to work. "In retrospect," Vivien later wrote, "I think this incident set the stage for what I consider our mutual respect throughout the years."[316] Willing to reveal his vulnerable "heart and spirit" not only to Dr. Blalock but also before an all-white audience of doctors and residents, Vivien consistently exemplified his willingness to reveal his vulnerability.

Vivien's attitude toward learning, knowledge and responsibility was the antithesis of manipulation. He became indispensable to Dr. Blalock, making profound contributions to research into high blood pressure and traumatic shock. Eventually, Dr. Blalock gained notoriety around the world, but it was Vivien's courage, creativity, intelligence and steady hands that provided the backbone of Dr. Blalock's work. Vivien invented the tools and devices for understanding shock and blood pressure, but he remained behind the scenes.

In 1941, Dr. Blalock was asked to become chief surgeon at Johns Hopkins University medical school. He was unwilling to move unless Vivien was included as part of his team. Vivien's family's lifestyle diminished in Baltimore, but he was compelled to move. Both men were stunned when they saw the ramshackle lab at the almighty Johns Hopkins, but they rose to the challenge, transforming the facility into a respected research lab. Together they made pioneering discoveries about the causes and effects of shock and the body's reaction to trauma. Dr. Blalock spent most of his time in the hospital while Vivien worked independently, never forgetting his lesson from his carpentry days. Vivien's intention was to work part time until he could return to Tennessee State. In Nashville, there were numerous black doctors who cared for their own, but his pay as a gifted laboratory technician remained at the level of a janitor because his skin color exempted him from a higher pay rate.

To earn extra money for his wife and two daughters, Vivien also worked as a servant at Dr. Blalock's dinner parties. Vivien never flaunted his importance to the medical school lab. He always followed the rules of the time, using the "colored" restrooms and cafeteria. Vivien wrote in his autobiography, "I knew I was something of a curiosity or an oddity at Hopkins."[317] With few token raises he practiced his well-retained carpenter lesson—do whatever needs to be done to accomplish the lab's goals. It was only in the privacy of the lab that the two men revealed their friendship. Little did they know that they were ushering in a new era of cardiac medicine. Ironically, Vivien's race precluded him from being medically treated in most hospitals, but he taught operating techniques to white staff surgeons. He even stood on a stool behind Dr. Blalock to coach his colleague as he performed surgery after surgery on "blue babies."

Dr. Blalock retired in 1964 and died four months later with Vivien remaining largely unacknowledged. Vivien had come to accept the harsh reality that his dream of becoming a doctor would never be fulfilled. But in 1971 his work was finally acknowledged by surgeons he had trained in the lab at Johns Hopkins. Vivien was honored at an unveiling of his portrait in the foyer of the Blalock Building at Johns Hopkins University School of Medicine along with Dr. Blalock's, and in 1976 he received an honorary doctorate degree.

Never boasting about his contributions, Vivien began his professional journey as a janitor and reached center stage at a formal presentation in honor of his contributions to medicine. In his remarks Vivien said, "I stated that I had lived with the personal inner satisfaction that I was helping to solve some of the numerous health problems that beset all mankind. I was now being publicly recognized as having played a significant role in research leading to these goals and the development of the skill of many surgeons."[318] Vivien continued to supervise the surgical research laboratory at Johns Hopkins until his retirement in 1979. Among surgeons, Vivien's work had become as familiar and respected as Dr. Blalock's

Sigmund Freud once said, "Out of your vulnerabilities will come your strength."[319] Vivien was vulnerable to both the times—when blacks were blatantly discriminated against—and the doctors—who originally included him only when they needed him. His vulnerability certainly was accompanied by pain, but his work in medical science and his clear purpose were more important than giving up his true Self. By standing in his honesty and true, guileless Self, recognition came to him, even though he did not seek it.

As noted previously, courage comes in a wide range of flavors. Consultant Joe Rei said, "I think too many men confuse demanding and authoritative with courage. I love to see the soft courage of the truly humble leader who knows his greatest vulnerability is that success and accomplishment rests in the hands of others. The application of courage simply takes hard work. The courage to:

- identify and state the problem in an open and honest way,
- seek out others with the expertise to help you overcome those problems, and
- share the problems and solutions with others on your team so that you all develop to the point that you're focused individually and collectively on your service to the world."

Living Death

Dolly, Arthur, Audrey, Barry, Lenny, Sally and Vicky each had their own style. Capricious and uncontrollable, they wreaked havoc and left paths of destruction in their wakes. Who were they? Hurricanes! While most of us will never experience the destructive force of a Katrina, we have all suffered the devastating effects of emotional storms, a concept Robin J. Bell understands completely.

> Since 2003 I feel like I have weathered many professional and personal storms, but I found my career. Professionally, I went through several different jobs just trying to make ends meet. I felt like I was the captain of a ship sailing to my destination, and from afar, I saw a storm approach quite abruptly.

> At that moment I had options. One option was to turn the ship around and never reach my true destination (the best career choice). This option would have created self-doubt and encouraged denial and grief. My second option was to jump overboard in a state of panic, sustaining a victim role. The option I chose was to address my fears as they arose, one storm at a time, one day at a time. This option allowed me to foster my courage and to continue to endure, knowing that the storm would end and peaceful waters would come.

> Another thing that helped strengthen my courage was something I heard when Martha Stewart got out of jail: "America loves a comeback kid." For some reason, that phrase connected with me, and that became my daily affirmation! In July 2005, I finally found a position that works with my strengths and challenges my weaknesses. What I know is "within each of us, spirit can achieve the impossible." I am finally enjoying those peaceful waters.

154

Robin had experienced career storms before. She had learned that docking at the port of a new job did not require her to stick it out if the emotional climate turned stormy. She also discovered that trying to manipulate stormy work situations is no more effective than trying to change the course of a real hurricane. Instead, Robin relied on the compass of her aspirations to navigate to the safe harbor of a fulfilling job.

"Spiritual confidence is the heaviest anchor in the midst of the unending storm that is life and death. It is an unshakable confidence in the inherent rightness of being here—confidence in the rightness of finding oneself in the very middle of the life process, even in all its chaos and complexity."[320] This type of courageous conviction comes from the heart—it is an internal intention to live in joyful self-fulfillment. What do you do when work-related storms gather? Have you recognized that manipulation is an obstacle that exposes you to the uncontrollable forces of emotional backlash? "Remember, that when you manipulate others, we are equally manipulated in return."[321]

No one is guaranteed a job anymore. Even if the company you work for is thriving, there is a creeping sense that no job is safe, which means heightened uncertainty and confusion that reinforce the reluctance to step up in courage and reveal vulnerability. But the storms that enter your work life offer opportunities for an honest assessment of your vulnerabilities. You discover that vulnerability comes in many forms, such as acknowledging unhappiness, learning to move on through disastrous events and learning not to manipulate failures or mistakes. "When we admit our downside, others cannot attack us there. As a consequence, we feel emotionally less vulnerable, and more safe and secure."[322]

"If you are able to fix your awareness on the quiet Center, the eye of the hurricane, you will be saved."[323] Where is your quiet place in the storm? Is it centered in your courageous heart and spirit? The more intense the circumstances, the more risky it seems to admit our vulnerabilities, especially in the context of work, but trying to manipulate these unsettled circumstances serves only the ego's need to feel in control and generally backfires, producing unnecessary suffering. Few people have the courage to reveal vulnerability and overcome it. Hopefully, you support your courage with some form of meditation. Meditation is the protective shelter from the ego's storms of emotion, and it is in passing through the storms that suffering is diminished.

As Parker Palmer asserts, "I believe that the God who gave me life wants me to live life fully and well. Now, is that going to take me to places where I suffer because I am standing for something or I am committed to something or I am passionate about something that gets resisted and rejected by the society? Absolutely. But anyone who's ever suffered that way knows that it's a life-giving way to suffer—that if it's your truth, you can't not do it. And that knowledge carries you through."[324]

Clean Up Those Missteps

Rather than focusing your energy on developing shrewd, manipulative schemes, consider admitting your vulnerabilities. Revealing your vulnerability demonstrates the courage and emotional maturity that accompany higher levels of personal development.. "When researchers and theorists speak about higher development, they are referring to levels or stages that go beyond Piaget's formal operational stage. Early formal operational thinking is typically acquired in adolescence. Many people reach this stage and happily live the remainder of their lives from it. In fact, polling across a variety of studies in the U.S. that include a wide range of socioeconomic backgrounds, roughly 79% of adults do not develop beyond this level. One can live and work successfully within the established roles and expectations of modern society."[325]

In *A New World*, Eckhart Tolle writes, "Your memories are invested with a sense of self, and your story becomes who you perceive yourself to be. This 'little me' is an illusion that obscures your true identity as timeless and formless Presence. Your story, however, consists not only of mental but also of emotional memory—old emotion that is being revived continuously … through grievances, regret, hostility, guilt.… Because of the human tendency to perpetuate old emotion, almost everyone carries in his or her energy field an accumulation of old emotional pain."[326] Steeped in adolescent immaturity, this human tendency to tote around bundles of emotional baggage keeps us stuck at an adolescent level of development. It represents an absence of courage and makes workplace harmony nearly impossible. It also keeps us from loving ourselves and the people around us.

Love is the most difficult and dangerous form of courage.
Courage is the most desperate, admirable, and noble kind of love.[327]

Do you confess your shortcomings and missteps? For example, if you lack knowledge about a topic, do you respond in a deceptive manner that keeps your protects your ego? The honest response would be to confess your vulnerability by admitting that you do not know the answer. A timely confessing made with positive intent is good for the spirit. The process helps us face the truth. We take responsibility for what is happening with our spirit and address those missteps that collect unhealthy energy. Yes, we invite potential trouble when we stand in our courage and confess our shortcomings, but more importantly, we hold ourselves accountable and establish our integrity. Even a corruption-tainted person should have the courage to confess! Confessing is a cousin to courage.

Damn, Bad Timing!

Theresa Hart originally identified herself as courageous. Taking her courage to work, she met feelings of vulnerability head-on, but she was also attached to the false scripts that kept her from taking care of herself. She was a courageous, competent, strong leader and role model, but she reached a point where she could no longer look only in the rearview mirror.

I had worked hard to obtain my position at a wonderful engineering company, but after five months, my doctor told me that I would need to have a hysterectomy and take a two-month leave of absence. "Damn, bad timing!" was the first thought that entered my head. With less than a year on the job and no accumulated vacation, I was extremely upset. The company's top executives had already witnessed me working long hours to meet demanding standards, but I was apprehensive. How would this news affect my status?

Facing the music (which is something I hate to do), I sat down with my manager to explain my situation. To my astonishment, he told me that I should consider having the surgery earlier. He asked if he could discuss the details with our director. The next day the director met with me and told me that I did not need to worry about my job and that he would be crazy to jeopardize the relationship with a productive employee. Quite frankly, I did not know how to react. Even though I perceived myself to be courageous, I had been afraid to show any vulnerability. And after my hysterectomy, I learned that my health issues were more significant than I had realized.

When forced to adapt to major issues such as health problems, our perspectives about ourselves change. Physical problem after physical problem left Theresa defenseless and motivated her to look internally. "With no control over my health situation, I felt exposed and raw. I was being forced to trust that things would work out. But because of my challenges," said Theresa, "I faced life and grew. Self-awareness is not an easy road if you are faint of heart, but ridding myself of the emotional shackles that controlled me allowed me to find inner peace."

Theresa was beginning to bathe in the lovely energy of self-awareness and self-healing rather than letting her ego prolong her suffering, and that is what courage consciousness is all about. Learning is about digging beneath the surface to reveal the roots of our personal limitations. Even though

Theresa had boatloads of courage, she uncovered emotional pain that the ego had repressed, and as Dr. Hawkins notes, "A person is vulnerable to emotional pain in exact relationship to the degree of self-awareness and self-acceptance. When people admit their downside, others cannot attack them there. As a consequence, one feels emotionally less vulnerable and more safe and secure."[328] Theresa had the innate courage to overcome her missteps— the heartaches that reveal unfulfilled visions hidden in disillusionment. "Self-healing is the willingness to love and forgive ourselves, to look at our vulnerability and call it our humanness."[329]

If you choose to live most often in the "yes" mode; then, like Theresa, you will expand your courage consciousness and awaken to unconscious viewpoints that keep you stuck. To claim your courage and take it to work entails a transformation process, a spiritual journey that demands a constant "letting go" of emotional obstacles and even attachments to the most enjoyable things. This process of self-surrender frees us from the residual of the false self. The ego no longer manipulates us to just "keep plugging away." Instead of trying to act out of love, we learn to *be* love. Eckhart Tolle expands,

> The ego believes that in your resistance lies your strength, whereas in truth resistance cuts you off from Being, the only place of true power. Resistance is weakness and fear masquerading as strength.... Until there is surrender, unconscious role-playing constitutes a large part of human interaction. In surrender, you no longer need ego defenses and false masks. You become very simple, very real.... What the ego doesn't know, of course, is that only through the letting go of resistance, through becoming "vulnerable," can you discover your true and essential invulnerability.[330]

Theresa learned that courage consciousness increases even during times of spiritual suffering and emotional pain. Regardless of the circumstances, we grow stronger and more courageous when we face the storms, accept the situation and surrender. "Surrender is not weakness. There is great strength in it. Only a surrendered person has spiritual power. Through surrender, you will be free internally of the situation. You may then find that the situation changes without any effort on your part."[331] Surrender, then, is not the negative act of admitting defeat that our competitive culture would have us believe. "It is the death of the false self, the egocentric life. It is the abandoning of the falseness to which our society habituates us."[332]

Vulnerability supports self-realization, underscoring a human being's essence—the true Self. Grow in the storms and the storms stop growing. "If you think about the things that created your character, created your ability to fight, and made a difference, in every case, it would be the storms."[333] John DePalma, a partner in a television production company summarizes this viewpoint: "Be true to yourself and accept those qualities you have that you want to keep and remove and replace the qualities you'd like to change. Recognize that no one is perfect and it's okay to be vulnerable and to be exposed from time to time. People want to be inspired by real people so recognize the fact that the only way you're really going to get ahead at an intrinsic level is to be yourself."

Focused Intentionality

"Whenever any kind of disaster strikes or something goes seriously 'wrong' ... know that there is another side to it, that you are just one step away from something incredible: a complete alchemical transformation of the base metal of pain and suffering into gold. That one step is called surrender."[334] With surrender comes acceptance, "not adding to or taking away from anything that is already there ... it does not fret or struggle. This complete assent is the foundation for any truly whole state of mind to which human beings can aspire, because not a fiber of our being says 'no,' and life becomes ours to live 100 percent."[335] The simple act of acceptance removes many of our masks and paves the way for vulnerability. The constant choice is to be present in the moment. Then, during vulnerable storms at work, what surfaces in presence is inner (and often outer) laughter. "We surrender to the attraction of interior silence, tranquility, and peace. We do not try to feel anything.... Without effort, without trying, we sink into the Presence, letting everything else go."[336] How can businesses possibly support this type of shift?

Nancy Hoffman, a Catholic nun and senior vice president of Mission and Ministry for Colorado's Centura Health, was interviewed for an article in *The Denver Post*. "There's so much frustration in the job market because people are not attached to their passion, or are disconnected from it.... It's time to make the workplace safe for you to ponder your spirituality."[337] In a follow-up interview, Sister Nancy added,

> It takes focused intentionality to bring spirituality into our professional world, and the invitation to do so presents itself every day we show up at work. This is where courage comes in. It takes courage to be present in such a way that we interact with others from a place of centeredness, a place of calm—from our essence. Courageous spirituality will help keep us from becoming entangled in the ever-present interplay of corporate egos. One has to have a clear determination to function as a spiritual person in the corporate world....

I also focus my journey from my essence rather than my ego, and this requires courage. While many people would not use the word spirituality to express what they are searching for, there is no doubt in my mind that people are hungry to find purpose and meaning in their professional lives as well as balance. People are waiting for leaders to inspire them. The ever expanding and new technologies create the danger of spinning us out of control, and technology is not the answer.

Heads of corporations will be courageous leaders when they bring balance back to the work place. These leaders will create opportunities for people to discover something new—what I call "their calling." In this process, employees will rediscover what gives their professional lives purpose and meaning.... One answer to this modern day dilemma is to have the courage, and the will, to bring a balance through reflection and silence.

Lawrence Diggs is an author and public speaker. His definition of courage is "the ability to make difficult decisions as a result of critical thinking." Unwilling to be manipulated by the circumstances, Lawrence's expanded definition of courage reveals critical aspects of his courageous willingness to reveal vulnerability. "It takes courage to admit a mistake when you know you will lose your job because of it. It takes courage to love with abandon, forgiving and loving those who seek to destroy you. It takes courage to allow for the human frailty of others at risk to your self. It takes courage to befriend an unknown or unpopular person or group or risk rejection and public ridicule to support an unpopular position. It takes courage to question the status quo or question authorities. It takes courage to say I am sorry. It takes courage to give to others when you are in need yourself."

Lawrence has had to overcome obstacles at work that required his courage. He recommends that you keep developing options for another job: "You may not accept the options, but you will feel more courageous, especially when you are the bread winner for your family. The company has you by the nose because it is not just about what will happen to you but what will happen to your family."

Lawrence feels this is especially true for men. "The economic pressure may be there, but the husband's family is not likely to bad rap the wife about not 'being a woman' and taking care of her husband and kids." So Lawrence suggests that you start looking for a new job as soon as you get one. "While this may not seem courageous, it is actually the most courageous. It is facing reality and facing yourself! Knowing that you have options will make it

160

easier to confront situations that demand taking a stand for or against something for the greater good. Courageous doesn't mean setting yourself up to be a loser. When it is known that you have options, people value you more and play fewer games with you. That means you have to play fewer games. Hopefully, you will never have to pull this sword from its scabbard because it may actually be more powerful in the scabbard. But all power is potential and when you have potential, i.e. options, outside of your job, you have more power."

Rather than attempt to manipulate situations, consider Lawrence's advice. Jon Kabat-Zinn writes in *Wherever You Go There You Are*, "If you are a strong-willed and accomplished person, you may often give the impression that you are invulnerable to feeling inadequate or insecure or hurt. This can be very isolating and ultimately cause you and others great pain."[338] Keeping the issue in simple perspective, Lawrence remains focused in his heart. "Simplicity of heart and life requires an appreciation of insecurity, vulnerability, marginality and detachment.… There is only the summons to transformation as part of human experience, and its requirements are universal."[339]

"Be Who You Really Are"

Easily distracted by our projections about people's personalities, we forget to focus on the main issues: getting results through collaboration. While preparing a presentation on courage leadership for a *Fortune 500* company, my client and I decided that having a panel of four internal employees (three women and one man) would be a great way to reveal situational courageous leadership within their organization. These four employees briefly shared a scenario about how they had uniquely displayed their courage at work. After they each shared their brief stories, an audience member asked the panel a question. Immediately, the male on the panel responded quite simply and strongly, "The bottom line is about getting results—that's all!" Results mean a profitable business, but manipulation makes getting the results even harder. What are the results you are trying to achieve? Does *reveal your vulnerability* need to be added to your Declaration of Courageous Intention?

With self-awareness, we begin to notice our personal forms of manipulation—from intimidation to indifference to passive aggressive behaviors. Facing a decisive moment provides an opportunity to reveal vulnerability. "The punishment imposed on us for claiming true self can never be worse than the punishment we impose on ourselves by failing to make that claim. And the converse is true as well: no reward anyone might give us could possibly be greater than the reward that comes from living by our own best lights."[340]

Revealing vulnerability allows our best lights to shine into the workplace. The difficulty arises from the ego mentality that refuses to believe this, insisting instead that vulnerability is a sign of weakness that must be hidden. "Real courage in the workplace is usually so quiet that it goes unnoticed," said Rob Gates. "Every day small business owners bid on jobs that could make or break the company without enough information or resources to be sure they haven't just signed a suicide pact. Every day people who are terrified of public speaking give speeches because that's the job that has to be done that day. There are countless things like that which take real courage."

While this may seem sensible in the workplace, the deeper truth is that revealing your vulnerability represents integrity and conveys your true identity. The alternative—hiding your mistakes and weaknesses—can only be accomplished through manipulation, which undermines your integrity, breeds distrust and stifles your true "heart and spirit" identity. Real estate broker John Gibbs keeps it simple when he says, "I believe by staying centered, close to your higher being and true to yourself, you can overcome any obstacle that faces you." As poet e.e. cummings wrote,

It takes courage to grow up and turn out to be who you really are.[341]

Courage Development Questions to Ponder

- When was the last time you revealed a weakness or a mistake at work? What was the response?

- When you contemplate your day-to-day interactions with fellow workers, do you see how you have manipulated situations and conversations to hide your vulnerabilities?

- Do you have a tendency to put mistakes behind you or face them head on?

- Take an inventory of the hurts being held in your psyche.

Chapter 12
Confront Uncomfortable Truths—
Denouncing Ambiguity

As human beings, our greatness lies not so much in being able to remake the world as in being able to remake ourselves.

— Mahatma Gandhi

How do *you* manifest the meaning of your work life? Your Declaration of Courageous Intention (DCI) is a summary that reflects your heart's intention. The DCI reveals the courage actions you naturally apply at work and the specific obstacles that hold you back on the job. Hopefully, after reading Chapter 1 you gave yourself permission to claim your courage. If so, you are finding that courage naturally grounds you in a simpler, more fulfilling and meaningful life that mirrors your true Self. If you continually commit to activities and people who fail to bring you fulfillment, how happy and fulfilling will your work life be over the years?

Make Courage Your Daily Legacy

It's hard to imagine a more fitting example of courage to conclude this book than Viktor Frankl. He made courage his daily legacy, and he still challenges us long after his death, asking the question, "What is the meaning of your life?" Few people can match Viktor Frankl's courage, and in a life rife with ambiguity he did not hesitate to

Confront uncomfortable truths.

Viktor faced ambiguity throughout his life:

- when people tried to discredit his *logotherapy* doctrine,

- when he helped keep young people from committing suicide,

- when he was imprisoned in Nazi concentration camps,

- when he remarried outside his faith, and

- when he spoke out against "collective guilt."

In the Foreword to the 2006 edition of Viktor's book, *Man's Search for Meaning*, Harold S. Kushner writes, "The greatest task for any person is to find meaning in his or her life. Frankl saw three possible sources for meaning: in work (doing something significant), in love (caring for

163

another person), and in courage during difficult times. Suffering in and of itself is meaningless; we give our suffering meaning by the way in which we respond to it."[342] Viktor knew that courage grows in choices and taking action.

After enduring three years in four different Nazi concentration camps, what would be the meaning of life for prisoner 119104? Viktor had the courage to confront an uncomfortable truth: under severe suffering, what is the meaning of my life? What's important is the attitude around suffering. Think of whatever is causing you to suffer right now—uncertain finances, lack of job security, unemployment …. Is there meaning in your life despite the suffering? "Persons facing difficult choices may not fully appreciate how much their own attitude interferes with the decision they need to make or the action they need to take."[343]

So how do you keep ambiguity at bay? Viktor found "sufficient proof that everything can be taken from a man but one thing: the last of the human freedoms—to choose one's attitude in any given set of circumstances, to choose one's own way … mentally and spiritually…. It is this spiritual freedom—which cannot be taken away—that makes life meaningful and purposeful…. The unemployed worker for example, is in a similar position [as a prisoner]. His existence has become provisional and in a certain sense he cannot live for the future or aim at a goal."[344]

Born in 1905 in a Jewish neighborhood near Vienna, Viktor had clarity about his future by the time he was three years old—he wanted to be a doctor. Ironically, not far from the Frankl's apartment lived a young man named Adolf Hitler. Austria's ethnic diversity sickened Hitler, who sought to live his dream in Germany with the race that aligned with his sensibilities. "[Hitler] began to believe that the financial success of Jews was responsible for his own poverty. In reality, many Jews were just as poor as Hitler was."[345] History tells Hitler's story, he was an angry and obsessed man who eventually moved to Germany to become their dictator from 1933 to 1945. Hitler provides a prime example of a person stuck in ambiguity, and his irrational fears led to the extermination of more than eleven million people, from Jews and gypsies to people like Dietrich Bonhoeffer.

Viktor, on the other hand overcame ambiguity even at a young age. Always somewhat lean and wiry, he was confronted by a group of boys who asked if he was a Jew. "Viktor felt they were about to use his heritage as an excuse to attack him. He replied with his own question, 'Yes, but does this mean I am not also a human being?'"[346] Viktor overcame ambiguity even in the concentration camps where the meaning of life might itself seem ambiguous at best. Constantly speaking up in the Nazi camps, Viktor helped many prisoners survive, and he helped many more die with meaning. Only by learning to express ourselves from our own courageous identities can we truly begin to confront uncomfortable truths.

The words on these pages were written as a guide for anyone willing to "face it"—face the meaning of *your* life. To find meaning in your life you must slow down, as I've written repeatedly between the covers of this book. Slowing to allow for quiet reflection is the way to invite courage into your life and allow meaning to unfold in your heart and spirit. Meaning for your life precludes ambiguity. Does ambiguity hold you back on the job? Be careful not to confuse ambiguity with uncertainty. Life is strewn with uncertainty—it's about how you hold yourself accountable that matters (Chapter 4). Ambiguity is the inability to confront brutal facts and act with conviction to resolve them.

After Viktor was released from the Turkheim concentration camp in 1945, he chose to face his horrific experience without cynicism by writing *Man's Search for Meaning*. To date, this small 160-page book has sold over twelve million copies. Why are so many people drawn to this book, and why is Viktor Frankl fit for the closing chapter?

What We Give to Life

Viktor's signature question, "What can be the meaning of my life?" has a different answer for every person who asks it. "First, he said that it is life that asks something special of each of us human beings, not we who ask life for meaning. In other words, what we give to life, not what we take from it, makes our lives meaningful."[347] Viktor gave tremendously to life.

- In 1924 Viktor entered the University of Vienna Medical School (while thirty-five-year-old Hitler was in jail). In a speech at the age of twenty-one, "Frankl came out and said that he believed that not all human behavior was motivated by [mental] illness. He stated that some behaviors might look like the symptoms of illness but could actually be expressions of one's innermost being, one's true self. For example, someone who showed symptoms of depression might actually be expressing dissatisfaction with her life, a need to find a more meaningful career."[348]

- Viktor had interests in a variety of medical specialties but ended up specializing in psychiatry and neurology because of his interest in psychoanalysis and psychological research. In Vienna he organized suicide-prevention centers for teenagers and treated thousands of depressed women on the verge of suicide. After his residency in 1937, his older brother and younger sister helped him start a private practice, but Jews soon lost their apartments, licenses and businesses. In 1940 Viktor became the chief of neurology at the Rothschild Hospital for Jews, which kept him out of the death camps for awhile. He met and married his first wife, Tilly Grosser, a nurse at the hospital.

- As Viktor's work and insights progressed, he was curious about a treatment he eventually called *logotherapy*—a therapeutic approach that stimulates the discovery of meaning in life and lifts the spirit. "In some way, suffering ceases to be suffering at the moment it finds a meaning such as the meaning of a sacrifice."[349] Viktor used his principles repeatedly in the camps to help himself and fellow prisoners survive. "He saw himself lecturing about the psychology of the concentration camps. This dream became his goal, and ironically, focusing on that dream, rather than survival, is what helped him survive.... He concluded that survival depended more on people's inner strength, on their ability to use this horrible experience to grow as individuals."[350] Amongst his psychiatric colleagues, Viktor's work became known as the *"human potential movement."*[351]

- Liberated from the Turkheim concentration camp by American troops from Texas on April 27, 1945, Viktor was forty years old. The remaining men who survived found their emotions deadened to the idea of freedom. Once out, Viktor learned that his wife, parents and older brother had died in the camps. Viktor fell into depression and had thoughts of suicide, but his own message kept coming back to him: he had something to contribute to life; his life had a purpose.

- Without his family, Viktor focused on his work. When he finished writing *The Doctor and the Soul* and sent it to his publisher, the accomplishment lifted his spirit, prompting him to write *Man's Search for Meaning*, first published in Austria in 1946. Writing rekindled Viktor's courage. Publishing the two books energized his spirit, and he returned to his work as a physician. He became the chief of neurology at Vienna Policlinic Hospital, where he met his second wife, twenty-year-old Eleonore Schwindt, a Catholic nurse working in the oral surgery department. They eventually married without a priest or rabbi in a civil ceremony, and over the years many people were judgmental toward his interfaith marriage.

- Married and with a new daughter named Gabriele, Viktor regained his happiness with his new family. He even returned to mountain climbing a favorite pastime that lasted until he was eighty (along with his love for Vienna coffee). At age sixty-seven, Viktor was thrilled when he obtained his pilot's license. He published his autobiography in 1977 and lived to the age of 92. As Viktor has written, "Life ultimately means taking the responsibility to find the right answer to its problems and to fulfill the tasks which it constantly sets for each individual."[352]

What Do You Communicate?

Do you feel life asks something of you but obstacles such as apathy, inertia, blame, manipulation, denial or any of the obstacles featured in this book seem to hold you back? Ask yourself these questions:

- Do you have a responsibility to step up and respond to the obstacles that hold you back on the job?
- Do you find meaning in expressing your true Self?
- What is your unique purpose and are you accomplishing it?
- Do you stumble over your obstacles or are they stepping-stones that you benchmark; hence, no regrets?
- How are you responding to the situation you are in right now?

People at work witness what we stand for, and straight talk gets attention because it is uncomfortable for most people. Speaking with courage means learning to speak with your own voice, to express the truth that flows from your own "heart and spirit." In fact, candor is a cousin to courage* (see montage of cousins to courage at the end of the chapter). Viktor never needed a "translator." His words expressed his true Self.

Quantum field theorist Danah Zohar's work on Spiritual Intelligence (SQ) confirms the importance of finding your courageous voice. "One of the main criteria for high spiritual intelligence is being what psychologists call 'field-independent'. That means being able to stand against the crowd, to hold an unpopular opinion if that is what I deeply believe.... High SQ requires us to have a functioning ego and a healthy participation in the group, but both must be rooted in the deep centre of ourselves.... I know who *I* am and what *I* believe. This is not egoism but true individuality, and it often requires great courage."[353]

For Viktor it meant communicating to the world about logotherapy, even when others saw it as self-promotion. Now many have said, "Viktor Frankl should be recognized as the father of the contemporary practice of positive psychology, which emphasizes working with the strengths people bring to life's difficult situations."[354]

Therapist Shane Holst confirms this value, "Nothing works better than communication. For example, I had a young woman say to me recently that she was frustrated by poor structure at meetings, i.e., red herrings, poor chairing, no or inadequate agendas and the like. She wanted to speak up but was afraid of offending her superiors. My advice to her (using nothing more profound than communication) was to say, 'I'm worried to say this for fear of offending some people, but I believe our meetings would be more productive if we had' ... etc. The point here is to speak the concern; voice the concern; reveal your concern; pre-empt your concern ... no matter what, please voice your concern or fear as exactly as it is." Only by learning to express our true selves can we confront uncomfortable truths at work and move beyond ambiguity.

You cannot step up unless you establish your personal "heart and spirit" identity and then stand unambiguously for what you represent. It takes practice, courage and the self-awareness to speak your truth *in spite of* the inevitable criticisms from ego-dominated personalities. How often do you posture your words with mixed messages? Do you need an incentive to tell the truth? Consultant Lee Livermore was moved by *Man's Search for Meaning* and said, "It was Viktor Frankl's realization that the one freedom that never could be taken away was the freedom of your response."

Viktor's was a courageous, unambiguous voice:

o   Each man is questioned by life; and he can only answer to life by answering for his own life; to life he can only respond by being responsible.

o   Love is the only way to grasp another human being in the innermost core of his personality.

o   When we are no longer able to change a situation—we are challenged to change ourselves.

o   What is to give light must endure burning.

o   Ultimately, man should not ask what the meaning of his life is, but rather he must recognize that it [is] he who is asked.

o   The one thing you can't take away from me is the way I choose to respond to what you do to me. The last of one's freedoms is to choose one's attitude in any given circumstance.[355]

Mixed Messages

A good deal of ambiguity comes from lack of clarity and direction. When we take responsibility for the roles we play and how we interact with each other, we set aside our differences and focus on the results, leaving no room for ambiguity. Dr. Marlene Caroselli's work as a trainer allows her to observe behaviors. Marlene said, "Expressing courage usually means taking a stand, and taking a stand is bound to get you noticed. Sometimes it's easier to go with the flow and not stand out. In this economy particularly, people are nervous about losing their jobs and thus are probably unwilling to deviate too far from the beaten path—whether that means not voicing an unpopular view or not offering an idea that is new and perhaps controversial. Keep in mind what Margaret Chase Smith had to say, though, about the down side of such suppression: 'Moral cowardice that keeps us from speaking our minds is as dangerous to this country as irresponsible talk. The right way is not always the popular and easy way. Standing for right when it is unpopular is a true test of moral character.'" Marlene also believes that "demonstrating courage is an incremental process." She suggests that an individual "find examples of courage that resonate within you."

Confronting an uncomfortable truth could involve something like confronting your boss when you learn that he does not think you can handle a difficult client or situation. While someone else might get to handle the important assignment, confronting your manager could reveal an uncomfortable truth (e.g., "I don't want to take a risk on a woman in this role"). As long as you are rooted in Being—in the truth of your heart and spirit—you are not identified or possessed by others' thoughts or consumed by your own. "The quicker you are in attaching verbal or mental labels to things, people, or situations, the more shallow and lifeless your reality becomes, and the more deadened you become to reality, the miracle of life that continuously unfolds within and around you."[356]

A client shared that she applies courage tips from my monthly courage newsletter "because they keep me honest." She understands that "truth cannot tolerate a contradiction."[357] Experiences fraught with ambiguity and contradiction merge into choices that reveal the principal danger of failed courage—corruption. Corruption encompasses far more than the unethical business practices that make headlines. Hypocrisy, for example, represents the corruption of your Being. It takes a courageous leader to wipe out ambiguity and the corruption it engenders at the personal as well as the corporate level. "The word 'courage' is the most difficult and most admirable trait of leadership."[358] In your work environment, do you experience a correlation between ambiguity, hypocrisy and corruption?

You have probably never heard of Pat Wyman because Pat is not famous. She is a therapist who believes courage at work is no different from courage in any other setting. She believes that "courage means holding to my truth, what I call 'radical honesty.' That means speaking my truth no matter the consequences (not to be confused with verbal abuse or character assassination). Secondly, courage means the willingness to step into the unknown, the untried, with the prospect of failure as a real possibility (knowing the lessons learned are worth the risk)."

Pat does believe that our culture trains and conditions women to be what others want them to be by perpetuating ambiguity so that "By the time we are adults, living our own truth is something we cannot even relate to."

Instead of agreeing to things that we don't want to do, we simply need to express our points of view without ambiguity. Christopher Witt, president of his own communication company, believes courage is developed over time through repeated choices to be true to oneself and do what needs to be done in spite of ambivalence. "I would say courage is the capacity for greatness. But what thwarts people from displaying their courage hovers around an issue I call 'mixed messages.' Mixed messages mean people tell you to speak your mind, to take a stand, to take risks. Yet they reward people who play by the book and play it safe. And they slap you down if your risk-taking doesn't pay off. I constantly have to stay true to myself and my convictions about speaking and speeches. I think it takes courage to speak the truth in love, not just to say something that is pleasing."

Do you follow your inner Truth? Think about the number of times you have withheld your personal beliefs from a co-worker (or loved one). Why did you not have the courage to converse directly and declare your intent? Choosing to accept an assignment from your boss (or a request from a loved one) requires you to execute it with renewed effort and accountability for the outcome. In essence, we are all sojourners seeking truth.

A former teacher and sports coach, Richard shared, "Most people will do anything to fit in, including lie about their core beliefs. Truth takes courage, because it will get you in trouble with the boss. Most people hide in a group and seldom expose their core beliefs. Being who you are and standing up for your core beliefs sounds easy. In the 'real world,' it takes courage. As Demaratus said to Xerxes: 'O King. Do you want a truthful answer or a pleasant one?'" It's difficult for most people to call a spade a spade because we define our relationships through our personal interactions and ambiguity creeps in when we choose the pleasant answer over the truthful one.

But failure to confront an uncomfortable truth in a work setting allows a subtle form of ambiguity to take root, producing a false person and undermining your potential. Lost potential is forgotten courage and represents the slow erosion of the spirit. In reality, the action taken (or lack thereof) reveals your courage quotient, and the outcome is usually better than our projections. Case in point, Travis W. Freeman is a wealth manager who faces obstacles with clients when they disagree with the way the relationship is working. Travis shared,

> One situation I will always remember involved a heated conversation with a client regarding the fees I was charging him. I charge all of my clients relatively the same fee for managing their wealth. This client in particular sent me a very hurtful email saying that I wasn't "worth the fee he was paying since the economy

was going down and some of his investments were losing value." He felt I should only be paid when his investments increased.

Insulted and hurt, I explained that I work each and every day to help him plan for his long-term financial goals, which encompasses much more than just managing his money. About thirty minutes later I had another email from this client with an even nastier message. By this time I had transitioned from feelings of insult to feelings of disgust. I had served this person for almost two years and felt as though all this time and work had toppled over like a building still under construction.

I called him right away and professionally let him know how I felt. "I have tried my best to be your partner and friend in this relationship. If I am trying to work as a team and you are working against me, maybe it is time that we part ways." The other end of the phone was silent for a long while. I waited. To my surprise, a subtle apology ensued. It made me feel better, but I was still upset. Our conversation did not last long, but I felt very relieved after making the phone call. Today, this person is a great client and no issues have risen since.

A Truth-Teller's Backbone

The movie *Another Woman*, written and directed by Woody Allen focuses on a woman's journey to recognize her inner ambiguous nature. Whether you are a man or woman you may have taken a similar journey. Gena Rowlands portrays "an accomplished philosophy professor who, upon turning 50, feels compelled to take emotional stock of her life.... Suddenly her quest for truth turns into a powerful and personal odyssey of self-examination, discovery and acceptance."[359] Her journey progresses through classic Allen vignettes in which she discovers her ambiguous nature and learns the direct truth about how people perceive her.

With each vignette, she becomes more conscious about her disconnect with her persona. Through the variety of exchanges she has with family members and friends, she slowly evolves into "another woman," overcoming ambiguity by manifesting the truth of her inner essence. It requires backbone to overcome ambiguity and confront uncomfortable truths, especially about ourselves. Before long, you will notice that people respond to you in a different way. Somehow, they recognize that you are real, accessible and centered in courage consciousness.

A male executive was going through his own transformation as "another man" when he wrote to me: "I have noticed that when I speak from my heart and not just from my head, the message gets through more clearly and with more effect. I usually don't say anything unless I feel moved to do so. Sometimes this works well, but other times I do have the regret that I didn't speak up. I have to do better about recognizing whether what I want to say is from the head or the heart!"

Notice when your voice fades, then start to monitor the missed opportunities. If you are not stepping up, you are probably sliding back into the old habits and scripts that have prevented your growth all along. People know the power of truthfulness; they know that when they give direct answers or confront a truth, they release positive energy, no matter how difficult that truth may be to accept. This verve is the backbone of courage, the opposite of the ambiguity that sets in when people are afraid to confront an uncomfortable truth. Do you mince words or tell it like it is?

Like painting or editing a book, remaining centered in your courage is not an exact science. The secret is to understand how to use the energy of the different courage action skills presented in each chapter and recognize that what you say and do creates and defines your world. The business environment changes continually, and a courageous leader knows how to go with the changing flow. Recall the last time you directly confronted someone at work with an uncomfortable but consequential truth you wanted to avoid.

Recognizing the delicate balance required during times of candor, John Gibbs, a real estate broker said, "We encounter many difficult people in this business, and the ability to work through those situations call on intense courage at times. We also are offered the opportunity to stray from the path of honesty and integrity on too many occasions. The courage to walk above this temptation has to be rock solid."

John gave an example from his business experiences: "If you have the courage to expose your inner feelings with honesty and integrity, then you have to beware of the path you may take the client on. For instance, if you are dealing in a divorce situation or a troubled relationship, your openness could be construed for something that is entirely not where you were headed in developing a professional client relationship. As a broker, the temptation to stray into this scenario can challenge many aspects of the typical man's ego thereby testing a man's true courage." In conclusion John shared, "I believe by staying centered, close to your higher being and true to yourself, you can overcome any obstacle that faces you."

First Red Flag
First red flag warnings are everywhere. People caught up in the falsehoods of ambiguity cannot help but reveal the deceptive facades projected by

their ego-dominated personas. A woman I will call Deb was preparing to speak at a conference when she got a big red flag in the form of a disturbing email from the association's education director. Meant for a staff member, the email was filled with sniping remarks about her! Believing she had a good relationship with the client, Deb was surprised by the unprofessional comments. Deb surmised that a rude conversation had taken place between the two co-workers at her expense. "Why would I want to speak at a conference when I'm being undermined behind the scene?" Deb asked. With courage, she replied to the director's email: "Did I miss a cue or is something wrong?"

The director quickly discounted the errant email by writing: "That email was one that people tell stories about in business magazines.... It was meant for...." Deb wanted to forget the incident but struggled for weeks with the nagging "first red flag" warning. In business for over ten years, she had learned the hard way that one red flag usually follows another, indicating a situation in danger of spiraling out of control. "Dramas of human error are of value because they serve as learning examples. Maturity often evolves through painful errors or mistakes."[360]

With the insight of her own past mistakes, Deb *hoped* she would be wrong but grew increasingly concerned. Needless to say, she was not surprised when her presentation did not go well, and she now has a stronger resolve to honor the first red flag. As Dr. Hawkins observes, "Everyone unconsciously knows when they are being lied to."[361] Ultimately, Deb learned a hard lesson: respond directly to the ambiguity represented by that first red flag warning. She also added, "Confront uncomfortable truths" to her DCI.

As you begin to design your own destiny and master a mix of courage action skills to overcome your personal obstacles, you amplify your level of courage consciousness and advance your career. You've read that stopping to reflect supports this process, allowing you to let go of false scripts and evaluate your progress. General Manager Curt L. Stowers summarizes the importance of confronting uncomfortable truths in the context of unreasonable goals. "The 'easy' approach is to nod one's head and ignore the situation in hopes that it will somehow work out. The more courageous approach is to confront the issue and deal with the short-term discomfort."

Have you stepped up in your level of courage consciousness? What insurmountable obstacle has you stuck right now? This book is your guide on your unique, purposeful journey. So whatever your biggest obstacle is at this point in your life, imagine how you will *FACE IT!* and live a fulfilled, courageous life!

Courage Development Questions to Ponder

- How often do you swallow your voice?

- Are you willing to have the courageous conversation that no one else is willing to have?

- What level of communication skills do you display when you disagree with someone?

* Courage cousins that accompany the courage actions: clarity, composure, consistency, carrying on, faith, controversy, concentration, compassion, commitment, contentment, confessing, and candor.

Reading Group Questions and Topics for Discussion

Courage and perseverance have a magical talisman, before which difficulties disappear and obstacles vanish into air.

—John Quincy Adams

1. Why is it important to recognize the obstacles that hold you back on the job?

2. If people like Victoria Woodhull, Dietrich Bonhoeffer, Golda Meir and Alexander Fleming were alive today, what do you think they would think about the progress people in organizations have achieved to date?

3. Share an instance where you have encouraged a peer to overcome his/her obstacles and move toward a courage-based identity.

4. What was the value of identifying where you are on the "Five Levels of Courage Consciousness" chart? Share your journey about stepping up to the next level.

5. There is often resistance to the practice of "stopping" and finding some form of contemplation to quiet the mind? With this understanding, how might you commit to integrating this critical practice into your daily life?

6. Review your Declaration of Courageous Intention (DCI) and assess your progress. Which obstacles are you finding to be the most difficult to overcome? What have you discovered about yourself?

7. Describe what the concept of not "facing it" has cost you. What obstacle(s) is holding you back?

8. What is the difference between courage and survival?

9. How have you learned to merge self-actualization and courage consciousness at work? What has been the response or result?

10. Where in your work life are you most able to be an observer of your scripts and the masks you wear?

11. Was there a particular interview or quotation in the book that moved you to action? If so, cite one of these examples that gave you particular insight. Explain.

12. Based on the original definition of the word courage ("heart and spirit"), why is it so important to *declare* your courageous intention?

13. How have you personally experienced abusive behaviors at work? Explain your viewpoints and response(s).

14. How might you begin to recognize everyday courage and use the word more frequently to identify defining moments in your work life?

15. Identify a person in your work life who has demonstrated everyday courage and analyze the obstacles s/he overcame. What skills identified in this book did s/he utilize?

16. What part does our culture play in keeping people from identifying and claiming their courage?

17. How has a fresher understanding of courage derived from the stories in the book affected your understanding of your own courage?

18. What immediate goal will you now create for your workplace to insure that you begin a plan to keep your courageous leadership alive and well?

About the Author

Everyday courage has few witnesses. It is no less noble
because no drum beats and no crowds shout your name.

— Robert Louis Stevenson

Sandra Ford Walston, known as The Courage Expert and innovator of StuckThinking™, is a learning consultant, corporate trainer and courage coach. Sandra's expertise allows her to focus on the tricks and traps of the human condition through recognizing and interpreting courage behaviors, courageous leadership and individual personality and leadership styles. As such, she is a sought-after speaker for companies and institutions seeking conscious change through personnel development. The internationally published author of bestseller *COURAGE* and an honored author selected for Recording for the Blind and Dyslexic, Sandra facilitates individuals and groups to discover the power and inspiration of their everyday courage.

Published in magazines such as "Chief Learning Officer," "Training & Development," "HR Matters," Malaysia and "Strategic Finance," she also provides skills-based programs for some of the most respected public and private blue-chip businesses and organizations in the world including Caterpillar, Inc., Auburn University Women's Leadership Institute, Procter & Gamble, Wyoming Department of Health Public Nurses, Farmers Insurance, Denver International Airport, Nolte Engineering, Virginia Commonwealth University, Teletech International, Wide Open West, Woodhull Institute, US Bank, IBM, Denver Health and Hospitals, Teletech, and Hitachi Consulting.

STUCK: 12 Steps Up the Leadership Ladder, Sandra's follow-up book to *COURAGE,* is directed at any woman, regardless of title or credentials, who wishes to grow professionally by introducing courage actions at work.

Sandra is qualified to administer and interpret the Myers-Briggs Type Indicator®, is a certified Enneagram teacher, and an instructor at the University of Denver. She can be reached at www.sandrawalston.com where she posts a courage blog and free courage newsletter.

Personal Acknowledgments

Writing the personal acknowledgments page is, for me, the best part of writing a book. Why? It's the last stage of birthing yet another book where I get to share my gratitude. Friends know that each book takes at least five years of research and gathering data. With each book I forget how they almost do me under. The self-sacrifice and discipline that is required summons all my courage to keep stepping up and overcoming the barrage of "no" — "no, I don't get the value of everyday courage!" So finally, I have the privilege of acknowledging some of the wonderful people who have provided support along the journey.

My incomparable and gifted personal editor, Joe Stone, understood my work from the beginning. Joe honored my voice, yet delicately inserted valued edits. Thank you to my creative web designer R. (Rahja) McKee-Cray for the Virgo-perfect layout of the manuscript. I can't thank enough my precious friend, Lauren Hildebrand for always dropping her work load to consult with me on the design elements of the book cover and coordinating everything with my talented graphic designer Christopher Bohnet.

Rene Reese gave me the kick-start I needed to complete God's calling — thank you for being there for me when I needed the helping hand. Thank you to the numerous professionals who took time to write insightful and heartfelt endorsements. Thank you also to "my" wonderful librarians at the Ross-University Hills Branch Library — you're the best!

And last, but not least, my wonderful colleague Daryl Conner for perceiving value in my research, writing skills and intention to awaken the Universe to this book's critical topic. Daryl wrote, "It may be that the only thing in shorter supply than courage itself is a proper understanding of what it really is." His Foreword was a blessing.

Words seem trite compared to the depth of my gratitude. Since this journey has taken longer than expected, I am well aware that I have left out other names — please forgive me and know you are deeply valued and loved.

For more information
about Sandra Walston's books,
lectures and programs, please visit
www.sandrawalston.com.

*The world of the ego is like a house of
mirrors through which the ego wanders,
lost and confused, as it cheers the images
in one mirror after another. The only way
out of the circuitous wanderings is
through the pursuit of spiritual truth.*

-- David R. Hawkins, M.D., Ph.D.,

Along the Path to Enlightenment

Citations

1 http://www.cnn.com/2009/WORLD/americas/07/05
costa.rica.happy.nation/index.html, (assessed July 6, 2009).

2 Parade Poll, *The Denver Post*, "Parade Magazine," January 9, 2011, 4..

3 Hawkins, David R., M.D., Ph.D., *Power vs. Force: The Hidden Determinants of Human Behavior*, Sedona: Veritas Pub, www.veritaspub.com, 1995, 68-69.

4 http://en.thinkexist.com/quotes/delmore_schwartz/, (assessed January 2006).

5 Hawkins, David R., M.D., Ph.D., *The Eye of the I: From which Nothing is Hidden*, Sedona, AZ: Veritas Publishing, www.veritaspub.com, 2001, 212.

6 Hawkins, David R., M.D., Ph.D., *Power vs. Force: The Hidden Determinants of Human Behavior*, Sedona, AZ: Veritas Pub, www.veritaspub.com, 1995, 180.

7 Tolle, Eckhart, *The Power of NOW*, Novato, CA: New World Library, 1999, 59.

8 Zohar, Danah & Ian Marshall, *SQ spiritual Intelligence the Ultimate Intelligence*, (London: Bloomsbury, 111.

9 Williamson, Marianne, *The Gift of Change: Spiritual Guidance for a Radically New Life*, San Francisco: Harper San Francisco, 2004, 92.

10 De Becker, Gavin, *The Gift of Fear: Survival Signals that Protect us from Violence*, New York: Little, Brown and Company, 1997, 10.

11 Iachetta, S. Stephanie, *The Daily Reader for Contemplative Living: excerpts from the works of Father Thomas Keating*, New York: Continuum, 2003, 238.

12 Teasdale, Wayne, *The Mystic Heart*, Novato, CA, New World Library, 1999, 2001, 18.

13 Tolle, Eckhart, *A New Earth: Awakening to Your Life's Purpose*, New York: Dutton, 2005, 220.

14 Tolle, Eckhart, *The Power of NOW*, Novato, CA: New World Library, 1999, 13 and 154.

[15] Tolle, Eckhart, *The Power of NOW*, Novato, CA: New World Library, 1999, 111.

[16] Tolle, Eckhart, *The Power of NOW*, Novato, CA: New World Library, 1999, 111.

[17] Tolle, Eckhart, *A New Earth: Awakening to Your Life's Purpose*, New York: Dutton, 2005, 257-8.

[18] Yogananda, Paramahansa, *Undreamed – of Possibilities: An Introduction to Self-Realization Fellowship*, Self-Realization Fellowship, 1982, 1997, 3

[19] Collins, Jim, *Good to Great*, New York: Harper Business, 2001, 210.

[20] Mary Oliver, http://storiesforspeakers.blogspot.com/2009/07/i-dont-want-to-end-up-simply-having.html, (assessed August 2, 2009).

[21] Hawkins, David R., M.D., Ph.D., *The Eye of the I: From which Nothing is Hidden*, Sedona, AZ: Veritas Publishing, www.veritaspub.com, 2001, 69.

[22] Aburdene, Patricia, *Megatrend 2010*, Charlottesville, VA, 2005, 4.

[23] Hawkins, David R., M.D., Ph.D., *The Eye of the I: From which Nothing is Hidden*, Sedona, AZ: Veritas Publishing, www.veritaspub.com, 2001, 30.

[24] Hawkins, David R., M.D., Ph.D., *I: Reality and Subjectivity*, Sedona, AZ: Veritas Publishing, www.veritaspub.com, 2001, 169.

[25] Tolle, Eckhart, *A New Earth: Awakening to Your Life's Purpose*, New York: Dutton, 2005, 8, 239-240.

[26] Hawkins, David R., M.D., Ph.D., *Truth vs Falsehood: How to Tell the Difference*, Toronto, ON, Axial Publishing Canada, www.veritaspub.com, 2005), xiv.

[27] Davis, Rennie, Lecture given by Rennie Davis, Denver, CO, RMCM Church, July 30, 2005.

[28] Tolle, Eckhart, *The Power of NOW*, Novato, CA: New World Library, 1999, 66.

[29] Pennington, M. Basil, *Why We Flee*, The Daily Dig, August 5, 2005.

[30] Zohar, Danah and Ian Marshall, Ph.D., *SQ: Spiritual Intelligence the Ultimate Intelligence*, London: Bloomsbury Publishing, 2000, 13.

[31] Marshall Goldsmith, "The Happiness Paradox," *Talent Management*, September 2010, 58.

[32] The Woodhull Institute, "Who was Victoria Woodhull?," www.woodhull.org/about/woodhull.html (assessed July 2004).

[33] McLean, Jacqueline, *Notable Americans Victoria Woodhull: First Woman Presidential Candidate* (Greensboro, NC: Morgan Reynolds, Inc., 2000), 32.

[34] Gabriel, Mary, *Notorious Victoria: The Life of Victoria Woodhull, Uncensored* (New York: Algonquin Books of Chapel Hill, 1998), 19.

[35] Chesler, Phyllis, *Woman's Inhumanity to Woman* (New York: Thunder's Mouth Press/ Nations Books, 2001), 429-430.

[36] Gabriel, Mary, *Notorious Victoria: The Life of Victoria Woodhull, Uncensored* (New York: Algonquin Books of Chapel Hill, 1998), front flap.

[37] Becket, Sister Wendy, *Meditations on Silence*, (London: Dorling Kindersley, 1995), 24.

[38] Zukav, Gary, *The Seat of the Soul* (New York: Fireside, 1989), 138.

[39] Ferrucci, Piero, *Inevitable Grace: Breakthroughs in the Lives of Great Men and Women* (Los Angeles: Jeremy P. Tarcher, Inc., 1990), 275-6.

[40] Pamer, Parker J., *Let Your Life Speak: Listening for the Voice of Vocation* (San Francisco: Jossey-Bass, 2000), 54.

[41] Hawkins, David R., M.D., Ph.D., *Truth vs Falsehood: how to tell the difference* (Ontario, Canada: Axial Publishing Canada, www.veritaspub.com, 2005), 244.

[42] Ferrucci, Piero, *Inevitable Grace: Breakthroughs in the Lives of Great Men and Women*, (Los Angeles: Jeremy P. Tarcher, Inc., 1990), 294.

[43] Ferrucci, Piero, *Inevitable Grace: Breakthroughs in the Lives of Great Men and Women*, (Los Angeles: Jeremy P. Tarcher, Inc., 1990), 143.

[44] Rilke, Rainer Maria, (translated by M.D. Herter Norton), *Letters to a Young Poet*, (New York: W.W. Norton & Co., 1962 Edition), 35.

[45] Ferrucci, Piero, *Inevitable Grace: Breakthroughs in the Lives of Great Men and Women*, (Los Angeles: Jeremy P. Tarcher, Inc., 1990), 307.

[46] Beckett, Sister Wendy, *Meditations on Silence*, (London: Dorling Kindersley, 1995), 26.

[47] Keating, Thomas, *The Daily Reader for Contemplative Living* (New York: Continuum, 2003), 128.

[48] Ferrucci, Piero, *Inevitable Grace: Breakthroughs in the Lives of Great Men and Women*, (Los Angeles: Jeremy P. Tarcher, Inc., 1990), ix.

⁴⁹ Ferrucci, Piero, *Inevitable Grace: Breakthroughs in the Lives of Great Men and Women*, (Los Angeles: Jeremy P. Tarcher, Inc., 1990), 2.

⁵⁰ Maslow, Abraham H., http://www.brainyquote.com/quotes/authors/a/abraham_maslow.html, (assessed May 2007).

⁵¹ Ferrucci, Piero, *Inevitable Grace: Breakthroughs in the Lives of Great Men and Women*, (Los Angeles: Jeremy P. Tarcher, Inc., 1990), 306.

⁵² Ferrucci, Piero, *What We May Be: Techniques for Psychological and Spiritual Growth*, (Los Angeles: Jeremy P. Tarcher, Inc., 1982), 139.

⁵³ Keating, Thomas, *The Human Condition*, (New York: Paulist Press, 1999), front flap.

⁵⁴ Ferrucci, Piero, *What We May Be: Techniques for Psychological and Spiritual Growth*, (Los Angeles: Jeremy P. Tarcher, Inc., 1982), 74-75.

⁵⁵ Palmer, Parker, *Let Your Life Speak: Listening for the Voice of Vocation* (San Francisco: Jossey-Bass, 2000), 32.

⁵⁶ Teasdale, Wayne, *The Mystic Heart*, (Novato, CA, New World Library, 1999, 2001), 93-4.

⁵⁷ Iachetta, S. Stephanie, *The Daily Reader for Contemplative Living* (New York: Continuum, 2003), 39.

⁵⁸ Keating, Thomas, *Open Mind Open Heart* (New York: The Continuum Publishing Company, 1986), 146.

⁵⁹ Tolle, Eckhart, *A New Earth: Awakening to Your Life's Purpose*, (New York: Dutton, 2005), 131.

⁶⁰ Chesler, Phyllis, *Woman's Inhumanity to Woman* (New York: Thunder's Mouth Press/ Nations Books, 2001), 37.

⁶¹ Teasdale, Wayne, *The Mystic Heart*, Novato, CA, New World Library, 1999, 2001, 142.

⁶² Durkheim, Karlfried Graf, *The Way of Transformation*, http://indranet.com/spirit/transform.html, (assessed August 2006).

⁶³ Tolle, Eckhart, *The Power of NOW*, Novato, CA: New World Library, 1999, 35.

⁶⁴ Tolle, Eckhart, *A New Earth: Awakening to Your Life's Purpose*, New York: Dutton, 2005, 129.

⁶⁵ Tillich, Paul, *The Courage to Be*, New Haven: Yale University, 1952, 14.

66 Yogananda, Paramahansa, *Undreamed – of Possibilities: An Introduction to Self-Realization Fellowship*, Los Angeles, Self-Realization Fellowship, 1982 and 1997, 5.

67 Tolle, Eckhart, *A New Earth: Awakening to Your Life's Purpose*, New York: Dutton, 2005, 134.

68 Teasdale, Wayne, *The Mystic Heart*, Novato, CA, New World Library, 1999 and 2001, 124.

69 Ferrucci, Piero, *Inevitable Grace: Breakthroughs in the Lives of Great Men and Women*, Los Angles: Jeremy P. Tarcher, Inc. 1990, 268.

70 Nin, Anais, http://www.quotationspage.com/quotes/Anais_Nin/, (assessed June 2006).

71 Tolle, Eckhart, *A New Earth: Awakening to Your Life's Purpose*, New York: Dutton, 2005, 276 and 281.

72 Teasdale, Wayne, *The Mystic Heart*, Novato, CA, New World Library, 1999, 2001, 82.

73 Einstein, Albert, http://www.zaadz.com/quotes/topics/opportunity, (assessed March 2006).

74 Unknown, http://www.heartquotes.net/Happiness.html, (assessed June 2006).

75 Teasdale, Wayne, *The Mystic Heart*, Novato, CA, New World Library, 1999, 2001, 120.

76 Tolle, Eckhart, *A New Earth: Awakening to Your Life's Purpose*, New York: Dutton, 2005, 103–105.

77 Tolle, Eckhart, *A New Earth: Awakening to Your Life's Purpose*, New York: Dutton, 2005, 224–5.

78 Tolle, Eckhart, *A New Earth: Awakening to Your Life's Purpose*, New York: Dutton, 2005, 273.

79 Yogananda, Paramahansa, *Undreamed of Possibilities: An Introduction to Self-Realization Fellowship*, Self-Realization Fellowship, 1982, 1997, 2.

80 Ferrucci, Piero, *Inevitable Grace: Breakthroughs in the Lives of Great Men and Women*, Los Angles: Jeremy P. Tarcher, Inc. 1990, 72.

81 Tolle, Eckhart, *A New Earth: Awakening to Your Life's Purpose*, New York: Dutton, 2005, 53.

[82] Tolle, Eckhart, *A New Earth: Awakening to Your Life's Purpose,* New York: Dutton, 2005, 87.

[83]Relyea, Kie, "Bully bosses: Couple works to pass laws to curtail the abuses," LSJ.com, November 15, 2003, www.lsj.com/news/business/p_031115bullypatch_7c-10c.html.

[84] Namie, Ruth and Gary, *The Bully at Work: What You Can Do to Stop the Hurt and Reclaim Your Dignity on the Job,* Naperville, IL: Sourcebooks, Inc., 2000 15-16 and 18.

[85] http://www.workplacebullying.org/docs/WBIsurvey2007.pdf, (assessed July 2010).

[86] http://www.workplacebullying.org/docs/WBIsurvey2007.pdf, (assessed July 2010)

[87] Teasdale, Wayne, *The Mystic Heart,* Novato, CA, New World Library, 1999, 2001, 142.

[88] Zukav, Gary, *The Seat of the Soul,* New York: Fireside Book, 1989, 237.

[89] Chief Joseph, http://en.wikipedia.org/wiki/Chief_Joseph, (assessed June 8, 2009).

[90] Moulton, Candy, *Chief Joseph: Guardian of the People,* New York: A Forge Book, 2005, 27.

[91] Hawkins, David, M.D., Ph.D., *Transcending the Levels of Consciousness: The Stairway to Enlightenment,* Sedona: Veritas Publication, 2006, 103.

[92] Keating, Thomas, *Open Mind Open Heart,* New York: The Continuum Publishing Company, 1986, 16.

[93] Zohar, Danah & Ian Marshall, *SQ spiritual Intelligence the Ultimate Intelligence,* (London: Bloomsbury Publishers, 2000), 225.

[94] Davis, Rennie, *Declaration for a New Humanity* online newsletter, 2007.

[95] Williamson, Marianne, *The Gift of Change: Spiritual Guidance for a Radically New Life,* San Francisco: Harper San Francisco, 2004, 133.

[96] Tolle, Eckhart, *The Power of NOW,* Novato, CA: New World Library, 1999, 43.

[97] Davis, Rennie, *The Great Turning: Evolution at the Crossroads,* MN: Galde Press, Inc., 2003, 73–74.

[98] Honore, Carl, *In Praise of Slowness: How a Worldwide Movement is Challenging the Cult of Speed,* San Francisco: HarperCollins, 2004, 122.

[99] Keating, Thomas, *Invitation to Love: The Way of Christian Contemplation*, New York: The Continuum Publishing Company, 2001, 3.

[100] Williamson, Marianne, *The Gift of Change: Spiritual Guidance for a Radically New Life*, San Francisco: Harper San Francisco, 2004, 91.

[101] Ferrucci, Piero, *Inevitable Grace*, Los Angeles: Jeremy P. Tarcher, Inc., 1990 294.

[102] Williamson, Marianne, *The Gift of Change: Spiritual Guidance for a Radically New Life*, San Francisco: Harper San Francisco, 2004, 95–96.

[103] De Becker, Gavin, *The Gift of Fear: Survival Signals that Protect us from Violence*, New York: Little, Brown and Company, 1997, 277.

[104] Apollinaire, Guillaume, http://en.thinkexist.com/quotation/come_to_the_edge-he_said-they_said-we_are_afraid/147797.html, (assessed January 2006).

[105] Zukav, Gary, *The Seat of the Soul*, New York: Fireside Book, 1989, 240.

[106] De Becker, Gavin, *The Gift of Fear: Survival Signals that Protect us from Violence*, New York: Little, Brown and Company, 1997, 277.

[107] De Becker, Gavin, *The Gift of Fear: Survival Signals that Protect us from Violence*, New York: Little, Brown and Company, 1997, 27.

[108] Breen, Bill, "What's Your Intuition?", *Fast Company*, September 2000, 292–300.

[109] Zohar, Danah & Ian Marshall, *SQ spiritual Intelligence the Ultimate Intelligence*, (London: Bloomsbury Publishers, 2000), 244.

[110] Lasater, Judith, Ph. D., P.T., *Living Your Yoga: Finding the Spiritual in Everyday Life*, Berkeley: Rodmell Press, 2000, 44.

[111] Bourgeault, Cynthia, *Centering Prayer and Inner Awakening*, Cambridge, MA: Cowley Publications, 2004, 87.

[112] Hawkins, David, M.D., Ph.D., *Power vs. Force: The Hidden Determinants of Human Behavior*, Sedona: Veritas Pub, 1995, 20.

[113] Tolle, Eckhart, *A New Earth: Awakening to Your Life's Purpose*, New York: Dutton, 2005, 294.

[114] Guglielmo, Connie, "No regrets, fired Fiorina says of her 5 years at H-P helm," *The Denver Post, Business*, May 11, 2005, 1C and 4C.

[115] Metzger, Joel, "Living with Intention, by Kay Gilley," ONN-Wisdom/6–88, September 8, 1999.

116 Metzger, Joel, "Living with Intention, by Kay Gilley," ONN-Wisdom/6–88, September 8, 1999.

117 Tolle, Eckhart, *A New Earth: Awakening to Your Life's Purpose*, New York: Dutton, 2005, 272.

118 Lewis, C. S., http://www.quotedb.com/quotes/350, (assessed January 2005).

119 Rumi, http://www.lucidmoonpoetry.com/bookreviews/fall2000.shtml, (assessed July 2006).

120 Chittister, Joan, "Envisioning Holiness," *Lutheran Woman Today*, June 2005, 18.

121 Teasdale, Wayne, *The Mystic Heart*, Novato, CA, New World Library, 1999, 2001, xvi.

122 Williamson, Marianne, *The Gift of Change: Spiritual Guidance for a Radically New Life*, San Francisco: Harper San Francisco, 2004, 215.

123 Bache, Christopher M, *Dark Night, Early Dawn: Steps to a Deep Ecology of Mind*, New York: State University of New York Press, 2000, 117 and 280.

124 Underhill, Evelyn, *Mysticism: The Development of Mankind's Spiritual Consciousness*, London: Bracken Books, 1911, 58.

125 Papasogli, Giorgio, *St. Teresa of Avila*, Boston, MA: St. Paul Books & Media, 1990, 419–20.

126 Hawkins, David, M.D., Ph.D., *The Eye of the I: From which Nothing is Hidden*, Sedona: Veritas Publishing, 2001, 68.

127 Lasater, Judith, Ph. D., P.T., *Living Your Yoga: Finding the Spiritual in Everyday Life*, Berkeley: Rodmell Press, 2000, 31.

128 Zukav, Gary, *The Seat of the Soul*, New York: Fireside Book, 1989, 236.

129 Chesler, Phyllis, *Woman's Inhumanity to Woman*, New York: Thunder's Mouth Press, 2001, 487.

130 Avila, Saint Teresa of, http://www.brainyquote.com/quotes/authors/s/saint_teresa_of_avila.html, (assessed June 2006).

131 Oprah, "What I Know for Sure," *O: The Oprah Magazine*, October, 2005, 350.

[132] Yogananda, Paramahansa, *Spiritual Diary: An Inspirational Thought for Each Day*, LA: Self-Realization Fellowship, 1986, January 23.

[133] Kabat-Zinn, Jon, *Wherever You Go There You Are*, New York: Hyperion, 1994, 196 and 198.

[134] Beckett, Sister Wendy, *Meditations on Silence*, London: Dorling Kindersley, 1995, 18.

[135] Stein, Edith, "The First Hour of Your Morning," *Daily Dig*, August 18, 2005, www.bruderhof.com, subscriber.

[136] Hawkins, David, M.D., Ph.D., *Power vs. Force: The Hidden Determinants of Human Behavior*, Sedona: Veritas Pub, 1995, 70.

[137] Cowan, Tom, *The Ways of the Saints: Prayers, Practices, and Meditations*, New York: Berkley Publishing Group, 1998, 415.

[138] Zukav, Gary, *The Seat of the Soul*, New York: Fireside Book, 1989, 205.

[139] Zukav, Gary, *The Seat of the Soul*, New York: Fireside Book, 1989, 136.

[140] Hawkins, David, M.D., Ph.D., *Truth vs Falsehood: How to Tell the Difference*, Toronto, ON: Axial Publishing Canada, 2005, 259.

[141] Hall, Thelma, r.c., *Too Deep For Words: Rediscovering Lectio Divina*, Mahwah, NJ: Paulist Press, 1988, 100.

[142] Chesler, Phyllis, *Woman's Inhumanity to Woman*, New York: Thunder's Mouth Press, 2001, 134 and 347.

[143] Avila, Saint Teresa of, http://members.aol.com/_ht_a/fatherpius/quotes7.html, (assessed June 2006).

[144] Tolle, Eckhart, *A New Earth: Awakening to Your Life's Purpose*, New York: Dutton, 2005, 40.

[145] Tolle, Eckhart, *A New Earth: Awakening to Your Life's Purpose*, New York: Dutton, 2005, 40.

[146] Hawkins, David, M.D., Ph.D., *Truth vs Falsehood: How to Tell the Difference*, Toronto, Canada: Axial Publishing Canada, 2005, 49.

[147] Tolle, Eckhart, *The Power of NOW*, Novato, CA: New World Library, 1999, 174.

[148] Tolle, Eckhart, *The Power of NOW*, Novato, CA: New World Library, 1999, 160.

¹⁴⁹ Davis, Rennie, *The Great Turning: Evolution at the Crossroads*, MN: Galde Press, Inc., 2003, 56.

¹⁵⁰ Teasdale, Wayne, *The Mystic Heart*, Novato, CA, New World Library, 1999, 2001, 123.

¹⁵¹ Yogananda, Paramahansa, *Spiritual Diary: An Inspirational Thought for Each Day*, LA: Self-Realization Fellowship, 1986, July 14.

¹⁵² Tolle, Eckhart, *A New Earth: Awakening to Your Life's Purpose*, New York: Dutton, 2005, 226.

¹⁵³ Kabat-Zinn, Jon, *Wherever You Go There You Are*, New York: Hyperion, 1994, 34.

¹⁵⁴ Tolle, Eckhart, *A New Earth: Awakening to Your Life's Purpose*, New York: Dutton, 2005, 45.

¹⁵⁵ Kabat-Zinn, Jon. *Wherever You Go There You Are*, New York: Hyperion, 1994, 55.

¹⁵⁶ De Mello, Anthony, *Awareness*, New York: Image Books, 1992, 134.

¹⁵⁷ Tolle, Eckhart, *A New Earth: Awakening to Your Life's Purpose*, New York: Dutton, 2005, 37.

¹⁵⁸ Flinders, Carol Lee, *Enduring Grace: Living Portraits of Seven Women Mystics*, New York: Harper Collins, 1993, 171.

¹⁵⁹ Tolle, Eckhart, *A New Earth: Awakening to Your Life's Purpose*, New York: Dutton, 2005, 45.

¹⁶⁰ Lasater, Judith, Ph. D., P.T., *Living Your Yoga: Finding the Spiritual in Everyday Life*, Berkeley: Rodmell Press, 2000, 84.

¹⁶¹ Bourgeault, Cynthia, *Centering Prayer and Inner Awakening*, Cambridge, MA: Cowley Publications, 2004, 137.

¹⁶² Tolle, Eckhart, *The Power of NOW*, Novato, CA: New World Library, 1999, 48–49.

¹⁶³ Williamson, Marianne, *The Gift of Change: Spiritual Guidance for a Radically New Life*, San Francisco: Harper San Francisco, 2004, 230.

¹⁶⁴ Ollala, Julio, "Gratitude," Newfield Networker Holiday Edition, December 2005, written permission granted.

[165] Ford, David and Rachael Muers, *The Modern Theologians: An Introduction to Christian Theology Since 1918, Great Theologians,* Massachusetts: Malden Blackwell Publishing, 2005, 45.

[166] Bonhoeffer, Dietrich, *A Testament to Freedom: The Essential Writings of Dietrich Bonhoeffer,* edited by Geffrey B. Kelly and F. Burton Nelson, New York: Harper-Collins, 1995, 5.

[167] Shepherd, Victor, http://www.victorshepherd.on.ca/Heritage/deitrich.htm, (assessed May 2009).

[168] Tolle, Eckhart, *A New Earth: Awakening to Your Life's Purpose,* New York: Dutton, 2005, 294.

[169] Ferrucci, Piero, *Inevitable Grace: Breakthroughs in the Lives of Great Men and Women: Guides to Your Self-Realization,* Los Angeles: Jeremy P. Tarcher, 1990, 269.

[170] Marden, Orison Swett, http://quotations.about.com/od/stillmorefamouspeople/a/OrisonSwettMar2.htm, (assessed September 2006).

[171] Gardner, David, "A Striking Interview, Part 2," *The Motley Fool,* http://www.fool.com/news/commentary/2005/commentary05121301.htm, (assessed November 2005).

[172] Italian Proverb, http://www.quotationspage.com/quote/26909.html, (assessed May 2007).

[173] McCrimmon, Cyrus, "Interview," *The Denver Post,* Business Section, April 2, 2006, 3K.

[174] Bruner, Jerome Seymour, http://www.quoteworld.org/quotes/1994, (assessed May 2006).

[175] Tischler, Linda, "Bridging the (GenderWage) Gap," *Fast Company,* January 2005, 86.

[176] Lovely, Sylvia L., "The True Meaning of Leadership," *The Day* New London, Conn., October 30, 2005, http://www.theday.com/eng/web/news/re.aspx?re=B8856A5A-8893-4814-B94A-68649B6A2C36.

[177] Marsch, Ann, "The Art of Work," *Fast Company,* August 2005, 78.

[178] Heffernan, Margaret, "The Morale of the Story," *Fast Company,* March 2005, 80.

[179] Beauprez, Jennifer and Kris Hudson, "Bernard Ascends at AT&T," *The Denver Post*, Business Section, 1 & 4C.

[180] Hillary, Sir Edmund, http://www.quotationspage.com/quote/4762.html, (assessed March 2006).

[181] Tolle, Eckhart, *A New Earth: Awakening to Your Life's Purpose*, New York: Dutton, 2005, 208–9.

[182] Albright, Madeleine K., Commencement Address, Mount Holyoke College, May 25, 1997, http://www.mtholyoke.edu/offices/comm/misc/albright/speech.shtml.

[183] Bernstein, Peter L., *Against the Gods: The Remarkable Story of Risk*, New York: John Wiley & Sons, 1996, 8.

[184] Hawkins, David, M.D., Ph.D., *Truth vs Falsehood: how to tell the difference*, Toronto: ON: Axial Publishing, 2005, 250.

[185] Ferrucci, Piero, *Inevitable Grace*, Los Angeles: Jeremy P. Tarcher, 1990, 287.

[186] Yogananda, Paramahansa, *Spiritual Diary: An Inspirational Thought for Each Day*, Los Angeles: Self-Realization Fellowship, 1986, September 3.

[187] West, Morris L., http://www2.bcinternet.net/~newman/Inspiration.htm, (assessed January 2006).

[188] Harburg, Fred "Learning How to Learn," *Chief Learning Officer*, September 2005, 22.

[189] Williamson, Marianne, *The Gift of Change: Spiritual Guidance for a Radically New Life*, San Francisco: Harper, 2004, 86.

[190] Tolle, Eckhart, *A New Earth: Awakening to Your Life's Purpose*, New York: Dutton, 2005, 236.

[191] Tolle, Eckhart, *A New Earth: Awakening to Your Life's Purpose*, New York: Dutton, 2005, 240.

[192] Maltz, Maxwell, http://www.quotelady.com/subjects/courage.html, (assessed June 2008).

[193] Teasdale, Wayne, *The Mystic Heart*, Novato, CA: New World Library, 1999, 2001, 108–9.

[194] Tolle, Eckhart, *A New Earth: Awakening to Your Life's Purpose,* New York: Dutton, 2005, 32–3.

[195] Tolle, Eckhart, *A New Earth: Awakening to Your Life's Purpose,* New York: Dutton, 2005, 260.

[196] Ferrucci, Piero, *Inevitable Grace: Breakthroughs in the Lives of Great Men and Women: Guides to Your Self-Realization,* Los Angles: Jeremy P. Tarcher, Inc. 1990, 93.

[197] "The Business of Being Happy," *O: The Oprah Magazine,* April 2003, 62.

[198] Bourgoin, Suzanne Michele and Paula Kay Byers, *Encyclopedia of World Biography* Second Edition, Detroit, MI: Gale Research, 1998, 135.

[199] King, Martin Luther, http://www.inspirationpeak.com/cgi-bin/search.cgi?search=Martin+Luther+King%2C+Jr.&I1.x=27&I1.y=3, (assessed April 2005).

[200] Rumi, Jalaluddin, http://sufistuff.blogspot.com/2006/01/to-know-ones-self.html, (accessed June 8, 2008).

[201] Heuerman, Tom, Ph.D, "Courage and Freedom," Pamphlet 53, December 5, 2001.

[202] Hightower, Jim, http://shetterly.blogspot.com/2005/07/americans-who-tell-truth.html, (assessed May 2007).

[203] Sittenfeld, Cutis, "no-brands-land," *Fast Company,* September 2000, 240-244.

[204] Keating, Thomas, *Open Mind Open Heart: The Contemplative Dimension of the Gospel,* New York: The Continuum Publishing Company, 1986, 1992, 95.

[205] Oprah, "What's True for You?", *O: The Oprah Magazine,* November 2002, 43.

[206] Walsh, Neale Donald, *CwG Weekly Bulletin #175:* "It's a New Day," Week of January 13, 2006, http://www.cwg.org/bulletins/Bulletin_175.html.

[207] Teasdale, Wayne, *The Mystic Heart,* Novato, CA, New World Library, 1999, 2001, 120.

[208] Emerson, Ralph Waldo, http://www.quoteworld.org/quotes/4519, (assessed May 2006).

[209] Rubin, Harriet, "What is Courage," *Fast Company,* February 2002, 98.

[210] Hawkins, David, M.D., Ph.D., *Transcending the Levels of Consciousness: The Stairway to Enlightenment*, Sedona: Veritas Publication, 2006, 314 and 329.

[211] Ferrucci, Piero, *Inevitable Grace: Breakthroughs in the Lives of Great Men and Women: Guides to Your Self-Realization*, Los Angeles: Jeremy P. Tarcher, Inc., 1990, 313.

[212] Berger, Melvin, *Famous Men of Modern Biology*, New York: Thomas Y. Crowell Company, 1968, 83.

[213] http://www.pfdf.org/knowledgecenter/journal.aspx?ArticleID=84, (assessed August 29, 2010).

[214] Frankl, Viktor E., *Man's Search for Meaning*, Boston, Massachusetts, Beacon Press, 1959, XIV.

[215] Keating, Thomas, "Shattered Vision," Contemplative Outreach News, Volume 16, Number 2 Fall/Winter 2002-2003, 1.

[216] http://thinkexist.com/quotation/it-is-the-lone-worker-who-makes-the-first-advance/362412.html 11/04, (assessed November 2010)

[217] Baker, Joel, http://www.quoteworld.org/quotes/975, (assessed May 2005).

[218] Teasdale, Wayne, *The Mystic Heart*, Novato, CA, New World Library, 1999, 2001, 102.

[219] Kabat-Zinn, Jon, *Wherever You Go There You Are*, New York: Hyperion, 1994, 21.

[220] Hawkins, David R., M.D., Ph.D., *Discovery of the Presence of God: Devotional Nonduality*, Sedona, Arizona: Veritas Publishing, www.veritaspub.com, 2006, 105.

[221] Breen, Bill, "The Hard Life and Restless Mind of America's Education Billionaire," *Fast Company*, March 2003, 84.

[222] Kabat-Zinn, Jon, *Wherever You Go There You Are*, New York: Hyperion, 1994, 208.

[223] Kabat-Zinn, Jon, *Wherever You Go There You Are*, New York: Hyperion, 1994, 53.

[224] Kabat-Zinn, Jon, *Wherever You Go There You Are*, New York: Hyperion, 1994, 76 and 78.

[225] Bronson, Po, "What Should I Do With My Life?," *Fast Company*, January 2003, 75.

226 Ferrucci, Piero, *Inevitable Grace: Breakthroughs in the Lives of Great Men and Women: Guides to Your Self-Realization,* Los Angles: Jeremy P. Tarcher, Inc. 1990, 123.

227 Tolle, Eckhart, *The Power of NOW,* Novato, CA: New World Library, 1999, 208.

228 Ferrucci, Piero, *Inevitable Grace: Breakthroughs in the Lives of Great Men and Women: Guides to Your Self-Realization,* Los Angeles: Jeremy P. Tarcher, Inc., 1990, 241.

229 Iachetta, S. Stephanie, *The Daily Reader for Contemplative Living: excerpts from the works of Father Thomas Keating,* New York: Continuum, 2003, 296.

230 Kabat-Zinn, Jon, *Wherever You Go There You Are,* New York: Hyperion, 1994, 44–45.

231 Tolle, Eckhart, *The Power of NOW,* Novato, CA: New World Library, 1999, 220–221.

232 Churchill, Winston, http://thinkexist.com/quotation/success_is_not_final-failure_is_not_fatal-it_is/150143.html, (assessed January 2006).

233 Rubin, Harriet, "Dr. Brilliant VS. The Devil of Ambition," *Fast Company,* October 2000, pages 254, 257 and 270.

234 DuTemple, Lesley A., *Jacques Cousteau,* Minneapolis: Lerner Publications Company, 2000, 12.

235 http://www.notablebiographies.com/Co-Da/Cousteau-Jacques.html, assessed July 4, 2009.

236 Palmer, Parker J., *Let Your Life Speak: Listening for the Voice of Vocation,* San Francisco: Jossey-Bass, 2000, 9.

237 Palmer, Parker J., *Let Your Life Speak: Listening for the Voice of Vocation,* San Francisco: Jossey-Bass, 2000, 5.

238 Olson, Geoff, "Love and its counterfeits," Common Ground, February 2006, http://www.commonground.ca/iss/0602175/cg175_olson.shtml.

239 Tolle, Eckhart, *A New Earth: Awakening to Your Life's Purpose,* New York: Dutton, 2005, 8, 14 and 73.

240 West, Rebecca, http://www.worldofquotes.com/author/Rebecca-West/1/index.html.

241 Tolle, Eckhart, *A New Earth: Awakening to Your Life's Purpose*, New York: Dutton, 2005, 8, 14 and 123.

242 *I Am That: Talks with Sri Nisargadatta Maharaj*, Translated from the Marathi tape recordings by Maurice Frydman, Revised and edited by Sudhakar S. Dikshit, Durham, North Carolina: The Acorn Press, 1973, Reprinted 2005, 8.

243 Ferrucci, Piero, *Inevitable Grace: Breakthroughs in the Lives of Great Men and Women*, Los Angles: Jeremy P. Tarcher, Inc. 1990, 301 and 266.

244 Palmer, Parker J., *Let Your Life Speak: Listening for the Voice of Vocation*, San Francisco: Jossey-Bass, 2000, 60.

245 Keating, Thomas, *The Human Condition*, New York: Paulist Press, 1999, 45.

246 Williamson, Marianne, *The Gift of Change: Spiritual Guidance for a Radically New Life*, San Francisco: Harper San Francisco, 2004, 178.

247 Kubler-Ross, Elizabeth, http://www.brainyquote.com/quotes/authors/e/elisabeth_kublerross.html.

248 Hawkins, David, M.D., Ph.D., *Discovery of the Presence of God: Devotional Nonduality*, Sedona, Arizona: Veritas Publishing, 2006, 102.

249 Hawkins, David, M.D., Ph.D., *Transcending the Levels of Consciousness: The Stairway to Enlightenment*, Sedona: Veritas Publication, 2006, 94.

250 Williamson, Marianne, *The Gift of Change: Spiritual Guidance for a Radically New Life*, San Francisco: Harper San Francisco, 2004, 178.

251 Hawkins, David, M.D., Ph.D., *Discovery of the Presence of God: Devotional Nonduality*, Sedona, Arizona: Veritas Publishing, 2006, 31.

252 Attributed to design expert Harold Nelson.

253 Ferrucci, Piero, *Inevitable Grace: Breakthroughs in the Lives of Great Men and Women*, Los Angles: Jeremy P. Tarcher, Inc. 1990, 96–7.

254 Pennington, M. Basil, "Why We Flee," Daily Dig, August 11, 2005, www.bruderhof.com.

255 Parker J. Palmer, *Let Your Life Speak: Listening for the Voice of Vocation*, San Francisco: Jossey-Bass, 2000, 70.

256 Keating, Thomas, "Homily for the Funeral of Dom Basil Pennington," *Contemplative Outreach News*, Volume 21, Number 2, Jan/June 2006, 12–13.

[257] Hawkins, David, M.D., Ph.D., *Transcending the Levels of Consciousness: The Stairway to Enlightenment*, Sedona: Veritas Publication, 2006, 331.

[258] Davis, Rennie, *The Great Turning: Evolution at the Crossroads*, MN: Galde Press, Inc., 2003, 46–48.

[259] Churchill, Winston, http://en.thinkexist.com/quotation/if_you_are_going_through_hell-keep_going/219081.html.

[261] Braiker, Harriet, http://en.thinkexist.com/quotes/harriet_beryl_braiker/.

[261] Lazerov, *Enciklopedie fun Idishe Vitzen*, 1928, #423.

[262] Iachetta, S. Stephanie, *The Daily Reader for Contemplative Living*, New York: Continuum, 2003, 175.

[263] Hawkins, David, M.D., Ph.D., *Power vs. Force: The Hidden Determinants of Human Behavior*, Carlsbad, CA: Hay House, Inc., 1995, 75.

[264] Felder, Deborah G., *The 100 Most Influential Women of All Time: A Ranking Past and Present*, New York: Citadel Press, 1996, 290.

[266] Hawkins, David, M.D., Ph.D., *Transcending the Levels of Consciousness: The Stairway to Enlightenment*, Sedona: Veritas Publication, 2006, 186.

[267] Felder, Deborah G., *The 100 Most Influential Women of All Time: A Ranking Past and Present*, New York: Citadel Press, 1996, 291.

[268] Graham, Katherine, http://www.brainyquote.com/quotes/quotes/k/katharineg166885.html, (assessed July 2005).

[269] Hawkins, David, M.D., Ph.D., *Power vs. Force: The Hidden Determinants of Human Behavior*, Sedona: Veritas Pub, 1995, 220.

[270] Andrew Cohen, "Spiritual Self-Confidence," *EnlightenNext*, June-August 2009, 112.

[271] Zukav, Gary, *The Seat of the Soul*, New York: Fireside Book, 1989, 142.

[272] Kennedy, Robert F.   , .http://en.thinkexist.com/quotation/only_those_who_dare_to_fail_greatly_can_ever/14582.html, (assessed May 2005).

[273] Zukav, Gary, *The Seat of the Soul*, New York: Fireside Book, 1989, 172.

[274] Hawkins, David, M.D., Ph.D., *Power vs. Force: The Hidden Determinants of Human Behavior*, Sedona: Veritas Pub, 1995, 193-4.

[275] Gerber, Robin, *Katherine Graham: The Leadership Journey of an American Icon,* New York: Penguin, 2005, ix.

[276] Teasdale, Wayne, *The Mystic Heart,* Novato, CA, New World Library, 1999, 2001, 141 and 151.

[277] Wintour, Anna, "Letter from the Editor, *Vogue,* September 2001, 86.

[278] Kearns, Linda Lou Rev., "Changing from the Inside," Florida Tampa Bay's *News Naturally,* March/April 2002 , http://www.altnewtimes.com/Articles/2002/e22llk.html (assessed June 11, 2008).

[279] Johnson, Cecil, "Katherine Graham's decades of struggle at the top of the Post," *Knight Kidder,* October 20, 2005, http://www.nj.com/printer/printer.ssf?/base/business-1/1130043197273880.xml&coll=1.

[280] Chesler, Phyllis, *Woman's Inhumanity to Woman,* New York: Thunder's Mouth Press, 2001, 219–20.

[281] Gottlieb, Annie, "The Radical Road to Self-Esteem, *O: The Oprah Magazine,* March 2001, 101.

[282] Jane Rule, http://en.thinkexist.com/quotation/my-private-measure-of-success-is-daily-if-this/380341.html, (assessed May 2006).

[283] Gottlieb, Annie, "The Radical Road to Self-Esteem, *O: The Oprah Magazine,* March 2001, 101–2.

[284] Sweets, Ellen, "in the eyes of the beholder," *The Denver Post,* The Scene, January 5, 2004, 1F.

[285] Ferrucci, Piero, *What We May Be: Techniques for Psychological and Spiritual Growth,* Los Angeles: Jeremy P. Tarcher, Inc., 1982, 110.

[286] Ferrucci, Piero, *What We May Be: Techniques for Psychological and Spiritual Growth,* Los Angeles: Jeremy P. Tarcher, Inc., 1982, 110.

[287] *I Ching,* http://www.wisdomportal.com/IChing/Hexagram29.html, (assessed July 2006).

[288] Krull, Kathleen and Kathryn Hewitt, *Lives of Extraordinary Women: Rulers, Rebels,* New York: Harcourt, Inc. 2000, 71.

[289] Felder, Deborah G., *The 100 Most Influential Women of All Time: A Ranking Past and Present,* New York: A Citadel Press Book, 1996, 126.

[290] Hawkins, David, M.D., Ph.D., *Power vs. Force: The Hidden Determinants of Human Behavior*, Sedona: Veritas Pub, 1995, 201.

[291] Ferrucci, Piero, *Inevitable Grace: Breakthroughs in the Lives of Great Men and Women*, Los Angles: Jeremy P. Tarcher, Inc. 1990, 10.

[292] Krull, Kathleen and Kathryn Hewitt, *Lives of Extraordinary Women: Rulers, Rebels*, New York: Harcourt, Inc. 2000, 72.

[293] Tolle, Eckhart, *A New Earth: Awakening to Your Life's Purpose*, New York: Dutton, 2005, 61.

[294] Dreamer, Oriah Mountain   , http://www.menstuff.org/books/byissue/affirmations.html, (assessed May 2006.

[295] Ulrich, Laurel Thatcher, http://www.wisdomquotes.com/002317.html, (assessed March 2006).

[296] Wendover, Robert, "Can You Teach Common Sense?", GenTrends Newsletter, November 2010.

[297] Claybourne, Anna, *Living Lives: Gold Meir*, Chicago: Heinemann Library, 2003, 42.

[298] Kinnel, Galway, "Reteach a thing its loveliness," *O: The Magazine, Live your best life*, March 2001, 47.

[299] Ferrucci, Piero, *Inevitable Grace: Breakthroughs in the Lives of Great Men and Women*, Los Angles: Jeremy P. Tarcher, Inc. 1990, 282.

[300] Teasdale, Wayne, *The Mystic Heart*, Novato, CA, New World Library, 1999, 2001, 51.

[301] Tolle, Eckhart, *A New Earth: Awakening to Your Life's Purpose*, New York: Dutton, 2005, 271.

[302] Bronson, Po, "What Should I Do With My Life?," *Fast Company*, January 2003, 76.

[303] Welch, Suzy, "Getting Unstuck, *O:The Oprah Magazine*, September 2005, 230.

[304] Emerson, Ralph Waldo , http://creatingminds.org/quotes/courage.htm, (assessed July 2005).

[305] Ferrucci, Piero, *Inevitable Grace: Breakthroughs in the Lives of Great Men and Women*, Los Angles: Jeremy P. Tarcher, Inc. 1990, 348.

306 Tolle, Eckhart *A New Earth: Awakening to Your Life's Purpose,* New York: Dutton, 2005, 262.

307 Monfort, Joyce, "Gifts," *Reflections on Life,* Self-published, 2001, 8.

308 Rohn, Jim, http://www.brainyquote.com/quotes/authors/j/jim_rohn.html, (assessed May 2005).

309 Tolle, Eckhart, *A New Earth: Awakening to Your Life's Purpose,* New York: Dutton, 2005, 277.

310 Tolle, Eckhart, *A New Earth: Awakening to Your Life's Purpose,* New York: Dutton, 2005, 186.

311 Zohar, Danah & Ian Marshall, *SQ spiritual Intelligence the Ultimate Intelligence,* (London: Bloomsbury Publishers, 2000), 285.

312 Eliot, George   , http://www.brainyquote.com/quotes/quotes/g/georgeelio161679.html, (assessed August 2006).

313 Bourgeault, Cynthia, *Centering Prayer and Inner Awakening,* Cambridge, MA: Cowley Publications, 2004, 102.

314 Thomas, Vivien T., *Partners of the Heart: Vivien Thomas and His Work with Alfred Blalock, An Autobiography by Vivien T. Thomas,* Philadelphia: University of Pennsylvania Press, 1985, 7.

315 Thomas, Vivien T., *Partners of the Heart: Vivien Thomas and His Work with Alfred Blalock, An Autobiography by Vivien T. Thomas,* Philadelphia: University of Pennsylvania Press, 1985, 16.

316 Thomas, Vivien T., *Partners of the Heart: Vivien Thomas and His Work with Alfred Blalock, An Autobiography by Vivien T. Thomas,* Philadelphia: University of Pennsylvania Press, 1985, 18.

317 Thomas, Vivien T., *Partners of the Heart: Vivien Thomas and His Work with Alfred Blalock, An Autobiography by Vivien T. Thomas,* Philadelphia: University of Pennsylvania Press, 1985, 64.

318 Thomas, Vivien T., *Partners of the Heart: Vivien Thomas and His Work with Alfred Blalock, An Autobiography by Vivien T. Thomas,* Philadelphia: University of Pennsylvania Press, 1985, 220.

319 Freud, Sigmund, http://www.bestinspiration.com/quotes-1/of/all/inspiration.htm.

[320] Andrew Cohen, "Spiritual Self-Confidence," *EnlightenNext*, June-August 2009, 112.

[321] Hawkins, David, M.D., Ph.D., *Healing and Recovery*, Sedona: Veritas Publication, 2009, 186.

[322] Hawkins, David, M.D., Ph.D., *Truth vs Falsehood: How to Tell the Difference*, Toronto, ON: Axial Publishing Canada, 2005, 238.

[323] Ferrucci, Piero, *Inevitable Grace: Breakthroughs in the Lives of Great Men and Women*, Los Angles: Jeremy P. Tarcher, Inc. 1990, 77.

[324] Krista's Journal, "The Soul in Depression," American Public Radio, "Speaking of Faith," October 6, 2005, http://speakingoffaith.publicradio.org/programs/depression/emailnewsletter.html.

[325] Debold, Elizabeth, EdD., The EnlightenNext Discovery Cycle, "Higher Development Research Project," June 13, 2009, EnlightenNext newsletter.

[326] Tolle, Eckhart, *A New Earth: Awakening to Your Life's Purpose*, New York: Dutton, 2005, 140.

[327] Schwartz, Delmore, http://en.thinkexist.com/quotes/delmore_schwartz/, (assessed October 2007).

[328] Hawkins, David, M.D., Ph.D., *Transcending the Levels of Consciousness: The Stairway to Enlightenment*, Sedona: Veritas Publication, 2006, 176.

[329] Hawkins, David, M.D., Ph.D., *Healing and Recovery*, Sedona: Veritas Publication, 2009, 382.

[330] Tolle, Eckhart, *The Power of NOW*, Novato, CA: New World Library, 1999, 216.

[331] Tolle, Eckhart, *The Power of NOW*, Novato, CA: New World Library, 1999, 83.

[332] Teasdale, Wayne, *The Mystic Heart*, Novato, CA, New World Library, 1999, 2001, 223.

[333] Tischler, Linda, "Vote of Confidence: Orlando," *Fast Company*, December 2002, 106

[334] Tolle, Eckhart, *The Power of NOW*, Novato, CA: New World Library, 1999, 220.

335 Ferrucci, Piero, *Inevitable Grace: Breakthroughs in the Lives of Great Men and Women*, Los Angles: Jeremy P. Tarcher, Inc. 1990, 77.

336 Iacetta, S. Stephanie, *The Daily Reader for Contemplative Living: excerpts from the works of Father Thomas Keating*, New York: Continuum, 2003, 31.

337 O'Connor, Colleen, "Spiritual life gives office pick-me-up," The Denver Post, "Style," Section L, January 30, 2005, 1L.

338 Kabat-Zinn, Jon, *Wherever You Go There You Are*, New York: Hyperion, 1994, 65.

339 Teasdale, Wayne, *The Mystic Heart*, Novato, CA, New World Library, 1999, 2001, 150.

340 J. Palmer, Parker, *Let Your Life Speak: Listening for the Voice of Vocation*, San Francisco: Jossey-Bass, 2000, 34.

341 cummings, e.e., http://www.quoteworld.org/quotes/3310, (assessed February 2005).

342 Frankl, Viktor E., *Man's Search for Meaning*, Boston: Beacon Press, 1959; 2006, x.

343 Frankl, Viktor E., *Man's Search for Meaning*, Boston: Beacon Press, 1959; 2006, 161.

344 Frankl, Viktor E., *Man's Search for Meaning*, Boston: Beacon Press, 1959; 2006, 66-67; 70.

345 Redsand, Anna, *Viktor Frankl: A Life Worth Living*, New York: Clarion Books, 2006, 13.

346 Redsand, Anna, *Viktor Frankl: A Life Worth Living*, New York: Clarion Books, 2006, 15.

347 Redsand, Anna, *Viktor Frankl: A Life Worth Living*, New York: Clarion Books, 2006, 19.

348 Redsand, Anna, *Viktor Frankl: A Life Worth Living*, New York: Clarion Books, 2006, 28-29.

349 Frankl, Viktor E., *Man's Search for Meaning*, Boston: Beacon Press, 1959; 2006, 113.

350 Redsand, Anna, *Viktor Frankl: A Life Worth Living*, New York: Clarion Books, 2006, 75.

351 Redsand, Anna, *Viktor Frankl: A Life Worth Living*, New York: Clarion Books, 2006, 31.

[352] Frankl, Viktor E., *Man's Search for Meaning*, Boston: Beacon Press, 1959; 2006, 77.

[353] Zohar, Danah & Ian Marshall, *SQ spiritual Intelligence the Ultimate Intelligence*, London: Bloomsbury Publishers, 2000, 289.

[354] Redsand, Anna, *Viktor Frankl: A Life Worth Living*, New York: Clarion Books, 2006, 126.

[355] Frankl, Viktor, http://thinkexist.com/quotation/each_man_is_questioned_by_life-and_he_can_only/203365.html, (assessed November 21, 2010).

[356] Tolle, Eckhart, *A New Earth: Awakening to Your Life's Purpose*, New York: Dutton, 2005), 26-27.

[357] Teasdale, Wayne, *The Mystic Heart*, Novato, CA, New World Library, 1999 and 2001, 47.

[358] Tan-Wong, Nellie, "Courage is the acid test of leadership," The Star Online—Business, December 25, 2005, 2.

[359] "Another Woman," Written and Directed by Woody Allen, Orion Home Video, 1989.

[360] Hawkins, David, M.D., Ph.D., *Truth vs Falsehood: How to tell the Difference*, Ontario, Canada: Axial Publishing Canada, 2005, 125.

[361] Hawkins, David, M.D., Ph.D., *Truth vs Falsehood: How to Tell the Difference*, Ontario, Canada: Axial Publishing Canada, 2005, 129.

Made in the USA
Charleston, SC
31 August 2011